ROLLINGSTONERAVES

ROLLING STONE PRESS

Quill · William Morrow · *New York*

What Your Rock & Roll Favorites Favor

Compiled by Anthony Bozza • Edited by Shawn Dahl

Preface by Matt Pinfield

A Rolling Stone Press book

Editor: Holly George-Warren

Senior Editor: Shawn Dahl

Assistant Editor: Ann Abel

Editorial Assistant: Carrie Smith

Library of Congress Cataloging-in-Publication Data

Rolling Stone raves : what your rock & roll favorites favor / compiled by Anthony Bozza;
   edited by Shawn Dahl; preface by Matt Pinfield;
   Introduction by Anthony Bozza. —1st. ed.
      p.   cm.
   Includes index.
   ISBN 0-688-16304-1
   1. Rock music—Quotations, maxims, etc.   2. Rock musicians—Quotations.   I. Bozza, Anthony.   II. Dahl, Shawn.
PN6084.R62R66   1999
781.66'092'2—dc21   99–24546
                                      CIP

Printed in the United States of America

First Edition

1 2 3 4 5 6 7 8 9 10

BOOK DESIGN BY BONNI LEON-BERMAN

www.williammorrow.com

www.rollingstone.com

contents

prefacebymattpinfield

IN THE SPRING OF 1983, I was attending Rutgers University and racking up more hours DJ'ing at the campus radio station than studying in any of my classes. As the music and promotion director, I sometimes had to get creative in my quest to land an interview with one of my favorite artists for my show. Although I haven't forgotten a single interview, one adventure stands out most in my mind.

The Cure were coming to New York City to promote their new release, *Pornography*, arguably their darkest record (and that's dark). With themes ranging from drowning to suicide, it was clear that songwriter Robert Smith wasn't in the brightest of spirits. The band's American label, Sire, hadn't invited anyone from my station to the Cure's press conference for college press. So I called their English record company, Fiction, and asked to speak with Chris Parry, who was the label head as well as the Cure's manager (I had gathered that information from reading the Cure's album liner notes). Surprisingly, I got Chris on the phone and convinced him to allow me a one-on-one interview.

One week later, I arrived at Sire Records and was escorted into a conference room full of college DJs and journalists. Robert Smith and drummer

Lol Tolhurst were trying to answer the questions—most of them redundant and absurd: "Do you think new wave will last?" or "Do you like American groups like the Romantics?" and "Why are you so depressed?" Lol looked appalled. Speaking very quietly, Robert soon buried his head in his hands. As the final questions were blurted out, the band looked out the window, silent.

While the record company publicist escorted the interviewers out, I boldly stayed in the room. I approached the band's tour manager, telling him I still had a few questions. He slowly walked over to Robert Smith and whispered in his ear. Robert looked up angrily, crushed the milk carton in his hand and threw it across the room.

I had to think fast. I walked up to Robert, bent down and spoke quietly: "Uh, Robert, I don't really give a fuck about the Cure. I just want to ask you about your mailman, the Cult Hero."

Robert raised his head. He broke into a smile and said, "How the fuck do you know about him?" The ice was broken. Robert and Lol lit up talking about "I'm a Cult Hero," a novelty single they had recorded with their mailman under the name Cult Hero. Luckily, I had asked Chris Parry about the single. "I'm a Cult Hero" was backed with "I Dig You" and, although it was a novelty record, "I Dig You" became a big radio hit on the few alternative stations operating back then. I had assumed there was a Cure connection, and it turns out that the band had lured their elderly and balding mailman (nothing wrong with being bald, of course!) into the studio one afternoon during his route to lay down some vocals. Since I knew about this, the Cure answered every question I had with respect and enthusiasm.

That day, I learned that knowing everything you can about an artist is essential to getting the most out of an interview. One of my favorite sources these days for such inside information is the Raves column in ROLLING STONE. I look forward to it in every issue because there is always something new to learn about a musician—even one I've met or interviewed myself. In the column, the artists are encouraged to let their thoughts run freely about their sources of inspiration and amusement. I assume that, like myself, serious music fans aspire to know as much as they can about an artist—particularly what has driven the artist to create.

One of the best things about working for MTV is the fact that it has enabled me to talk with many of my heroes—a rock child's dream come true—from Lou Reed to U2. And I've gotten to ask the questions that have always plagued me, such as knowing the source for David Bowie's fictional character Ziggy Stardust. Along with the Beatles, the Stones and the Who, it was David Bowie who converted me from a singles-oriented lad to an album-oriented enthusiast: *The Rise and Fall of Ziggy Stardust and the Spiders From Mars* was one of those life-changing albums for me. A couple of years ago, when I was invited to dinner with David Bowie, I was a bit anxious because there were so many myths I hoped to unravel. We spoke for hours that night about everything from his Davey Jones and the King Bees phase to the late, great Mick Ronson. One of the most interesting stories was about the Ziggy character. Bowie explained he had based him on an Australian pop singer named Vince Taylor—the equivalent of America's Fabian and England's heartthrob Billy Fury. Many such teen idols popped up around the world during Elvis's GI days, reigning supreme on the charts. Vince Taylor started to believe his own hype, and beyond that—he became convinced that he was the messiah. Things deteriorated; Vince went completely mad and was almost killed at one of his shows when the crowd turned on him and beat him badly. Then the Beatles and Stones came along and took care of all the teen idols' sorry asses.

That night I told Bowie that he had turned me on to Jacques Brel as a teenager when he covered Brel's "My Death" and "Amsterdam." Had it not been for Bowie's versions, I'm sure many young Brits and Americans would have never heard of Brel or many of the other artists Bowie paid tribute to on his 1973 all-covers album, *Pin Ups*. Metallica is doing the same thing for Nineties kids, by the way, with their recent double-CD *Garage Inc.*

when anthony bozza called to interview *me* for his Raves column, I was blown away. To be included in the pages of ROLLING STONE, which I had read since I was a child, was yet another dream come true. As I'm sure it was for the musicians included in this book, it was extremely hard to narrow down my list of the things I like to rave about to only a few. So I gave Anthony a long list of albums, films, books, etc., and asked him to make the decision about which we would discuss. We met at a Mexican restaurant in Times Square and I had the greatest time talking about all the records that changed my life. To be able to reflect on some of my passions was one of the most rewarding experiences I've been through.

As such a huge music fan, I want to know what the artists who affect me emotionally do with their spare time—what movies they watch, what books they read, what they eat, what they remember from childhood, what they think about other musicians. I want to know about their best gigs and biggest fears. I want to feel a spiritual and soulful connection to the songwriters who touch my life with music. In a simple but beautiful way, the Raves column has done that for me—leaving me hungry for more.

And *more* is what you will find in these pages—the unedited (and unexpurgated) responses of the artists here represent the director's cut of the soundtrack to our lives. Read on and get closer . . .

M A T T P I N F I E L D

A Cohiba cigar after a Peter Luger steak is about as good as it gets—uh, really good sex, *then* a Peter Luger steak. All right—really good sex, then a Peter Luger steak, with a Jack & Jill ice-cream sandwich for dessert and a fine Cuban cigar. *That* produces probably the most euphoric, mellow, alive buzz there is.

—John Popper of Blues Traveler, for Raves interview, 1998

IN 1993, ROLLING STONE launched a column called "Raves," to provide an outlet for the editors to enthuse about a few of their favorite things—obscure bootlegs, public-access television and cult films, for instance—that didn't logically fit anywhere else in the magazine's coverage. The very first enthusiast was senior editor David Fricke, who, in the July 8–22, 1993, issue raved about a bootleg CD of a 1973 New York Dolls rehearsal and seven other albums, a concert (Robyn Hitchcock doing an a cappella version of "Kung Fu Fighting") and a book about 'zines. Soon enough, artists took notice and wanted to get in on the action, starting with Lenny Kravitz in the

November 11, 1993 issue. The column became a well-loved staple for our readers, who flipped to it for new insights into the artists, as well as a short list of books to devour, records to buy and movies to see.

When I took over the column in 1994, rather than having artists answer questionnaires, I conducted interviews—strange and uncharted territory. My first subject was the infamous Ozzy Osbourne, who had matured from his rowdy dove-biting days (see the chapter "You Take the High Road and I'll Take the Low" for the gruesome evidence) into a man of wealth and taste. "I like to walk in the woods on my property," he told me. "I'll sit on an old log and smoke a Havana cigar."

One thing is for certain: As soon as artists start discussing topics dear to their hearts, they loosen right up. John Popper of Blues Traveler, for example, was a regular Raves ticker-tape (witness quote above), holding forth for thirty minutes in a busy bar with scarcely a pause for breath, prompted only by one question: "So, what are some of the things that you're into?" Conversations meant to be brief sometimes stretched as long as an hour and a half, ranging over topical hill and dale. Melissa Auf der Maur of Hole, who collects clothing and paintings from the turn of the century, ended up giving me advice on the proper way to hang a shawl on a wall (a complicated science that she approaches with the precision and ingenuity of McGyver). Sean "Puffy" Combs started our interview giving props to Cyndi Lauper and ended up endorsing a four-hours-a-night sleep regimen—as you may know, Combs has a lot to do during the other twenty. Greg Graffin of Bad Religion, one of the few punk rockers with a Ph.D., chatted about his former day jobs before floating my way an impromptu lecture on the finer points of geology. Unfortunately, as any loyal reader knows, the Raves column isn't exactly the size of *War and Peace*. Within the pages of ROLLING STONE, it's the perfect quick hit. It seemed such a shame, however, to let these telling tidbits go to waste. We've gathered them up and presented them for you in categories and in the back, you'll find an index of the Raves by artist, so you won't miss any of your favorites' favorites. In addition, we combed the magazine's archives to find raves of yore. Since its beginning in 1967, ROLLING STONE has probed artists for their likes and dislikes. We've retrieved in-depth interviews and Q&As with Jim Morrison, Jimi Hendrix, John Lennon and others to glean their "raves." You'll notice how in thirty years passions have changed—and remained the same.

the idea for this book was originally developed two years ago with Eric Flaum, who was ROLLING STONE's beloved production manager for many years. Eric, a zealous music fan who loved the Grateful Dead as much as the Ramones, told me Raves had always been one of his personal raves, and that it was high time that ROLLING STONE collect the column into a book. Most of all, Eric was struck by the fact that artists from such different backgrounds gravitated toward the same things. It's true: Polly Jean Harvey, Lenny Kravitz and Sean "Puffy" Combs are all inspired by the Bible. Rappers love Brian DePalma's *Scarface,* but so does Mick Jones (of the Clash and Big Audio Dynamite). Dave Matthews and Björk are members of the same book club, and it ain't Oprah's—both raved about Georges Battaile's dark and sensual *Story of the Eye.*

Over beery "meetings," Eric and I dreamed up chapter titles, cross-referenced the voluminous material and mused on how we would fill a column of our own raves. Sadly, our friend Eric passed away on March 8, 1996. This book is dedicated to him. It is our hope that ROLLING STONE *Raves: What Your Rock & Roll Favorites Favor* is imbued with Eric's enthusiasm and that you discover within these pages as much about your favorite artists as we have about our own.

there are a few other people who helped to make this book happen: I owe a debt of thanks to ROLLING STONE art director Fred Woodward for inspiring me to do my best. He once told me to think of every article and interview, no matter how small or how short, as one more page in a larger book of work. As you can see, I listened.

Thank you to Noah Tarnow. He did an amazing job of combing the vaults for this book. Many thanks also to the interns who lent me a hand—especially Andrew Simon and Lauren Brown. I also owe a big thank you to Ann Abel for the copious overtime she put in on this book. Her editing skills and attention to the book were very much needed and appreciated.

I thank my mother and grandparents for their unequivocal love, nurturing and support.

And thank you dearly Jancee Dunn for your love, support and more shared laughs per day than I thought humanly possible.

ANTHONY BOZZA

acknowledgments

People are always raving about something at ROLLING STONE. In my early years at the magazine, I'd adamantly defend my late-night (um, early-morning) clubbing because of the thrilling, pounding, fast, thump-thump-thump of techno (a.k.a. *rave*) music moving my soul and feet for hours and hours. In 1992 I actually *enjoyed* sitting next to three RS writers whose very different tastes I found intriguing. At any moment, I'd hear Public Enemy, Guns n' Roses and Nirvana emanating from the nearby cubicles of, respectively, Alan Light, Kim Neely and Chris Mundy. In 1993 I started working with Holly George-Warren at the magazine's newly revived book division, Rolling Stone Press. Her musical passions (and expertise) ranged from classic honky-tonk to poetic punk songstresses, which exposed me to a lot of music I might otherwise have scorned. By 1996 I'd begun playing catch-up on jazz history (Rolling Stone Press was creating the new ROLLING STONE *Jazz and Blues Album Guide*) and listened almost exclusively to jazz at work. This past Christmas I gave about ten people a copy of Miles Davis's recently remastered album *Kind of Blue*. Even though something of a neophyte, I don't hesitate in calling it the best jazz album ever recorded (and I'm certainly not the first or only one to say that).

Within these pages, you'll find such declarations—raves—from more than 250 musicians. Compiling all this information was a daunting task: About half the raves are derived from transcripts (hundreds of pages of interviews! hours of rock-star chat!) that ROLLING STONE's Anthony Bozza acquired in the past couple years as the magazine's Raves editor and Random Notes columnist. While I gleaned the tidbits, more raves were being uncovered via three decades' worth of the magazine's Random Notes, artist profiles and interviews. This keen detective work was conducted by Anthony and Rolling Stone Press's excellent editorial team of Ann Abel and Carrie Smith, as well as interns Tim Siefert, Susan Yusef and Ann Zeidner. They all read countless pages, and I'm grateful for their exhaustive research—and absolutely indebted to every RS writer for getting the quotes we've excerpted here. I especially appreciate Holly's encouragement and guidance in my shaping the manuscript. In addition, Carrie conducted a pair of interviews specifically for this book and pestered every record company publicist to get us many more raves. We'd like to cite Carole Campbell, Steve Martin, Lisa Millman, Heidi Robinson, Sage Robinson, Mark Satlof and Chris Sharp for taking Carrie's calls! Others who have helped along the way: Laura Sandlin, Hannah McCaughey, Michele Shapiro and Roo Reath. Jancee Dunn and Mark Kemp shared their unexpurgated Beck interviews—a pleasure to read, difficult to edit down. Writer Kara Manning compiled and edited the first incarnation of the Raves column, from 1993 to 1995, and Noah Tarnow and Liza Ghorbani have taken over where Anthony left off. Thanks for keeping our inquisitive minds satiated and for getting us some primo material for this book. Rolling Stone Press has many others to acknowledge: ROLLING STONE's Jann S. Wenner, Kent Brownridge, John Lagana, Fred Woodward and Evelyn Bernal; our agent Sarah Lazin, with Tana Osa-Yande, for championing our projects; Eric Flaum for being our guiding light; Russell Anthony Trunk for providing the "drawings of the stars by the stars"; and William Morrow's Paul Bresnick for getting the project rolling and our editor Ben Schafer for heralding the book to the rest of the company. Last but not least, I'd like to give kudos to Anthony Bozza for recognizing the Raves column's potential and for collaborating with us on turning the work into a book.

—Shawn Dahl
March 1999

ROLLINGSTONERAVES

UNDERTHEINFLUENCE

So much music has been made under the influence . . . of other artists. Patti Smith heard the voice of her generation in Bob Dylan's "Like a Rolling Stone," and later had the same effect on Michael Stipe. Jerry Garcia cited John Coltrane as a major influence, and John Popper points to Beethoven's Ninth. Sometimes, however, it goes much deeper than that.

chrissie hynde of thePretenders

I listened to *Moby Grape* a couple of hundred times in 1969, but when I heard it again after it was recently reissued, it blew my mind. I realize how influenced I was by it. It's been in my subconscious the whole time. **1994**

meredith brooks

I have a really strong funk background, but my strongest influence was Chrissie Hynde and the Pretenders. I love Bonnie Raitt, the Ohio Players and Earth, Wind and Fire. Aretha Franklin has easily the greatest voice. My new thing is Edith Piaf. I can't stop. Love her. **1997**

isaac hayes

B.B. King was one of my early influences because he was a blues man and Memphis was a blues town—blues and jazz. A guy named Lucious Coleman, who's a brother of jazz saxophonist George Coleman—also from Memphis—was kind of like my musical mentor. He taught me a lot about Bird and Diz and Miles. I listened to a lot of singers like Nat King Cole and Perry Como and people like that. I was listening to Billie Holiday. And when I was a teenager I sang jazz at a local club in Memphis. I'd see blues bands in the rural areas of Mississippi and Arkansas. One of the first things I heard on the radio, actually, was hillbilly music, which is now country music. But the first orchestra I heard just totally blew me away. All the bows moving the same way—it was just fascinating. I just loved it—all the *sounds*. **1998**

rick nielsen of CheapTrick

Jeff Beck is my favorite guitarist all around. Style, technique, tone. The only things I don't like about him are that he doesn't make enough records and I'm not as good. Not anywhere near. Boy, that kid can play. **1996**

billy corgan of SmashingPumpkins

[Black Sabbath with Ozzy Osbourne]—that's the sonic obsession. Those are some of the best-sounding records ever made. You can argue about the ethics behind them, but that doesn't matter. *Masters of Reality* sounded pretty awesome to my wee ears, with the doubled Ozzy vocals. Right there you pretty much have the Pumpkins' sound: that voice cutting through the thick guitars. **1995**

john wozniak of MarcyPlayground

"Bold as Love" has always been my favorite Hendrix song. The sonic texture, the playing and the lyrics—they're brilliant. Everyone talks about his guitar playing, but his lyrics are so . . . four-dimensional. Incredible voice, too. Listen to "Spanish Castle Magic." **1998**

moby

"I Can See Clearly Now," by Johnny Nash, is my favorite song right now because it's so depressing. I envision some guy going through a self-help class, completely at wits' end and ready to blow his brains out, but he keeps repeating the words to the song, trying to convince himself that things are okay. If you listen to it, it's so desperate. The quality of Nash's voice and everything. I imagine some guy in a one-room apartment in Tulsa, he's the janitor at the local hospital, and his girlfriend left him and he's broke and he's got seven thousand dollars in credit-card debt and his mother is sick with lymphoma or whatever and he's sitting in his apartment trying to tell himself everything's going to be okay. **1997**

montell jordan

Curtis Mayfield's old stuff I love because he had that dope falsetto voice. "Ain't nuthin' said/'Cause Freddy's dead." I was *feeling* it. My song "Irresistible" is kind of a tribute to Curtis. **1998**

bootsy collins

James Brown was in control of everything that was going down with him, and I dug him for that. It was like a big school with James, like psychotic bump school, only deeper. **1978**

darryl "d.m.c." mcdaniels of Run-D.M.C.

Run-D.M.C. gives all honor and praise to the Cold Crush Brothers. When we heard their tapes, it put the heart and fire into Run-D.M.C. **1998**

busta rhymes

George Clinton should be everybody's favorite funkster. He's one of the only originals. Roger Troutman is my man, too. Them is two different types of funks. George Clinton is definitely the father of this whole shit, though. I did a coupla records with him and I sampled him a lot growing up. He made soul shit, he made shit that was jazz feeling, he made shit that was rock feeling. He was a very creative motherfucker, man, and his range of creative abilities was spread between many different areas. **1997**

ben harper The way Bob Marley reached and affected the world— that's why I sing. **1995**

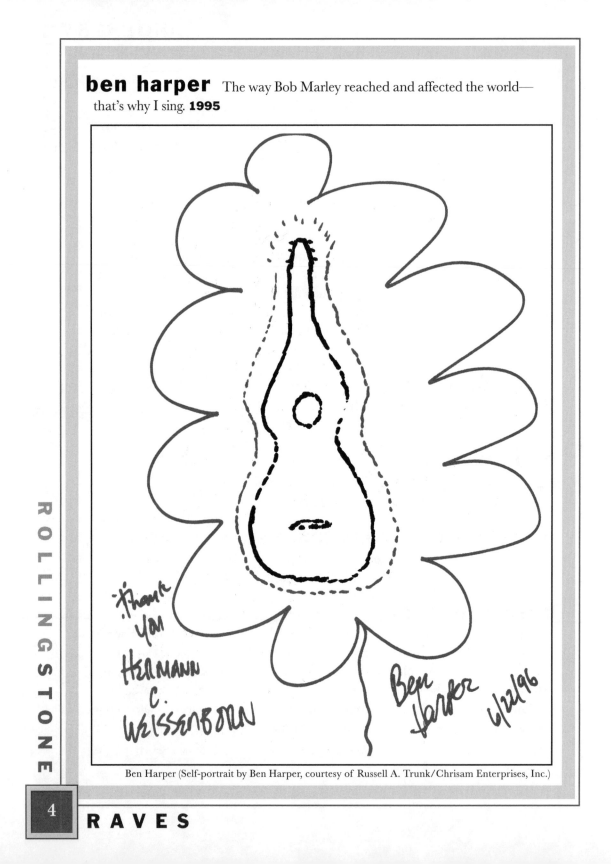

Ben Harper (Self-portrait by Ben Harper, courtesy of Russell A. Trunk/Chrisam Enterprises, Inc.)

sinéad o'connor
Bob Dylan's *Slow Train Coming*, which I heard at thirteen, totally changed my life, made me want to be a singer. It was sexy religious music, which is why I like Bob Marley, too. For an Irish Catholic girl, it was great to hear music that did not separate sexuality from religion. **1997**

john lennon
I still love Little Richard, and I love Jerry Lee Lewis. They're like primitive painters. . . . Chuck Berry is one of the all-time great poets, a rock poet you could call him. He was well advanced of his time lyric-wise. We all owe a lot to him, including Dylan. I've loved everything he's done, ever. He was in a different class from the other performers, he was in the tradition of the great blues artists but he really wrote his own stuff—I know Richard did, but Berry *really* wrote stuff, just the lyrics were fantastic, even though we didn't know what he was saying half the time. **1971**

joni mitchell
At first I thought [Bob Dylan] was a copycat of Woody Guthrie. For a while his originality didn't come out. But when it hit, boy, oh, boy. I said, "Oh, God, look at *this*." And I began to write. So Dylan sparked me. **1991**

johnny cash
Dylan is going to influence anybody that is close to him, I think, as a writer some way or another. He's a powerful talent. **1973**

lou reed
I always go out and get the latest Dylan album. Bob Dylan can turn a phrase, man. Like his last album [*Down in the Groove*], his choice of songs. "Going ninety miles an hour down a dead-end street"—I'd give anything if I could have written that. Or that other one, "Rank Strangers to Me." The key word there is *rank*. . . . For language, Dylan kills me to this day. **1989**

jerry garcia of theGratefulDead
I can only do so many love songs without feeling like an idiot. Dylan's songs go in lots of different directions, and I sing some of his songs because they speak to me emotionally on some level. Sometimes I don't even know why. Like that song "Señor." There's something so creepy about that song, but it's very satisfying in a weird sort of way. Not that I know anything about it, because you listen to the lyrics, and you go, "What the hell is this?" . . . It's like Dylan has written songs that touch into places people have never sung about before. And to me that's tremendously powerful." **1991**

chris barron of SpinDoctors

Bob Dylan and Leonard Cohen—big influences. Dylan and Cohen gave the language of rock a lot of credit. Cohen's really sad. I think he comes closer to poetry, whereas Dylan is more of a performer. Not that Dylan isn't literary, but he's more in an oral tradition than Cohen is. **1994**

patti smith

When [Bob Dylan's] "Like a Rolling Stone" came out, I was in college—I think I was a freshman. It was so overwhelming that nobody went to class. We were just roaming around, talking about this song. I didn't know what Dylan was talking about in the song. But it didn't matter. It needed no translation. It just made you feel like you weren't alone—that someone was speaking your language. **1996**

ana da silva of theRaincoats

It was twenty years ago that I got Patti Smith's *Horses*. I wanted to play it all the time, but I didn't want to get sick of it, so I ended up playing the first half in the morning and the last in the evening. **1996**

michael stipe of R.E.M.

Patti Smith's *Horses* was really visceral. It grabbed me like nothing else I'd heard before. There was something that was very real, very no-bullshit. And in 1976, there wasn't much of that around. **1996**

dan wilson of Semisonic

I try to learn from R.E.M. a little bit in terms of lyrics. If a line in a song can mean two really different things and can hide some of what the song's about, I think it all turns out for the best. If there's something to discover later and it's not all too straightforward. I tried to learn that from listening to Michael Stipe a lot. I definitely didn't learn that from Prince—"We can fuck until the dawn." **1998**

jim kerr of SimpleMinds

The first album I bought was David Bowie's *The Rise and Fall of Ziggy Stardust and the Spiders From Mars*. It sounds like overdramatizing to say this record changed my life . . . but it did. **1995**

joan jett

When I got into the glitter stuff and I moved to California with my family, I got even more into David Bowie, T. Rex, Sweet. Suzi Quatro was a huge thing to me, 'cause I never had seen a woman play rock & roll. And to see her with her bass, screaming, really inspired me. I thought, well, if she can do it, I can do it, and if I can do it, then there's got to be other girls out there that are thinking about doing this. **1997**

stevie nicks

Joni Mitchell's *Court and Spark* was a very big influence. My relationship with Lindsey [Buckingham] was coming to an end. Not only was it music I loved to listen to, but she really helped me put everything into perspective. She wrote songs that were perfect for me while I was trying to figure out what I was going to do. **1994**

paula cole

Kate Bush's *Hounds of Love* was influential to me at that pivotal point in my life when I was wondering if I was going to be a jazz singer struggling financially through life in depressing lounge gigs or I was going to write my own music. After hearing *Hounds of Love,* it became clear that I should choose the latter. She made it acceptable to be audacious and bizarre and passionate. **1998**

k.d. lang

Patsy Cline goes without saying. She really initiated the whole first era of k.d. lang—the whole country-punk thing. Her early stuff was kind of rockabilly with a sense of humor: "I love your money, I love you honey, most of all I love your automobile"—stuff like that. She'd also do some swing and a little bit of jazz. For that day and age, it was quite different. She was a little bit hipper than the rest of the country people at that time. A bit of a shit-disturber. **1997**

erykah badu

I was greatly influenced by the Seventies music that my mom listened to. Stevie Wonder, Chaka Khan, Miles Davis. She had good taste. I heard these things from the womb, so I just came out a soulful baby. **1997**

ian thornley of BigWreck

Folk was my big thing growing up. My mother had a real taste for sweet melodies—certain Beatles stuff and a lot of Supertramp. So that was at my disposal for listening pleasure. The first rock record I bought was *Led Zeppelin III*—the acoustic mellow one. That got me into rock because a few tunes on that album really kicked. **1998**

polly jean harvey

Blues is what I grew up listening to. I was very lucky to have parents with a fine, fine record collection. God knows what I'd have turned out like if I didn't. I was brought up listening to [John Lee] Hooker, to Howlin' Wolf, to Robert Johnson and a lot of [Jimi] Hendrix and [Captain] Beefheart. So I was exposed to all these very compassionate musicians at a very young age, and that's always remained in me and seems to surface more as I get older and have more experience myself. **1995**

billie joe armstrong of

GreenDay

Elvis Presley's *The Sun Sessions* was the first record I ever bought. I lucked out with that one. I remember I wanted to buy an Elvis record because I had just seen one of his movies and he looked the best on the

Polly Jean Harvey (Maria Mochnacz/Island)

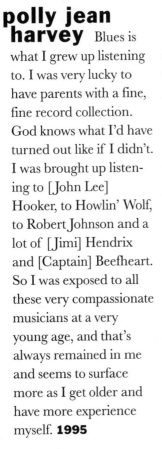

cover of *Sun Sessions,* so I got that one. The pompadour—that was the coolest part. **1998**

dicky barrett of theMightyMightyBosstones

For my eighth birthday my brother gave me Aerosmith's *Toys in the Attic.* If you listen to it, you'll see how it would appeal to an eight-year-old. The songs are really catchy. Plus it had toys on the cover. As soon as I put it down I went and played with my toys—what a way to get into rock & roll. **1997**

lisa loeb Queen's *Night at the Opera* was the first album I obsessed over. It is

the perfect children's album: super-dramatic, every song sounds different than the one before it, and the cover is white with an embossed crest on the front that has a lot of pink in it. Pink is my favorite color, so that was very thrilling to me. **1997**

edwyn collins The Buzzcocks' *Spiral Scratch* was an inspiration and

an aspiration for me and my first band, Orange Juice. It had a breakdown of the recording costs on the sleeve, and it only amounted to a couple of hundred pounds. Self-produced, self-packaged and very crude, it made the mystique of records suddenly accessible. **1995**

tommy lee of MötleyCrüe

Two things made me want to be a musician: Kiss's *Alive* and Van Halen. Kiss weren't on the radio that much, but that album, with its double gatefold, I saw these fucking freaks and bombs blowing up and this drum set that was bigger than anything I had ever seen—it freaked me out. That was the beginning of the end. Shortly after that I remember Van Halen's debut record. Eddie Van Halen's guitar fucking freaked me out. Eddie Van Halen had me air-guitaring, and Peter Criss's drum set flipped me out. That got me doing the cardboard boxes and setting up these pretend drum sets and thinking I was just the full-blown rock star. I was that guy, jumping up and down on my bed in the mirror thinking I was Eddie Van Halen or with my drumsticks up in the air like I was Peter Criss. Fucking weird, huh? **1997**

steven page of BarenakedLadies

I was fifteen when Elvis Costello's *Blood and Chocolate* came out. I remember lying in bed late at night listening to "I Want You." I was transfixed; I was paralyzed. It

9

still sounds so great, so raw, so urgent. I've had the opportunity to meet him three times, but I've shied away. What's he gonna say to me: "Good luck with your little band"? **1998**

29Sept/94

Steven Page of Barenaked Ladies (Self-portrait by Steven Page, courtesy of Russell A. Trunk/Chrisam Enterprises, Inc.)

stephan jenkins of ThirdEyeBlind

David Bowie's Ziggy Stardust era and Camper Van Beethoven were a huge influence on me. Camper Van Beethoven is underrated. I would go to their concerts and it was like church, and other people were like, "It sucked." I couldn't believe it. I loved the sense of whimsy and wild possibilities and joy. David Lowery's lyrics were so amazing. I am on a quest to get them to re-form—help me in this—and come on tour with us. That's my goal. Actually, the name Third Eye Blind comes from Camper Van Beethoven. It's a play on words and I liked the whole wit, the snappy name. There's their album *Eye of Fatima* so Third Eye Blind came from that. I took that tape, a Walkman and a backpack across Europe, plus Jane's Addiction's *Nothing's Shocking*. That's all I listened to. **1997**

rupaul

I have two copies of Cher's *It's a Man's World*, the European one and the American one. The European one came out first. On the American one, they remixed a lot of the songs. I like the European one better. It has more songs and is a little more rocking. She was on my show once and as soon as she hit the stage, we were just yapping and yapping so they just let the cameras run and it turned into two shows. One was a proper show and the other was uncensored with bits of us just *doin'* it. She's like a long-lost friend. We hit it off like gangbusters. More than with any other idol I've ever met. With Cher, you can be yourself: You can say *fuck* and *shit* and *pussy,* and that's how I talk anyway. At one point we were taking some pictures and she didn't like the way her face looked in one because she was scowling, so she said, "Ru, say something funny." I said, "Pussy." And she just busted up. We had a great time. She's a no-bullshit person, and the most rocking cool chick you ever want to meet. **1997**

chris whitley

I heard Nat King Cole's "China Gate" once, years ago. I couldn't remember the title and I looked for it for years—I knew it was China something. I found it later on his soundtrack album *At the Movies*. It was from this 1957 Vietnam movie of the same name. It's supposed to be a fucked-up antiwar movie—it came out before the Vietnam War, even. It's so deep. Really slow and really sparse. His singing is great. There are Chinese instruments and a giant, dark symphony. His voice is such a killer. Nat King Cole is my male role model. **1997**

aretha franklin

My father used to play Oscar Peterson and Dorothy Donegan records for me, and what he was trying to get me to do then is just beginning to come out now. He really put the big bad ones on me—Erroll Garner and Art Tatum, too. **1971**

whitney houston Being around people like Aretha Franklin and Gladys Knight, Dionne Warwick and Roberta Flack, all these greats, I was taught to listen and observe. It had a great impact on me as a singer, as a performer, as a musician. Growing up around it, you just can't help it. I identified with it immediately. It was something that was so natural to me that when I started singing, it was almost like speaking. **1993**

coolio Aretha Franklin sang her songs like she wrote them—even though she mostly didn't. She was just really feeling what she was saying. And I love everything Al Green's ever done. The raw edge to his voice. He's a natural. **1995**

bob seger I don't think anything ever killed me like Little Richard's *Greatest Hits* did—the energy of his voice! He's one of my all-time favorite artists. I always wished I could sing like him. **1996**

jewel Ella Fitzgerald really got me into perfecting my voice—just listening to her ability, her skill. Ella Fitzgerald's voice I enjoyed more than Billie Holiday's, because it was more versatile and more playful. It just made me feel better to listen to her. **1997**

flea of theRedHotChiliPeppers
I liked Dizzy Gillespie and Louis Armstrong because I wanted to be a trumpet player. I heard rock music, but it sounded stupid to me. . . . But when I met Hillel [Slovak, the Chili Peppers' first guitarist, who died in 1988] he started playing lots of rock music for me, and I got into Led Zeppelin and Jimi Hendrix. And for rock music, the Sixties was without a doubt the most innovative, expressive time. To me the greatest thing that happened after that was punk rock. You can't be a relevant rock musician today without knowing punk rock and understanding it. **1994**

fatboy slim The Jungle Brothers are really a big, big influence on me. They are the dons as far as I'm concerned. I kiss the stage they walk on. **1998**

noel gallagher of Oasis
The first band I felt a part of were the Jam. I was a teenager, and they were the

best group in England. Paul Weller was the coolest pop singer. Totally. The Jam always had a single out every three months, which is what Oasis tries to emulate. **1995**

duncan sheik I'm a huge David Sylvian fan. The late Talk Talk records are really very important to me. And things like the Blue Nile and the Cocteau Twins are sort of where I come from. **1997**

Duncan Sheik (Nitin Vadukul/Atlantic)

nick hexum of 311

Hearing the Clash was the first explosion in my frontal lobe. It was the first album that I liked that my parents made me turn off. That was part of the appeal. **1997**

mix master mike of InvisiblSkratchPiklz and theBeastieBoys

I love Miles Davis's "Autumn Leaves." Old, cool jazz. I study the patterns, the way he plays his notes, and incorporate that into my scratching. The silence is key. **1998**

jerry garcia of theGratefulDead

I've been influenced a lot by [John] Coltrane, but I never copped his licks or sat down and listened to records and tried to play his stuff. I've been impressed with that thing of flow, and of making statements that to my ears sound like paragraphs. **1982**

john popper of BluesTraveler

Beethoven's Ninth is arguably the finest piece of music ever written. Musically, there is so much to steal from it. I listen to it in my car and I keep finding something new—melodies, countermelodies, harmonies. The way he moves his phrases throughout. There's a ton of countermelodies you don't even notice—you have to keep listening, and they're in there. **1998**

billy joel
Beethoven was writing rock & roll before there was such a thing, in terms of the passion and the sex drive, even his playfulness with rhythm. He was very heavy-handed, too. **1999**

sean lennon
I really like jazz, Brazilian music, funk. Those are things my dad wasn't into. I can imagine him saying, "Why are you doing this fake jazz shit on your record? What is this crap?" . . . My mom's sixty-five. She doesn't come from the Sixties. The music she grew up listening to was not the Beatles. She grew up listening to *Three Penny Opera*, and that's what she turned me on to. Schönberg. Wagner. Some serious shit. "Listen to John Cage, prepared piano." That's the stuff that was important to her. **1998**

aphex twin a.k.a. Richard James

I quite like Karlheinz Stockhausen a lot. He's a German avant-garde experimenter from the Fifties, and it's fucking awesome. It's like generators and tapes, and I have a feeling it's the first of its kind. It sounds completely twisted. The thing is with most old music, you have to think going in, this is from the Sixties or whatever—you have to know the time period to understand how amazing it sounds. But Stockhausen's stuff is art that is seriously insane. You put it on and you'll just go like, "What's this?" You *don't* need to say, "It was done in the Fifties," to make it sound amazing. But when you realize that as well, then you know this bloke is completely nuts. **1997**

art alexakis of Everclear

One of the things I keep coming back to, over and over again, are the Pixies. I knew at the time how influential they were, but no one else seemed to. *Doolittle* is fucking phenomenal. I loved *Surfer Rosa* and when *Doolittle* came out, I was working an office job in San Francisco—a suit-and-tie job. I wasn't really happy in my life. I couldn't get a band going and I was bumming out. On my lunch hour I walked to this pretty shitty record store downtown and saw *Doolittle* on sale for like fifteen bucks for just the cassette. I didn't care; I bought it, man. I threw it in my Walkman, started walking back to work listening to "Debaser." I got to right around the corner from work and I called in sick and got on a bus. I fucking just took that bus all over San Francisco for like three hours, listening to that album over and over. When I got home, I told my wife, "Look, this is bullshit. I'm starting a band tomorrow." **1996**

alec empire of Atari Teenage Riot

Underground Resistance's *Riot* EP is a very important record to me—it even influenced Atari Teenage Riot, which was just forming at the time it came out, after the Los Angeles riots. *Riot* was really the only good thing that happened in techno because Underground Resistance linked statements to the records. It has such a spontaneous sound to it, which I miss on most of the electronic records today—perfectly programmed, but missing the vibe. **1997**

mark mcgrath of Sugar Ray

I'm the trendiest music fan ever. I look at myself as a fan before being a musician. And not in some garage, staring at the wall, coming up with some song that I think everyone wants to hear, because I want to hear the world's songs. I'm a fan. If you look at my record collection, you can document my musical inspirations. I liked So. Cal. punk in the early Eighties, and then rockabilly for a couple of months, and then I was into Mod, and then I got into death rock with Specimen and the whole Bat Cave club bullshit. Then, like, heavy metal just ripped my ass apart—I became a freak with long hair, wristbands and everything. Then *Nevermind* destroyed heavy metal for everybody. It was over. I loved metal, the late Eighties—the Sunset Strip. I got into hip-hop along the way. I used to be a break dancer. I'm just a trendy, kooky music fan. But every time I went to a new trend I never threw away all my records. I kept listening to them. If you look at my record collection, I can put on Lords of the New Church, G.G. Allin, Figures on a Beach, Trixter, Loudness and Public Enemy. I've ripped off everybody I know to form Sugar Ray—I'm not a musician, I'm just a guy that borrows a lot. **1997**

Mark McGrath of Sugar Ray (Self-portrait by Mark McGrath, courtesy of Russell A. Trunk/Chrisam Enterprises, Inc.)

RAVES

OHTOBEACHILD

hildhood, that most tender and impressionable phase of life, brings to mind hazy remembrances of a more innocent time. Pony rides, imaginary friends, marbles, *Thin Lizzy*—these are the things a rock child's dreams are made of.

kim thayil of Soundgarden

In school, if someone did something bad in class and the teacher wanted to know who did it, I was always the kid whose eyes started shifting around: "Maybe it *was* me. Was it me? I don't *think* I did it, but maybe it was me." She keeps looking at me. "Fuck, I *did* do it, she thinks I did it . . . " **1994**

terence trent d'arby

I had very vivid memories at two. I remember running around the house and singing the Beatles' "She Loves You" and "I Want to Hold Your Hand." Butt naked. **1994**

dave matthews The Beat-

les made me dream about making music when I was five or six. I started not thinking about Little League or any of that. All I did from when I was five to when I was about ten was listen to the Beatles; I was obsessed. **1996**

erykah badu One of my

momma's favorites was Deniece Williams's *This Is Niecy*—I played it yesterday. I love her voice and what she sung, especially in the song "Free": "I just got to be free/Got to be me." I was digging that, even as a kid. It made me want to spin around and spin around and spin around until I fell down. I'd usually be outside in the backyard doing that by myself. The trees would be haloed over the garage and over the whole yard, I would look through the branches while I was spinning around while the song would be playing through the back door. That was real cool. **1998**

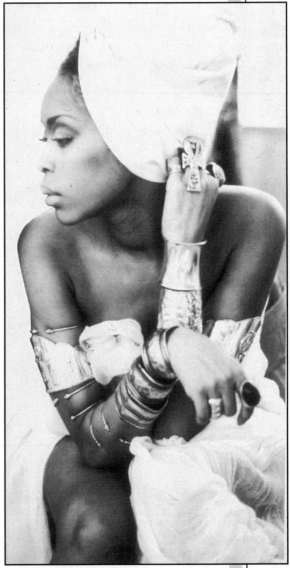

Erykah Badu (Imari Dusauzay/Kedar Entertainment)

lenny kravitz

I was lucky because my parents were into music. So I've seen everybody from Duke Ellington to Count Basie to Ella Fitzgerald to Sarah Vaughan to Miles Davis to Bobby Short at the Cafe Carlyle to James Brown at the Apollo to opera. But my first musical memory is that song "Born Free." My grandmother said I used to love that record when I was about two years old. **1994**

"weird al" yankovic

"Mama Get the Hammer (There's a Fly on the Baby's Head)," by Bobby Peterson is a song I heard in my childhood and it's been stuck in my cranium ever since. That and "You Light Up My Life" by Debby Boone. Which is similar in an odd way. **1997**

janet jackson

The Secret Life of Plants is one of my favorite Stevie Wonder albums, the one that made me feel like I was drowning in beauty. When I'd get home from school, I'd pop this puppy on the stereo, slap on the headphones and just soak up the gorgeous melodies. Escaping. **1993**

van morrison

I remember my father took me into town one day, and there was this jazz band playing on the back of a truck. I was, like, five. I got into it, because I saw people blowing horns and saxophones and singing. I thought it was great that people could do that. So I suppose in terms of why I got into it, it would be for all the wrong reasons. It wasn't about being a star or wearing certain clothes or having a certain image. It was just the idea that people could get up and sing and play. **1990**

elvis costello

The first records I ever owned were "Please Please Me" and "The Folksinger," by John Leyton. I was at a little bit of an advantage because my father was still with Joe Loss [Orchestra] then—he used to get quite a lot of records because they would cover the hits of the day. He'd often have demonstration copies, even acetates; as late as 1966, Northern Songs would still send Beatles acetates out to the orchestras to garner covers for radio play. I've got them at home. I was into singles, whatever was on the radio—the Kinks, the Who, Motown. It was exciting. . . . I was in the Beatles fan club when I was eleven; I used to buy the magazines. The one kind of music that I *didn't* like was rock & roll—as a distinct [classic] form. . . . My dad went a bit psychedelic around the edges, about 1968. He grew his hair quite long; he used to give me Grateful Dead records and [Jefferson Airplane's] *Surrealistic Pillow*. I'd keep them for a couple of weeks, and then sell them at the record exchange and buy Marvin Gaye records.

When I went to live in Liverpool, I discovered everyone was still into acid rock—and I used to hide my Otis Redding records when friends came around. I didn't want to be out of step. At the age of sixteen it's really crucial that you're in—and I tried hard to like the Grateful Dead. **1982**

noel gallagher of Oasis

The Beatles' Red and Blue compilations [*The Beatles 1962–1966* and *The Beatles 1967–1970*] are my favorite records because they were the first ones I ever had as a kid. **1995**

sean "puffy" combs a.k.a. Puff Daddy

I grew up in the prime time of hip-hop, when it was just getting off the ground. From Run-D.M.C. to KRS-One to the Beastie Boys to L.L. Cool J. I was there. I seen that. I would be twelve years old, and sometimes I'd be out until three, four in the morning, seeing the music. I had to sneak out to do it, but I was doing it. **1997**

tori amos
I would get lonely sometimes when other children didn't want to come and play with me. I had millions of friends from the other world. As a little girl, you play with who you can, and if they're not in human form, they're still very real to you. Let's put it this way: It's never lonely in my Toyota 4-Runner. **1998**

rufus wainwright
Melissa Auf der Maur [of Hole] and I grew up together. I was in love with her and she was in love with me when we were about twelve. We were the same height at that point, which was quite small. We were nervous and embarrassed and just never expressed it. The world was too fast for our love. She had a massive growth spurt and was two feet taller than I was the next year. She was developing all sorts of little toys and suddenly I went from her true love to the mascot for her and her cool friends. I was her beast of burden. She had me along when she needed little jobs done and then disappeared. We're friends now, though, of course. **1998**

steven tyler of Aerosmith

For the most part, to be creative you gotta be a child. You gotta be true to the crib. **1994**

RAVES

marilyn manson

In many ways, I wish that I could start all over and once again appreciate the taboos. It would be great to be innocent again. . . . I was never afraid of what was under the bed. I wanted it. I wanted it more than anything. And I never got it. I just *became* it. **1997**

liz phair

I believe in ghosts. I used to think I was a witch when I was little. I had a lot of magic in my life when I was a kid. And I refuse to lose it, because it isn't something that was just a game. It was how I knew my place in the universe. **1994**

madonna

I used to dance in front of my mirror to the Isley Brothers, to "Who's that lady, beautiful lady, sexy lady," but I just assumed I was that sexy lady. Of course, I was desperate for that to be the truth. **1994**

mike d of theBeastieBoys

The greatest education that I got was at my own dinner table. I look at the true privilege of how we grew up not being so much economic—there's no question we

Beastie Boys: Adam Yauch, Adam Horovitz and Mike Diamond (from left) (Danny Clinch/Grand Royal/Capitol)

were very fortunate—but the privilege really came out in an intellectual and geographic way. We were constantly exposed to these total New York characters. **1994**

isaac hayes

I'm from Memphis. It's a musical town. As a young kid—around ten, eleven, twelve years old—I stood on garbage cans and looked in clubs and watched the jazz and blues musicians there. We had picnics outside our church when I was a little kid. Guys were playing flutes with a bass drum and snare drum and I was just so fascinated by it. I was maybe six or seven years old. Of course, I grew up in the church and I would see my cousins play piano and the choir singing. I was fascinated with that, too. **1998**

bonnie raitt

From the time I was seven or eight, I was a tomboy with a vengeance. When you are the one girl in a family of boys, and your dad relates to the boys well—well, I just couldn't stand the way girls got the second best of everything. They couldn't throw as far. They weren't paid as much. To me, it was the same as black people getting treated as second-class citizens. So I always stayed out and played longer and hit the ball farther and had tough hands and all that. **1990**

gwen stefani of NoDoubt

My dad used to read Dr. Seuss books to us all the time. And probably one of my favorite songs is "Rainbow Connection," sung by Kermit the Frog—it's such a great song—the banjo and the words. I think of it and I get shivers. The original *Muppet Movie* rules. It's that same story I love, you know, "I'm gonna make it." That's my favorite story. **1996**

lil' kim

When I was a little girl, I read *Rainbow Jordan*, by Alice Childress. It's about a young girl that's seen a lot in her life and patterns herself after her mom. She just grew up hard, straight from the streets. Basically, I identified with her. I really felt her. She goes through a real real tough time and at the end she gets herself together. **1997**

lisa loeb

A lot of my childhood memories are associated with food. Like the *Sesame Street* episode when Ernie ordered thirty-one flavors of ice cream and they put them on in the wrong order so they had to flip them over again. Or like the math problems you learned by counting how many pieces of pizza there were. And I loved the pie chef and the cake, and the chocolate cake part with Ernie and Bert. **1997**

jerry garcia of theGratefulDead

[My mother] was a registered nurse, but after my father died, she took over his bar. He had this little bar right next door to the Sailor's Union of the Pacific, the merchant marine's union, right at First and Harrison, in San Francisco. It was a daytime bar, a working guy's bar, so I grew up with all these guys who were sailors. They went out and sailed to the Far East and the Persian Gulf, the Philippines and all that, and they would come and hang out in the bar all day long and talk to me when I was a kid. It was great fun for me. I mean, that's my background. I grew up in a bar. And that was back in the days when the Orient was still the Orient, and it hadn't been completely Americanized yet. **1991**

perry farrell of Jane'sAddiction and PornoforPyros

I had older brothers and sisters, and the best times I remember are when they'd crank up the radio or play records out on the balcony where we lived in Queens [New York]. I'd hang out with them, and I could dance pretty good. I remember thinking, "These guys are cool." In high school [in Florida], I was into David Bowie and Lou Reed, but I didn't know they were punk rock. It wasn't labeled yet, but these guys were fucking out there. When I got to California, I saw it firsthand. Pretty awesome. **1995**

graham nash of Crosby,StillsandNash

My father [took] pictures as an avid amateur photographer. He used a little dark-room, which was my bedroom, and he would block out the windows with a blanket and go to it. I saw beautiful images of giraffes, elephants, my mother pregnant, and all sorts of family things permeating my consciousness from a very early age. The vision and smell of all that magic has been with me to this day. **1979**

nick cave

I was riding my bicycle home from school, and I found this dead guy in an alley just by the river that went past the school. I had a few moments to poke around at the body before I raced back to tell the teachers about it. **1996**

huey of FunLovin'Criminals

There was a kid in my neighborhood on the Lower East Side we called Skisuity. His mother used to dress him up in a ski suit—it was blue with white stripes down the arms and legs—and when he would walk down the street, everyone would shout out, "SKISUITY!" One day he threw a kid out his window and then moved down to Chinatown with his family. We used to go down there on our bikes and see him and shout, "SKISUITY!" And he'd flip out and chase us and try to kill us. He was, like, ten, when he threw that kid out. He was really pressured, though. Imagine that, summer, winter, fall, spring—"SKISUITY!" I almost wrote a song about Skisuity. But he's a grown man now. Imagine he's in a bar, hanging out with some girl, and he hears "SKISUITY!" He starts screaming, runs off, maybe jumps off a building, I didn't want to be responsible for that. There was a guy named Blue Boy, too, who had a birthmark on his hairline, but it came down over his ear and it was, like, bluish. We'd shout, "BLUEBOY!" **1998**

eric clapton
There was a funny Saturday-morning radio program for children, with this strange person, Uncle Mac. He was a very old man with one leg and a strange little penchant for children. He'd play things like "Mule Train," and then every week he'd slip in something like a Buddy Holly record or a Chuck Berry record. And the first blues I ever heard was on that program; it was a song by Sonny Terry and Brownie McGhee, with Sonny Terry howling and playing the harmonica. It blew me away. I was ten or eleven. **1985**

lindsey buckingham of FleetwoodMac
We were in the fifth grade, my friend and I, and we had a little section of my backyard that was just all woods. Very small. My friend and I had just been to Disneyland, and we went on the jungle cruise. When we got back, we went out into the backyard and dug a little river, filled it with water from the garden hose and made our own jungle. It was great—we even had sound effects. I dragged a speaker from the record player out there and put on a sound-effects record so we'd have noises: *Oooook ooook akkkk!* Jungle noises. I don't think many kids did things like that. **1980**

scott weiland of StoneTemplePilots
I was a pretty apathetic and lonely kid. I guess I never felt that I was liked very much. When I was younger, the only friend I really had was an imaginary friend named Poogus. I used to blame things on him. **1993**

whitney houston
The disadvantage of growing up with two boys is that you can't do *anything*. If they saw me with a boy, it was like . . . "Who's *that?*"

RAVES

I was totally like, "Oh, God, *please,* just go away. The advantage was that I knew all the raps. I knew all the shit that guys could lay on you from A to Z. I got to hear how guys talk about girls. **1993**

babyface
As a small boy I played out my love fantasies by pressing a guitar to my heart and strumming little stories. I'm still doing that. It's just that more people are listening. **1994**

m. doughty of SoulCoughing
When I was a kid, my life was about going home and lipsynching to Thin Lizzy records. **1996**

neil diamond
I was a Brooklyn cowboy. When I was a teenager, I used to take people riding at the Brooklyn Riding Academy. And I always loved the singing-cowboy movies. And on the back of comic books there was always that ad where kids could get free gifts if you sold enough greeting cards, and my eyes always went right to that guitar—there was always a guy on a horse with a cowboy hat and a guitar. **1988**

luther vandross
I remember I was thirteen years old and I was living in [New York, in] the Alfred E. Smith projects downtown, near Chinatown. Murray the K was the big DJ of the day. And at a place called the

Neil Diamond (Neal Preston/©1998 Neil Diamond)

Brooklyn Fox Theater he would give shows every Easter and every Christmas and they would have the Four Seasons, the Shirelles, Patti LaBelle and the Blue Belles, etc., and the Angels with "My Boyfriend's Back." I was sitting there, the next act was about to come on and the music started. Then all of a sudden you hear *"hmmm, hmmm, hmmm."* And this woman with a very exotic look and a red spaghetti-strap dress—chiffon—started singing, "Anyone who ever loved, could look at me and all that I love." It was Dionne Warwick. She single-handedly is the reason why *I* wanted a career singing. No male singer has ever influenced me— only female singers, and she was the first. The sheer beauty of her voice carried me—and her—away. The way she pierced me with what she was putting down on that microphone and to that audience was something I wished one day I would be able to do. **1997**

john tesh When I was in school, every weekend I was one of those guys who used to go to wherever Jethro Tull was. That's the band to see, if you're going to see a band live. They're all brilliant musicans. Anyone that can play flute like that, standing on one leg. **1997**

boy george of CultureClub

I remember as a kid, we never really went on any kind of exotic holiday, we usu-ally went inland. The first time I left England was with Culture Club. I never flew before I was about twenty. A lot of my friends went to Spain and all these places and I'd sort of go to a local seaside resort. I can remember being a kid—I came from quite a big family—and we would sort of go to the beach and then we'd go to the fairgrounds. And there was never really enough money for everyone to go on everything, so whoever shouted the loudest got their own way. **1998**

sean "puffy" combs a.k.a Puff Daddy

My biggest childhood idols were Muhammad Ali and my mother. The best advice she gave me was "Better go beat him up." One day I came home and I was crying and told her how this little boy hit me. She told me I better go back out there and beat him up and don't come back home until you do. I mean it's a big part of life, you gotta fight to survive in this world, man. You can't just let nobody beat you up without beating him up back. I was maybe eleven. You know what it really was, though? He stole my skateboard. I didn't actually go beat him up. I got one of my older friends to help me, to be honest. **1997**

method man of Wu-TangClan

We was terrorists on Halloween. We'd go egging and candy-bag snatching all day. There was a motherfucker who owned a corner store and he never liked to give niggas groceries for free when they needed a little help, never hired anybody from the community either. He'd get rushed every time. We'd steal all the eggs up out his joint. If he had been decent with the community, we wouldn't a fucked with him. **1998**

michael stipe of R.E.M.

There was a fellow in Texas named Mr. Pemberton, who had a record store. He was really old and looked really mean. But he was really nice, and he used to give me and my sister the singles he didn't need anymore, the ones that wouldn't sell. So we got Tammy Wynette, the Beatles and Elvis. And Roger Miller—he had a song called "Skip a Rope." That song had a profound influence on me. **1992**

tina turner My role model was always Jacqueline Kennedy Onassis.
My taste was high. So when it came to role models, I looked at presidents' wives. Of course, you're talking about a farm girl who stood in the fields, dreaming, years ago, wishing she was that kind of person. But if I had been that kind of person, do you think I could sing with the emotions I do? **1986**

WOULDYOULIKEFRIESWITHTHAT?

Everyone's got to start somewhere. Even Brian Wilson. Even Ann Wilson. Instruments cost money and those bar gigs never pay much. Nothing wrong with a job on the side—it doesn't mean sacrificing an iota of artistic integrity. Plus, four out of five studies show that crap jobs kick careers into gear faster than hefty advances.

mike ness of SocialDistortion

My first job was at a porno shop, as a clerk. I loved that job. Sunday nights I would turn on Rodney on KROQ, order a pizza and a six-pack of beer and "study" the world of pornography. **1998**

steven tyler of Aerosmith

I worked the land. I used to mow the lawn, build roads and dig out ponds. That's why I still have the frame I have—from getting up early and busting my hump. **1979**

brian wilson

My first job was working at Vic Tanny's Gym. I went to the gym at night, after it had closed, and vacuumed the floors. When I was eighteen years old, I was hired to stack lumber at some company in Hawthorne, California, where I grew up, and that was the worst job I ever had. All I remember is my hands full of splinters. After two months I had to call it quits. Thank goodness I did. Our first hit came about nine months later, so I saved my hands for playing music with the Beach Boys. **1998**

Brian Wilson (Neal Preston/Giant)

stephen malkmus of Pavement

I painted curbs in suburbia. It was totally under the table—the guy didn't have a real business license. That was fun—my high school summer job on the hot streets of Stockton, California. **1997**

billy joel

I went to the West Coast. I just disappeared. I really didn't want to leave, but I had to get out of these contracts [with Ripp and Paramount], and I didn't want these people to know what I was doing. I used the name Bill Martin and got a gig in a piano bar for about six months. It was all right. I got free drinks and union scale, which was the first steady money I'd made in a long time. I took on this whole alter identity, totally make-believe; I *was* Buddy Greco, collar turned up and shirt unbuttoned halfway down. The characters that Steve Martin and Bill Murray did as a goof, I was doing too, only people didn't know I was kidding. They thought, "Wow, this guy is really hip!" **1980**

perry farrell of Jane'sAddiction and PornoforPyros

I worked delivering liquor, and that led to a job at a strange private club in Newport Beach. They asked me to "model and dance." They were also pushing prostitution. I had to wear a Speedo. It was pretty sleazy stuff. I bullshitted my way into being the star attraction every weekend. Then I wanted to try singing, because there's not many things I'm better suited for. I don't know—I just *look* like a singer. I feel like I'm a prostitute or an erotic dancer—I go out there and the vibe is really a sex vibe. **1991**

billy idol

In England I worked as a postal worker at night in between college. It was pretty easy, and I liked working at night. But basically, all jobs seemed unromantic, undramatic dead ends. One night I was singing to myself, "Don't Be Cruel," by Elvis Presley, or a Lou Reed song, "Vicious" or something, and a bloke said the classic, "Don't ever try singing for a living." Eleven albums and a career spanning the world and I can still hear him saying it to me. Ha ha! **1998**

andy partridge of XTC

The first job I had was in a newspaper office running messages from desk to desk. Most of the day was spent getting hangover cures for the reporters. The last job I had was painting posters in a department store. At the time we were already touring around Britain. I'd be in Dundee or something and call in and say, "I've got a cold." It just got to be too much; I couldn't come up with any more illness excuses. But, then again, it wasn't a stressful job. I'd sit there painting posters, drinking beer, listening to music. And trying to seduce the young girls in the window-dressing department. One day two men came in, they were reps trying to sell some product. About ten minutes later, one of these beautiful girls from window dressing came up and said, "There's a man in my office having a shit in my waste paper bin." And we were like, yeah, right. She came back five minutes later and said, "Honestly, he's gone now, but he's had a shit in my waste paper bin, one of these men in the suits." And sure enough, one of them had walked into her office and shit in her bin. **1998**

david cassidy
My first and worst job was working for a textile company in the mailroom when I was eighteen years old. I had just graduated from high school and moved back to New York. There were six other people working in the mailroom with me, four men and two women. They made me cut my hair, which at the time was shoulder length, and in the late Sixties, it was my shield. The youngest person besides me was a forty-eight-year-old woman who had two sons my age. One of them had been electrocuted while playing by the railroad tracks and survived. She insisted on telling me over and over about his horrible misfortune. There was another guy who had worked in that mailroom since he was twenty-three, and he was seventy-eight. They paid me two dollars an hour and I cleared $38.80 a week—pretty grim, huh? **1998**

eddie izzard
My first job was selling ice creams in a kiosk in Bexhill-on-Sea, a seaside town in England. No one would buy any ice creams, as everyone in Bexhill is about eighty years old. I would spend all day in the kiosk just staring out and going slightly mad. Then I hit on the idea of eating all the ice creams myself, so things got a lot better and I got a lot fatter. **1998**

elvis costello
I graduated from secondary school in 1973. It was the first year in recent times of one million unemployed in England—in Liverpool, anywhere up north, it was worse. I was very lucky to get a job as a computer operator, which happened to be comparatively well paid: about twenty pounds a week. I'd just put tapes on the machines and feed cards in, line up printing machines—all the manual work the computer itself doesn't have arms to do. **1982**

dean wareham of Luna

When I used to have to put on a fucking tie and go to work and get on the subway at nine in the morning in the worst of the New York summer heat, I was pretty miserable. I used to temp doing word processing at, like, Chase Manhattan, wherever I was sent. **1996**

jon spencer of theJonSpencerBluesExplosion

My first real job was working as a busboy at the Hanover Inn, which is in the town where I grew up—Hanover, New Hampshire—and, you know, it wasn't that bad. It only turned me off breakfast. I mean, you couldn't get away from the smell of syrup. I've done a lot of different things. You know, I painted houses. I'm not one of those people who complains about working too much. I worked in a head shop, I worked in a frame shop, I worked at a lot of different magazines doing production work [including ROLLING STONE], I worked at a medical library. The medical library was the worst because they were throwing away a lot of the books. They were kind of going through everything and tossing the old stuff, so most of the day I was just in the stacks—these rooms with shelves and shelves of books— going through, pulling the stuff they didn't want. It was in the summer. I think it was at Columbia's medical school, I'm not sure. But it was in Manhattan, way uptown, and there was no air-conditioning. I was pulling down all these books, the air was really musty, there was a lot of dust, and it was very, very hot. **1998**

beck

I had a job in a garment factory unloading sixty-pound steel rods. I didn't know what they were going to do with them, but every day I'd go up and there'd be a new semi full of these rods. I've been fired from a few jobs, too. At one, they said they didn't like the way I dressed. Not that I was dressing outrageously or anything. They just didn't like my style. I didn't really understand, because I was just wearing jeans and a shirt from Sears. You couldn't get more bland. I was a stock boy. I don't know. They had, like, high expectations for stock positions. But I couldn't really afford the latest fashions with what they paid me. **1996**

annabella of BowWowWow

When I was thirteen, I needed pocket money. My mum was a single working mum with four children to bring up, so she didn't have a lot to spare. I decided to get a job on Saturdays and almost got one in a cake shop, but my mum said I'd get fat working there. About a week later she told me the local dry cleaners was looking for someone to help out, and this became my first job. I was very nervous, but within a couple of weeks, I learned how to bag and ticket clothes and how to work behind the counter. It was a happy environment because a Jamaican guy worked alongside me pressing the clothes, drinking Newcastle Brown Ale and smoking weed! The radio was always on, and one day this guy walked in, heard me singing along to it, and asked if I'd go to audition for a band. At first, I thought he was trying to pick me up, but after he explained that I could bring a friend and it would be during the day, I decided to go. After the audition I worked in the dry cleaners until Malcolm McLaren, the manager of the band and the man who'd auditioned me, got me fired. He said the band I'd auditioned for—Bow Wow Wow—had been booked to go out on tour. **1998**

Annabella of Bow Wow Wow (James A. Steinfieldt)

mike simpson of theDustBrothers

My first job was when I was fifteen—I was a busboy at Straw Hat Pizza. After six months, I was told I was going to have to take a polygraph test because someone had been stealing from the restaurant. I was interrogated for three hours but never actually hooked up to the machine. As it turned out, I was the only employee who wasn't stealing. **1998**

tracy bonham
I worked at Taco Time in Eugene, Oregon—I was nineteen and I lasted three weeks. I also worked at the Pillar House in Wellesley, Massachusetts. The owner hated me because I was happy. He eventually made life miserable for me and I had to quit. **1998**

patti smith
I was a baby-buggy-bumper-beeper inspector. You know those beepers on the buggies? I had to beep them to make sure they worked. But I kept getting demoted. I actually liked my lowest job—I had to inspect the pipes they used for the handles on the buggies—because I could take my copy of [Rimbaud's] *A Season in Hell* down in the basement and read. I only worked there in summers. I wanted to make money to go to college. It was just a schoolgirl thing. **1996**

robyn hitchcock
My first job? Throwing live turkeys over a fifteen-foot electric fence. Few survived. **1998**

cia soro of Whale
My worst job was chasing away hobos from the street outside a twenty-four-hour hamburger bar. I had to use a broom. I was thirteen years old and worked till three in the morning. I did that and sliced onions, so I always had this horrible odor of dirt and onion. **1998**

prince be of PMDawn
I worked at Kentucky Fried Chicken for about six months. I said, "Oh, I can get a job." I quit school; I went there, I worked there. It was so horrible. Luckily, September came around and I went back to school after that. **1998**

ann wilson of Heart
The summer I graduated from high school I knocked around Bellevue, Washington, like a bored and balky calf, not knowing what to do. I would attend art college in the fall, but I was eighteen and three months was an eternity. My best friend had a job at a drugstore, and it earned her all kinds of respect, as well as money, so I decided to try working. I needed that weekly ten bucks it cost then for a lid, not to mention cigarettes and music. The local KFC—then called Colonel Sanders's Kentucky Fried Chicken—was hiring. It was the first place I applied, and they snapped me right up. I was flattered. I figured I was overqualified and

that the work would be a walk in the park. I was so wrong! It was one of the grossest experiences of my life—this is from an experienced woman of the world who has worked in the music industry for more than twenty years. They said, "Be sure to wear *sneakers* to work." For comfort? No, for stability while skating around on the grease in the kitchen. My job was to stand between two barrels. One was full of whole, unwashed, fat chickens, and I'd pull the visible fat off the carcasses, discard it in the second barrel, cut up the chickens according to a chart mounted on the wall, and collate the pieces in organized containers. One container for breasts, one for drumsticks and so on. Then, I dipped the pieces in the secret batter (made that morning by another flunky) and spread them out on a huge cookie sheet, ready for the oven. When my stomach was settled again, it was time to bake the biscuits, which came in mammoth flats covered in plastic. I remember the biscuits made me strangely sad. I had always believed that they were good, and homemade. The slaw, mashed potatoes and gravy were equally impersonal, and by the first day's end, I was already debating ever returning. I did come back for another day, and learned to follow another chart to fill orders, but I didn't know how to run a cash register, and the public just weirded me out. Many of them were rude and pushy, and it bothered me that they believed the myth of the biscuits. So by the end of the second day, I'd had it. I took off my apron and greasy sneakers for good. I could not work on the hog farm. For someone else it would have just been a summer job, but for me the sensual imagery was too awful. The sad part, of course, is that even though I still have a skill for cutting up chickens, I could never again believe in the biscuits. **1998**

wyclef jean of theFugees

Me and Pras worked at Burger King on Route 46, in Jersey. I worked there, like, a year. I had cousins that was pushin' big Lexuses; they'd pull up to the window and go, "Gimme twenty Whoppers! Yo, Clef. What you doing here, man? Let's go!" But I'd be like, "That's all right. I'll stick to my legal job." It was cool cuz I always was writin' songs while I was fixin' Whoppers. We had a friend whose parents was rich; he lived fifteen minutes from work. Sometimes me and Pras would pull up to the Burger King; we'd see three buses outside. That's, like, 130 Whoppers! We not going in. So we hung out at my friend's house, go in the pool and have a good time. There'd be a lot of Deadheads; there was music and bud. Then late night, all the babes would come through. Knowing that you gotta be back home at a certain time—it kept the whole thing exciting. Later, we'd put our Burger King outfits back on and go back home to our parents. **1998**

Wyclef Jean of the Fugees (Kwaku Alston/Ruff House/Columbia)

IT'SAFAMILYAFFAIR

A pet is truly a musician's best friend. It won't argue about song-writing credit, ask for a divorce, quit the band to start a solo career or divulge secrets to the press. Of course, human family is important, too.

gwen stefani of NoDoubt

I can remember my older brother was my biggest influence as far as bringing music into our house. He heard Madness's song "Baggy Trousers" at a club one night and he went out and got the record. It became our family obsession. He

Feb 28 – JOY!

Gwen Stefani of No Doubt (Self-portrait by Gwen Stefani, courtesy of Russell A. Trunk/Chrisam Enterprises, Inc.)

collected every Madness single and poster, it didn't matter if it was the same song and same recording, if it had different artwork, he would collect it. We had this one compilation tape of interviews and all their videos, and I swear to God all four of us—I have a little brother and little sister—used to sit and watch it every single day. And we'd memorize parts of it. It's silly, I know. But we were really into them and they brought a lot of joy to our lives. I actually got to meet them, too. I went to a KROQ baseball game against Madness. My parents took us to that. We were a family outing kind of family. We got to take pictures with Madness. They were really nice to my little brother and sister, who were very young at the time. **1996**

roni size
When I was young, I couldn't afford to buy records, so I'd go through my brother's collection, like, nonstop. When he was about sixteen and had started dating girls, he'd buy all these smooth records to play in his bedroom with his girlfriend. When he went out, I'd go through his records. I'm crazy about Grover Washington Jr. Definitely *Winelight*. Alphonse Mouzon—ever heard of him? Brazilian jazz. Really different—early jazz funk. What attracted me to Herbie Hancock was "Rockit." When I started looking for break beats, I'd go back through my brother's Bo Diddley and Bernard Purdie records and stuff like that. Then I got into Grandmaster Flash and the Furious Five. They were my boys. You've seen *Wild Style*, the movie, yeah? Grandmaster Flash showed me what I wanted to do with my life: two turntables and a mixer. **1998**

mike d of theBeastieBoys
My parents were very, very good about not separating us as kids from their adult friends. So on any given night, we'd have, like, this kind of freak show—artists and art dealers coming over. And these are the people I feel like I learned from. **1998**

emmylou harris
My daughter's learning to drive straight stick because we have to in our family. It's like when you throw a baby into the water to teach it how to swim. We're taking Route 66 with the occasional smaller road. It's fabulous. Everybody should be required as an American citizen to drive across country. I've got one of my four dogs with me, all taken from an animal shelter. He's a mutt. A poodle mix that looks like he was drawn by Dr. Seuss. His name's Bonaparte. He's lanky, has great big feet and floppy ears. His tail does a dip and he's black. **1996**

kim thayil of Soundgarden

My dog is black and white, we call her Salvador Doggie because her whiskers curl upward like Salvador Dalí's mustache. And her face is white, but it's black around the muzzle. She's part terrier and shepherd—Australian and English and mixes. Her ears are black and floppy and hang down like Dalí's hair, so if she's looking right at you, she looks like Salvador Dalí dog. **1996**

ozzy osbourne

My passion and my love of life are the six dogs I have at home. I absolutely adore them. I have two bullmastiffs, a mastiff, a British bulldog, a German shepherd and a boxer. Baldy, Sugar, Sonny, Raider, Buster and Phoebe. I've got forty or fifty acres of land in the forest and when I get the opportunity, I take my dogs and go sit on an old log with them. My dogs are so cool, man. I really love them. My dog Baldy is the king of the manor. If I go in and my boxer, Sugar, is all wagging her little stumpy tail at me, he'll trudge up—he's a British bulldog and he's got, like, a big miserable face—if I don't show him undivided 100 percent affection, he gets miserable and pissed off. He turns his head and looks at the other dogs. He doesn't make a growl, he doesn't make a squeak or anything, but they all know. They're all like, "Okay, man, we get the vibe, we understand, 'Don't fuck with him, he's mine.' " **1995**

aaliyah

My father's my manager, my mother's my comanager. It's a family business because my uncle is the head of my label. It's good to have them there watching my back, protecting me. And they give me my freedom. I just turned eighteen, if I want to go to a party, they let me go as long as I have security. It's really cool, I wouldn't have it any other way. **1997**

usher

My mother was musically inclined. She guided me into becoming a singer, and now she's my manager. She was the youth director in Chattanooga. She is a positive woman that keeps me in a positive vibe. I respect that. Who knows, maybe eventually we'll do a song together and everybody will see how good she can sing. She can blow—my mother's got tone to her. She can get to you sometimes, but I love her, though. Now that I'm nineteen, though, I got my own little thing—I ain't really worried. She come by and beat me up every so often, but it's cool. **1997**

janet jackson

When we were kids, and played games like Scrabble, it was our mother—not our father—that gave us all that sharp edge of competition.

We were taught to win. Michael and I aren't very happy with anything less than first place. **1993**

liam gallagher of Oasis

I don't think there is a difference between me and Noel. He's a cunt, I'm a cunt. Don't let him spin you; he's a cunt, I tell you. I'm the one who is made out to be the cunt, but he makes me be the cunt. He pushes me into that cunt zone. **1996**

paul mccartney

For me, life at home is what is interesting now. I have two kids, a wife of one year and everything at home. I love being at home and I love music. That is largely what interests me and I am not looking for anything else to interest me. **1970**

sean lennon

I have a lot of memories of just talking with him [John Lennon], hanging out and watching TV. Saying "Good night" to me was an intimate moment. It was just me and him. There was something so soothing about his voice. And he did this really cute thing: He would flick the lights on and off in rhythm to whatever he would say. He would say, "Good night, Sean," and the lights would go [*makes clicking noise*]. It just made me feel so cozy. **1998**

Sean Lennon (Tamra Davis/Grand Royal/Capitol)

mya

I never looked at singing and dancing as a career, but my parents did. My entire family is musical. I'd be up late doing schoolwork because of all my activities, and my mom was always there for me. She taught me to work hard, which, I think, is why I have so much energy. I mean, I graduated high school at sixteen. **1998**

montell jordan

My daughter is twenty-one months old going on, like, ten years. She's a video fanatic. Her favorites are my "Let's Ride" video,

Master P's "Make 'Em Say, Uhh." She loves Destiny's Child, "No No No." She'll put up her finger and say *no no no*. She does the little dance they do. She goes around the house singing Wyclef Jean's "Gone Till November." She loves Usher's "Nice and Slow." I'm gonna have to give him a piece of my mind when I see him. **1998**

pete townshend
The whole incredible thing about my parents is that I just can't place their effect on me, and yet I know that it's there. When people find out that my parents are musicians, they ask how it affected me. Fucked if I know; musically, I can't place it, and I can't place it in any other way. **1968**

flea of theRedHotChiliPeppers
Being a good father is pretty much my number-one concern in life. **1995**

art alexakis of Everclear
It might sound trite if you don't have kids, but having a daughter has totally changed my whole priority system. She's the funniest person I know. She makes me laugh more than anyone. How I view everything—music, food—everything is different since I've had her. A lot of men are dogs. They'll have children and they don't raise them. My dad was kinda like that. I just can't understand it. It's such a special thing. It's one of the things that's gotten me through the rough spots of the last few years. She's three and a half. Beautiful. Pain-in-the-ass brat, spoiled rotten by her daddy, no doubt. But that's all good. She and my wife are coming to Europe to meet me; it's a big deal for both of them. She's excited about going on an airplane, so my wife keeps asking her, "What games do you want to get?" You know, so she's occupied on the plane, and the other day she looked up kind of sullenly and said, "Mama, I don't want to talk about it right now. You wouldn't understand." She said that to my wife! She's a three-year-old! She scares the hell out of me. **1996**

chris whitley
One time I played at Brownies in New York, my daughter sang a couple of songs. That was a blast. She sings really great. It was midnight when we walked in and she said, "Daddy, when are we gonna play, I'm gettin' sick of waiting." I'm used to feeling older than everyone in a club—and my daughter was the young one. She was like, "You guys are old." That was fun. **1997**

rick nielsen of CheapTrick

My son got a golf scholarship to Miami of Ohio. My mother-in-law asked him what his favorite course was and I blurted out "Intercourse." Everyone thought it was pretty funny, I mean, they laughed. **1996**

dick dale

My son is four and he's already beating my computer at chess. He plays four notes on my trumpet and drums at my concerts. He's been playing since he was twelve and a half months. He's sponsored by the Zildjian cymbal company as the youngest drummer in the history of their company. Prairie Prince of the Tubes and Jefferson Starship gave him his drumsticks when I did *Tribal Thunder*. He's been playing with full-sized sticks since he was twelve months. We started him just rapping on cymbals, just *du-du-du-du-taka-taka-taka-taka*. He would show up and play on all the drums when we were breaking down the stage. He's either Damien or a man in a boy's body. People freak out when they watch him. He's no-nonsense. He's better than some drummers I've had. And then, of course, I'm teaching my wife, she's twenty-eight, I'm fifty-eight, we've been together nine years. I'm teaching her drums. I build my music around percussion. That's why I play like that on the guitar. I bring her up in all the encores. She plays like a man. So the whole family will be onstage. I'll have, like, three drummers. **1996**

dave mustaine of Megadeth

It's a rush. It's amazing. Every day this little guy wakes up and he's one day smarter. He's somehow figured out another way to challenge everything that he's been taught and everything that he's learned so far. I think what it is about growing up is that you wanna be your own God, you want to be your own judge and jury and make decisions for yourself. And within those decisions, someone's gotta be there to let you make those decisions and also be there to keep you from making bad ones. It's kinda like, you know, the first time your knee ever hit a piece of concrete, there was an exchange. The concrete got some of your skin and your skin got some of the dirt from the concrete. So no matter what you do in life, you're always going to have an exchange with the influences that you come across and someone needs to be there to set a good example and help. It's not so much about beating kids, but it's also not about being these chickenshit people who are afraid of parental abuse. When my son got out of line when he was growing up, I would give him one spank on his behind to get his attention. I would talk to him and reason with him, and I remember the first time I went to give him a spanking, I forgot that he wasn't wearing diapers anymore and he was wearing training underwear, and I smacked him on the behind and he looked at me and screamed as loud as he possibly could. And I just went, "Aw, man, well, you're gonna remember next time, aren't you?" **1997**

whitney houston

Having Bobbi Kristina . . . I could never do anything that could top that. There's been nothing more incredible in my life than having her. God knows, I have been in front of millions and millions of people, and that has been incredible, to feel that give-take thing. But, man, when I gave birth to her and when they put her in my arms, I thought: "This has got to be *it*. This is the ultimate." I haven't experienced anything greater. **1993**

tommy lee of MötleyCrüe

I'm just tripping out being a dad, and my son now is walking and talking. He wakes up in the morning and goes, "Daaa-daaa," and opens my eyelid when I'm asleep to wake me up. It's the cutest thing, I think, I've ever seen in my entire life. He'll be a year old next month. He wakes up at night for feedings and stuff and sometimes my wife will just put him in bed with us in the middle, and he gets up pretty early—earlier than Dad, that's for sure. He's starting to wake me up now; he's like, "C'mon, let's roll, Dad." It's cute, and he's playing his drums. He's got a little kit. He freaks. I do realize that with all little kids, you put a drumstick in their hand and they love to just bang on anything, but he has this extra fire in his eyes when he sees anything that resembles a stick because his whole world is a drum right now. He likes to play on anything. If there's no sticks in sight, he plays with his hands on a table or the floor. But he definitely has the tools here if he wants to become something musical—there's musical instruments all over the place: drums, piano, little guitars, it's all here. We're crazy, we play all the time. Recently, now that he's standing up on his own, he can actually stand there and *bap-bab-bab-bab-bab*. For a while we'd sit on the floor and put drums on the floor and he'd sit down and go crazy. He's got a little bass drum, his hi-hats are two tiny splash cymbals put together on a hi-hat stand, a twelve-inch snare drum, two toms, one floor tom, a little ride cymbal and two little crashes. He's got it all. Yeah, he's ready. I had the guys who build my drums make a tiny little version of my drums for him, so he'll be able to thrash on this for years and he'll never break it. Built for speed. Pamela loves it. She freaks, man. She loves the fact that he loves music. When music comes on around the house, he immediately starts dancing or bob-blin', wobblin', rockin' out. She loves it because it's a musical household around here. **1997**

billie joe armstrong of GreenDay

Goodnight Moon, by Margaret Wise Brown, is the classic children's book. My wife and I read it to [our son] Joey every night. **1998**

john wozniak of MarcyPlayground

My wife and I have a little boy. He's eighteen months. He's awesome. My wife's brother was over for dinner one night when she was pregnant and he said, "You should name him after the singer from the Smashing Pumpkins, Billy Keegan." We were like, "Okay . . . " We slept on it and we thought Billy Corgan wasn't exactly appropriate, but Keegan was cool. **1998**

shaun ryder of HappyMondays and BlackGrape

I met a lot of famous, nice people. I have lots of friends and I'm trying not to meet a lot of people in this business. You know, like, when you start meeting other musicians and shit, and you've liked them and you find out they're assholes. But there's people like Donovan, me wife's dad, he's a fucking great. He's still Mr. Mellow in the Sixties, you know what I mean? He's really cool. He's like the teacher on fucking *Beavis and Butt-Head* [*imitates him*]. "Your money goes. Oh, what you been doing now, you been taking drugs." He's terrible funny. He's a nice man. **1996**

busta rhymes

The music sometimes keeps you away from your family, and I got a son. There are plenty of times when I be wantin' to get with him, but *work*—know what I'm sayin'? The work creates a bad taste not just in his mouth, but in mine because I'll be feelin' like I'm letting him down if I don't come when I say I'm gonna come. I've been working that whole shit out because that's the least that I could do. I can't be letting my son down. Everything gotta stop. When it comes to my son, everything gotta stop. None of this shit more important than him. He'll be five soon. Word. So he's gettin' into that mind state where he's remembering shit and focusing in on shit. I want to make sure we're in sync as far as our energy and our vibe. It gets hard because music ain't just my love, it's the bread and butter for my family. I got to stay busy so that everything is thoroughly taken care of. But then at the same time, everything can be taken care of except your relationship with your child if you don't put in the time. And time ain't got nothing to do with money. To a degree it do because if the money ain't there so that you can make time, it's like, shit, I can't afford to sit down right now because

Busta Rhymes (Dean Karr/Elektra)

we gotta eat. I've been trying to communicate that on a level that my son under-
stands now because he sees me on TV and hears me on the radio, so he knows
that this is what I do. He's also got to understand that this helps me, him and his
mother. **1997**

eddie van halen of VanHalen

My son Wolfie's environment is music, and he's already written a couple of ditties
himself on piano. He starts humming along to this little bit. He's so into Sonic the
Hedgehog, it was probably about that. I forget what he called it. He hangs around
me and he's always like, "I want to play like you, Daddy. What's that you play
that's not chords?" It's improvising. So that's what he's into. That was when he
was in kindergarten, and so in music class at school, he started improvising when
they were supposed to be singing Halloween songs. The teacher gave him a time-
out for not doing it right, and he picked up a pumpkin and threw it at the teacher
and said, "My daddy said it's okay!" So I got a call from the principal. I asked him
what he was doing and he said singing a different melody. I told him next time,
aim better—no, I'm kidding. I was gonna pull him out of the class because I don't
want anyone telling him that there is a wrong and right when it comes to music. I
don't want him taught that way. **1998**

MYGENERATION

People try to put them down, just because they get around. Or used to get around. The so-called Generation X resents the Baby Boomers; the Boomers see only shiftless kids. It's an age-old quarrel—perhaps a man of many generations named Bowie can make some sense of all this.

pete townshend One of the things which has impressed me most in life was the Mod movement in England, which was an incredible, youthful thing. It was a movement of young people, much bigger than the hippie thing, the underground and all these things. It was an army, a powerful, aggressive army of teenagers with transport, man, with all these scooters and with their own way of dressing. To be a Mod, you had to have short hair, money enough to buy a real smart suit, good shoes, good shirts; you had to be able to dance like a madman. You had to be in possession of plenty of pills all the time and always be pilled up. You had to have a scooter covered in lamps. You had to have, like, an army anorak to wear on the scooter. And that was being a Mod, and that was the end of the story. The group that you liked when you were a Mod were the Who. That's the story of why I dig the Mods, man, because we were Mods, and that's how we happened. That's my generation, that's how the song "My Generation" happened, because of the Mods. **1968**

kim thayil of **Soundgarden**

There's millions and millions of people in their forties who think they're so fucking special. They're this ultimate white-bread, suburban, upper-middle-class group that were spoiled little fuckers as kids because they were all children of Dr. Spock. Then they were stupid, stinky hippies. And then they were spoiled little yuppie materialists. Now they're all at the age where they produce films and news reports, and it's the same nostalgia trip with *that*. And we get *their* understanding of history. They're denying other age groups their own memories. . . . They thought they had a monopoly on rock & roll, and all of a sudden, they realize they don't. It belongs to someone else now. But they just won't let it go. **1994**

joan baez Woodstock was wonderful. I mean, it wasn't any fucking revolution; it was a three-day period during which people were decent to one another because they realized that if they weren't, they'd all get hungry. **1983**

joni mitchell A lot of hippie politics were nonsense to me. I guess I found the idea of going from authority to no authority too extreme. And I was supposed to be the "hippie queen," so I had a sense of isolation about the whole thing. **1998**

bonnie raitt I took to wearing a peace symbol around my neck when I was eleven, around 1961. It represented my whole belief! And I used to wear olive green tights and black turtlenecks and I had a pair of earrings—my mother wouldn't let me pierce my ears, but I had a pair of hoop earrings. I'd grow my hair real long so I looked like a beatnik. **1975**

stevie wonder When I think of the Sixties, I think of two things: I think of Motown and I think of the Beatles. Those are the major influences. I just listened to the compact disc of *Sgt. Pepper* and the compact discs of a lot of Motown stuff, and it all sounds really great. It sounds timeless. The Beatles made me feel that I could do some of the ideas that I had. Every time one of their records came out, I wanted to have it, particularly after "Eleanor Rigby" and all that stuff. But we all influenced each other. That's really what it's all about. **1987**

john lennon I like rock & roll, man, I don't like much else. That's the music that inspired me to play music. There is nothing conceptually better than rock & roll. No group, be it the Beatles, Dylan or Stones have ever improved on "Whole Lot of Shakin'" for my money. Or maybe I'm like our parents: That's my period and I dig it and I'll never leave it. **1971**

art garfunkel *Boogie Nights* got me out of the house. I think it says very interesting things about America as I remember it in the late Seventies and early Eighties. There's one girl who's snorting and another who's saying, "I can't keep up with the speed of all these changes." And I was thinking, that's exactly right! In 1983, if you were a historian trying to keep track of what the Sixties meant as they moved into the Seventies, by around '83, you'd say, "I give up." It's spinning out of orbit now. And when that happens you just roll up the bill and go for another snort. It's like, if I can't keep my house in order, I'll get married to chaos. That's what I think. So for me, the Seventies were a real deflation. I'm kind of a disappointed Sixties guy. **1998**

david bowie There is a real natural need for ritual and theater in people. To have problems or supposed problems played out for them on a stage is just such a part of how man continually educates himself about himself. The idea of mythology is so inherent in us. The need for moral and amoral story lines is so incredibly a part of our personas. There is a real hunger for that. I guess it will emerge in these particularly disturbing times—disturbing more than anything else that there's no sense to be made out of the past anymore. It seems that events arise and move so quickly that it's hard to retain a little perspective on what's happened in the past and how we piece history together to make any sense of today and to give us some lead into what the future may or may not be like. We have been cast adrift a little. And I think that bands like Marilyn Manson play out those fears very adequately. I think that they're the opportune thing at the right time. Whether it's witting or unwitting. I think that society throws up the things it needs. They're there for when we need them. We'll provide them somehow. I don't know how Marilyn thinks about what he's doing, but I remember so distinctly at the time that I used to get so hostile about the idea of integrity and all that. It was like, fuck it, artifice is the thing for me. That is a true rebellious stance. All this realness and all that, I just don't buy it. It's not how we puzzle out our lives' problems. And I think our whole group of us felt that way. That we were rebelling absolutely against exactly that. I would feel that possibly the same type of feeling is evolving again, that this earnestness has become a career opportunity. It's not for real any more. That realness. The new realness is let's make it something really theatrical, let's put our problems up on a theatrical stage. And for a bit, that will be the new reality. **1997**

method man of Wu-TangClan

You can tell all you need to know about a nigga by looking him right in the eyes. If the eye's weak, other niggas gonna eat you alive. Only the strong survive. When you see a nigga out on the street wearing sunglasses all the time, that's what he trying to do. Hide the eyes 'cause they weak. **1998**

bo diddley
At sixty-nine years old, I'm still goin'. I write in a young person's vein. I can write in an old person's vein. I can write way back to Muddy Waters, when I first started, if I feel like it. But I'm writing what I feel like is gonna sell records. I wanna sell records, I don't want them to sit in the back room and get moss on them. I want them in people's homes. So therefore I found out, in order to do this, you gotta be able to roll with the punches. The new kid on the block, the new things that they're buying and the stuff that DJs are playing, you've got to figure out how to get your toe in the door. And hope that you went in the right door! Because I find you have no idea what kids are going to go after. My mother did tell me that I was sick one time. I started wiggling and carrying on and everybody thought I was the worst thing to hit the stage, because I was wiggling. Me and Elvis—he started his legs wiggling. We weren't doin' nothin'. They put

ideas in my head. Old folks don't know a lot of times, when they say something to kids, they start them to thinking. It was a lot of old people back then, which I can not blame them, because they were taught that way. So they passed it on to us, you shouldn't pat your foot, because if you pat your foot and it ain't a church song, you pattin' your foot to the devil. You dig? Our ancestors were taught this. So I don't blame Mama and Daddy for getting upset when this new music came out. Things got to move on. You take jazz, the way it is played today is the way it was played twenty, thirty years ago. The one thing I can say, jazz has remained jazz. Rock & roll has went into something I don't understand myself. **1996**

Beck (Charlie Gross/Geffen)

beck   The so-called Generation X is an easy target. Most of Generation X can't even defend themselves. They don't know how to put the words together to bring out their inner experience. That's a loss—a big loss. And then when somebody does come out full of angst—which is something commonly associated with this generation—it's written off simply as whining. As if it's not real. I'm a traditionalist in a lot of ways. A lot of what my generation is into, what it represents, I'm totally against. I think a lot of my generation has been fed a culture that's disposable. A lot of simple techno stuff—it's going to look stupid ten years from now. It might look fresh and new and exciting now, but it's going to look old and stale as time goes by. **1997**

tori amos   Our generation has an incredible amount of realism, yet at the same time it loves to complain and not really change. Because if it does change, then it won't have anything to complain about. I think our generation loves our pain, and if you dare fucking take it away from us, we're going to kill you. We like our pain. And we're packaging it, and we're selling it. **1994**

53

foxy brown Being seventeen works and it doesn't. I got pulled over by the cops yesterday. They had the lights flashing simply because they saw a '97 Benz with a young girl drivin'. I was with my boyfriend. I didn't have my license with me and I was like, shit, we're finished. But all my papers were legit. The cop was like, "Hey, are you Foxy Brown?" I'm like, "Yeah." He was like, "Nah, I'm gonna let you go." So it works in the way that people feel sorry for you. Then it works like, okay, you're not supposed to drink, you're not supposed to do this, you're not supposed to do that. And you know, I'm more mature than seventeen. Like if we hung out, you would never even think I was seventeen. I always tell my mother, that seventeen-year-old—the kind in dark, long dresses—is over with. This is a whole new era. Word. **1997**

EVERYDAY I READ THE BOOK

The written word has toppled governments, started wars, opened minds and inspired reams of lyrics. Sometimes one book can touch (really touch) folks as diverse as Björk and Dave Matthews. Dostoyevsky—love those murder scenes!—did it for Nick Cave. And it's always interesting to find out who's reading the Bible.

beck I read the dictionary a lot. I take it on tour with me. **1996**

"weird al" yankovic My favorite book is probably the Los Angeles Yellow Pages. I have probably read that more than any other book. Of course, the plot development leaves a little bit to be desired. But I can overlook that. It's just so comprehensive. **1996**

9/25/96   "WEIRD AL" Yankovic

"Weird Al" Yankovic (Self-portrait by "Weird Al" Yankovic, courtesy of Russell A. Trunk/Chrisam Enterprises, Inc.)

david bowie   *The Wild Boys,* by William S. Burroughs, was a really heavy book that had come out around 1970. It was a cross between that and *Clockwork Orange* that really started to put together the shape and the look of what Ziggy and the Spiders were going to become. They were both powerful pieces of work, especially the marauding boy gangs of Burroughs's *Wild Boys* with their bowie knives. I got straight on to that. I read everything into everything. Everything had to be infinitely symbolic. **1993**

juliana hatfield   I like *The Last Gentleman,* by Walker Percy. I always fall in love with the guys in Percy's books. They're really lost and sad—but hopeful. Kinda confused, like me. But they're nice. **1995**

tina weymouth of **TalkingHeads and TomTomClub**
The Book of Changes and the Unchanging Truth, by Hua-Ching Na, is a great I Ching book. Many Chinese people consult it every day. They read it for the wisdom within. The foreword has a wonderful exploration of the cosmos. *Women's Bodies, Women's Wisdom,* by Christiane Northrup, is a must for women. If they don't take care of their bodies, they're hopeless. They're just messes, but when they're together, they're goddesses. And they just raise their men up, they're just fantastic for their men, themselves, or their women. *Shadows of Forgotten Ancestors: A Search for Who We Are,* by Carl Sagan and Ann Druyan, is a good one for ignorant racists. It's the first of a trilogy. Ninety-nine point six percent of our DNA is like chimpanzees'. It's a great help to understanding our own makeup. Chimpanzees are very aggressive, tribal, xenophobic and ethnocentric. They kill those of other tribes, just like we do. All the stuff about race that the Victorians made up is total bullshit. Pan-troglodyte was the classification for chimpanzees. They don't even live in caves. Man, the hominids, is really supposed to be classed with apes, but they really didn't go and do it because of religion. Before that, they'd just say a person was from Africa, or wherever they were from. We are actually all one race, the human race, and what makes us different is our tribe. *Crosstown Traffic: Jimi Hendrix and the Post-War Rock 'n' Roll Revolution,* by Charles Shoar Murray, is not a bullshit book. He's such a great writer and has a great overview. He just truly loves music. It's not only the story of Jimi Hendrix, but of the blues. It goes all the way back to Jimi's roots, to Robert Johnson and everything. It doesn't dwell on the sordid side at all. The drugs are only a fact of Jimi's death, not the crux of Jimi's life. Another rock & roll book, *I Need More,* by Iggy Pop with Anne Wehrer, has marvelous photographs, and it's really honest. In one chapter, he tells us how Nico taught him to give really good head. *The Buddha of Suburbia,* by Hanif Kureishi— he's English and Pakistani—is insightful about rock & roll in the Eighties. It's a

funny, enjoyable story about coming of age in the suburbs, then moving to London and eventually New York. Henry James's *The Awkward Age*—he wrote it after a strange period in his early fifties. It's not like his other writing. Still a good read a hundred years later. You realize that the important books that stay with you have a persona that is parallel to a persona in your own psyche. Like in fairy tales. As we go through life these things gain meaning as to who we are. *Possession: A Romance,* by A.S. Byatt, is incredibly romantic and erudite. You must refer back to mythology to understand the poetry in it. I find it infinitely erotic. She speaks to me, but I'm a woman, so it could be a chick thing. **1996**

jewel Pablo Neruda was the biggest influence on me at a younger age. I was into philosophy before I was into poetry. I was really into reason and the brain and abandoning emotions to know truth. Then I read Neruda and it completely changed everything. I quit writing essays and all those things and started writing about the heart and feeling that I could know humans better and myself better by doing that. A lot of the poets I had read before then—and I wasn't well versed— were kind of sappy, had kind of a meaningless air. The substance just didn't touch me for some reason. But when I read Neruda's political writing as well as his love poetry, they seemed synonymous, and it was really touching. You can't know truth without knowing your heart, and I sort of learned that through Neruda. I've also always been a huge fan of Charles Bukowski. My writing style changed a bit after reading him. I had these really lush images like in my poem "Wild Horse," but I started to get drier and straighter. It was like being given permission. I got to meet Bukowski's widow at a party. A mutual friend introduced her to me—I didn't know who she was at the time—and he had me sing her "Painters." She was sobbing. Later on, she showed us these books that she had put out posthumously with pictures of her and Bukowski traveling and stuff, and it just struck me that all she has left are those words. **1998**

janis joplin I always did have a very heavy attachment for the whole Fitzgerald thing, that all out, full-tilt, hell-bent way of living, and [Zelda] and F. Scott Fitzgerald were the epitome of that whole trip, right? When I was young I read all of his books; I've reread them all: autobiographies, *The Crack-Up,* all the little scribblings . . . and she was always a mythic person in his life; you also have the feeling that he destroyed her. You always get the feeling that she was willing to go with him through anything and that he ruined her. But in the book [*Zelda*] you find out that she was just as ambitious as he was, and that they sort of destroyed each other. He wrote her a letter one time in which he says, "People

Jewel (Self-portrait by Jewel, courtesy of Russell A. Trunk/Chrisam Enterprises, Inc.)

say we destroy each other, but I never felt we destroyed each other, I felt we destroyed ourselves." **1970**

tori amos
I wrote "Cornflake Girl" because of what Alice Walker's *Possessing the Secret of Joy* inspired. I feel that genetic memory gets passed down. Walker talks about this. Women have a hard time holding their mothers accountable, because mothers have had such a hard time. It's not about blame, but taking responsibility. **1994**

emmylou harris
The Living, by Annie Dillard, is the story of ordinary people settling the Northwestern territory in the mid to late 1800s, made extraordinary by their day-to-day struggle to survive. Dillard's writing at times can take your breath away. I read it a couple of years ago, but it still comes back to me. **1996**

ana da silva of theRaincoats
Buffalo Girls, by Larry McMurtry, is about the last days of the Wild West and some of the characters then: Calamity Jane, Annie Oakley, Sitting Bull. The funniest thing for me was that after reading it for hours and getting involved in a very faraway and exotic life, a few of the characters get in a boat with Buffalo Bill's Wild West Show and come to England. In no time, they're in Earl's Court in London—two subway stations away from me. **1996**

Emmylou Harris (Matthew Barnes/Eminent)

sarah mclachlan
I feel so drawn to what Rainer Maria Rilke says in *Letters to a Young Poet*—there are things that resonate strongly inside me that I haven't even recognized yet. **1994**

terence trent d'arby
I carry the complete Whitman wherever I go. He is one of my heroes. **1994**

simon le bon of DuranDuran

I'm reading *Corelli's Mandolin*, by Louis de Bernières; it's funny and really happy. It's set during the war on a Greek island, south of Corfu. It's about how they cope with being invaded by the Italians. These Italians don't want to be at war, though, particularly Captain Corelli. I'm dreading getting near the end, you know? *The Master and Margarita*, by Mikhail Bulgakov, is a story about the devil coming to Moscow for a weekend of fun and arriving with all his minions, one of whom comes in the guise of a six-foot cat smoking cigars. There's a beautiful book, *Gabriela, Clove and Cinnamon*, by Jorge Amado, that's set in Brazil and it's a lovely love story. *Birdsong*, by Sebastian Faulks, is hard, it's very tough on you, it really takes you. It starts in the First World War and comes up to the present day. **1997**

roni size

At the moment, I'm reading *The Alchemist: A Fable About Following Your Dream*, by Paulo Coelho. It's about a shepherd adapting to the sheep—or are the sheep adapting to him? Basically when he wakes up, the sheep wake up. And when he walks, the sheep walk. Or is it the other way around? When the sheep wake up, does he wake up? When they walk, does he walk? It's all about adapting. The book is very short and the object of it is to read it not once, but five or six times, because you're always going to miss something. So you go backwards and forwards and you start to read into things differently every time. The book doesn't tell one story, it's about twenty different stories depending on how you read it. **1998**

billy gibbons of ZZTop

Empire of the Ants, by Bernard Werber, is an in-depth study of the entire ant world. Two stories run parallel—some see it as fiction, others as an enlightening educational tool for learning about the world. One puts it down chapter by chapter feeling a little closer to these unusual russet-colored critters that surround us. Also, check out Haruki Murakami's *Hard-Boiled Wonderland* and *The End of the World*, which are set in modern-day Tokyo. There is this sort of cataclysmic, geometric collision of Western images meets old Japan. It's science fiction—a dreamlike, ethereal, chapter-by-chapter surprise attack to be met with Ferraris, Lamborghinis, American hot-rod Fords, pasta, piles of liquor, cigarette smoke, computers and tumbling refrigerators. What a concept! It's just wicked great reading. **1996**

Garbage: Duke Erikson, Butch Vig, Shirley Manson and Steve Marker (from left)
(Joseph Cultice/Almo Sounds)

shirley manson of Garbage

I read *Corelli's Mandolin,* by Louis de Bernières, from cover to cover on a recent plane ride to the U.S. from Scotland and barely noticed the weirdo next to me who kept talking into a plastic phone! It left me elated. Although it exposes the ugliness of human nature, it illuminates the beauty, too. **1996**

michael hutchence of INXS

The White Hotel, by D.M. Thomas, is a mind fuck. You're taking a ride in your mind, and there are all these channels going on at the same time. Endless possibility. You choose, but some things are chosen for you. You actually have no control—the dynamic of life. **1994**

tanya donelly of ThrowingMuses and Belly

Oranges Are Not the Only Fruit (and other books) by Jeanette Winterson. She has a very weird, warped, fairy-tale style as a writer. **1994**

fred schneider of theB-52's

I'm rereading Edgar Rice Burroughs's three Martian Series novels: *Thuvia, Maid of Mars*, *Chessman of Mars* and *Mastermind of Mars*. It's always good to take a mental vacation to another planet. **1996**

dave matthews
I read this really weird, freaked-out book that someone gave me in Woodstock called *Story of the Eye*, by Georges Bataille. You have to stop every once in a while and either have a cold shower or drink a couple of shots of whiskey or masturbate. It's demented. But it's cool. It's beautifully written. The only really fat book that I've ever been able to get through is *A Confederacy of Dunces*, by John Kennedy Toole. It was the only postmortem Pulitzer Prize–winning novel. The guy blew himself away in the Sixties and the book was published in 1980—his mother found it. I've always tried reading James Michener. He writes those epics that cover a time period of five hundred years. That guy, fuck him. I try to read those books, I get in there and will be all into it, then I just drop it. They're impossible to finish. **1996**

björk
Story of the Eye, by Georges Bataille, is an antimorality on-the-road book that changed my life. A boy and a girl go on a mission to do everything they want to do. Books like that proved to me that I wasn't mad. I read Tove Jansson's children's books to my son, Sindri, who loves them. She writes about this valley with elves. Her books have a lot of anarchy in them. **1994**

john wozniak of MarcyPlayground

The Neverending Story, by Michael Ende, is a work of art. It's about a kid who goes into a bookstore and steals a book called *The Neverending Story*, which happens to be a magical book that transports him to the world of stories. It's unbelievable. It's like a cross between J.D. Salinger's *Catcher in the Rye* and C.S. Lewis's *Chronicles of Narnia*. It's absolutely for kids but also it's for adults. **1998**

lisa loeb
I love Spanish magical realism like Fíderico García Lorca and Isabel Allende. She brings these wild stories to explain the truth in a way that's really visual and leaves you not knowing if it's a story or the truth. Roald Dahl does the *Twilight Zone*–style in a really cool way. *Kiss Kiss* is futuristic, but not like spaceship science fiction. It's creepy horror—like your baby is a furry bee. **1997**

63

gaz coombes of Supergrass

I remember reading *The Wonderful Story of Henry Sugar and Six More,* by Roald Dahl. I was quite young, but it wasn't like a kids' book. It was some of his more severe stuff. It's twisted. I was just fascinated. I read it again about a year ago and enjoyed it just as much. **1997**

d'arcy of SmashingPumpkins

I read children's books more than adult books. Dr. Seuss—I cried when Dr. Seuss died. I was distraught, it was terrible. Wonderful man. I bring a copy of Lewis Carroll's *Alice in Wonderland* with me wherever I go and open it to wherever and start reading. It's also twisted. Shel Silverstein's *Where the Sidewalk Ends.* Oh, and I love, love, love Maurice Sendak so much. He's so awesome. I don't know if Edward Gorey is for children—but his cartoons are great and twisted. **1996**

john popper of BluesTraveler

I was in the eighth grade when I read *The Amityville Horror Conspiracy,* but, *man,* that thing kept me in suspense from word one to the end. I had nightmares. I'd fall asleep and hear the pig and hear the marching band sort of walking through. **1998**

carnie wilson
I like Stephen King—books that keep me on the edge, like *The Dark Half.* That scared the shit out of me. This is gonna sound so lame and womanly, but my favorite book is *Fried Green Tomatoes at the Whistle Stop Café,* by Fannie Flagg. It's the best book about friendship. Any self-help books, psychology books are good—Barbara De Angelis, Wayne Dyer, Leo F. Buscaglia. **1997**

nick cave
My father read me the murder scene out of *Crime and Punishment.* He said, "Look, if you're going to read this other trash, here's a murder scene that's beautifully written." It was, and it is. **1996**

polly jean harvey
The Bible—everything is possible as far as I'm concerned, and nothing is impossible. I enjoy reading it for that. It's like, if you want to let your imagination run wild, dip into a few Bible stories. Why take a trip on acid when you can read the Bible? **1995**

lenny kravitz
The Bible. Eternal Knowledge. **1993**

sean "puffy" combs a.k.a. Puff Daddy

The Psalms are my favorite stories in the Bible, and the story of St. Lazarus. Lazarus rose from the dead. That's why I wear a St. Lazarus piece around my neck at times. I rose from the dead a couple of times, just through all this stuff I've been through, man. It's rough on your brain. I'm like Dennis the Menace, man. You know, he don't mean no harm, he didn't do nothing, it's just that when everybody walks into the room, he's there and the room's turned upside down. They left him at home and they come home and the house is burned down. He didn't even do nothing. I'm that guy. **1997**

dave mustaine of Megadeth

The Book of Job was always a book that I really dug because it's about patience and no matter how hard things go, that there's always gonna be a pot of gold at the end of the rainbow, so to speak. I've got a lot of self-help books, but for me getting help for myself and my finite knowledge compared to the infinite wisdom of my creator is a mismatch. There are some books written by guys like M. Scott Peck and Joseph Campbell that I have enjoyed for their uplifting value, but nobody really has the secret. I read *The Prince*, by Machiavelli, stuff like that, and all kinds of autobiographies. **1997**

john tesh
Spontaneous Healing, by Andrew Weil, is this book about helping your body heal itself. Everything from garlic to colloidal silver to all that stuff, which I'm very much into. About every year or so, I reread *The Road Less Traveled: A New Psychology of Love, Traditional Values and Spiritual Growth*, by M. Scott Peck. An amazing book. "Life is difficult" is the first line. The whole philosophy of this book is that people go through life thinking that everything should be easy and cool, asking "Why am I not happy?" and "Don't I deserve more?" This whole book says, "You're fucked." Life sucks, and as soon as you realize that, you can work on finding a way to not get around it, but embrace it and live your life. He makes that point, then goes on to tell you how life sucks and how it's going to suck even worse every day. **1997**

rupaul
Marianne Williamson's *Return to Love* has influenced me more than any book I've read. I read it three times consecutively, and still read it from time to time. I deal with positive energy and great love, so I use it to trigger things in my mind. I don't do soliloquies on positive energy or love, I *project* it. All that schlocky spirituality shit, I've always been into it. Like *The Celestine Prophecy*, by James Red-

field. We're all on this planet to learn and evolve and to be more godlike. Those books help. They've helped me so much. Each of us has such incredible energy, and once you understand it, the party really begins. My focus now is to learn how to meditate and really concentrate and focus. **1997**

ziggy marley
I have many different kind of books. Mostly books about spirituality, books about, like, juicing, because I'm health-conscious. Lots of books like the Bible. Books about spirituality, enlightenment, reincarnation. I've checked out some Indian stuff. There are a lot of versions of the Bible, so I have many different Bibles. The King James version, some from the original Eastern manuscripts, the Jerusalem Bible. I would advise getting many different versions. People should realize now that we are the children of the most high. It's what we need to do. It's a spiritual experience. **1997**

paula cole
Siddhartha, by Hermann Hesse, is totally influential in my life. I've read it probably four times. I don't see it as Buddhist. I see it in that Joseph Campbell sense of the journey of the soul. Hesse borrows obviously from Buddhism, but to me it spans all cultures. To me, it was the journey of this individual, and I just saw it as a metaphor for my own life. First of all, leaving your home and your parents, you know. Going out into the world. Trying to become more ascetic. Trying to dig in your inside world and become deeper spiritually, and then going into the outside world and having sex and taking drugs. Experimenting and living and crashing and burning. And then finally somehow marrying all of the extremes and finding it all as the middle way in life. But it just got me starting to think about different issues in life back in high school. **1998**

luther vandross
I think my favorite book is one that I read way back in high school called *Death Be Not Proud: A Memoir,* by John J. Gunther. His son Johnny Gunther was a teenager who developed a brain tumor and the book is about how Johnny coped with it. It touched a place in me that I never forgot. **1997**

erykah badu
One of the most influential books that I've read is *Behold a Pale Horse,* by William Cooper. Having been in Navy Intelligence, Cooper had access to secret naval records and documents, which he reveals in the book. He even realized that he might be killed. And last year, he was. It's about silent weapons, the quiet wars, AIDS, UFOs, the "new world order" protocol of the

RAVES

Elders of Zion, treason in high places, secret government and secret organizations and societies. My favorite quote is "No matter what you believe, what the powers-that-be believe will affect you." So it's good to know this information, no matter how peaceful you believe everything is. On a lighter note, another book that I've enjoyed is *Heal Thyself*. And that's by Queen Afua. It's for health and longevity. I don't think a woman, man or child should be without this natural-healing book. It tells you about your diet, about how to purify your blood, how to heal yourself with baths, how to heal yourself with fruit, how prayer meditation can help heal. It's good for someone in a business or anybody in day-to-day life that has to deal with a lot of different people's energies and things. The book deals with exercise, massage, yoga, sex—everything. **1997**

pat smear of theGerms and FooFighters

Inventing the AIDS Virus: The Truth Behind the World's Greatest Miscalculation, by Peter Duesberg, and *Scandal of the Century,* by Jon Rappoport—I support any books and articles that expose AIDS as the medical, pharmaceutical and governmental cartel's cruelest hoax of our lifetime. I'll never forgive them for killing Freddie Mercury. **1996**

thom yorke of Radiohead

I picked up this history book by Eric Hobsbawn, *The Age of Extremes.* The whole conclusion is that this has been the most brutal century ever for human beings. So either we go down in flames, or we start doing something about it. All we really need to do is have a marketplace with a moral framework. What we've got now in the marketplace is completely amoral anarchy. Our politicians and governments aren't in control. I don't believe that the American government is in control of America; I don't believe that the British government is in control of Britain. I haven't believed that for, like, five years now. The global market, you know, the global nationalists are in control. It's the way that greed works. The average consumer doesn't take responsibility for their actions, because they don't care and today they're almost not given a choice. **1998**

jay-z

I just read *Nigger: An Autobiography,* by Dick Gregory. Goddamn, he had it hard. You look at your own situation like, "I'm *living.*" They couldn't eat, struggling for food—even just the bare necessities. They had to wear the same clothes, it was a big thing to get a pair of pants. Just ridiculous. Before they had food stamps, you had to sign a book at the supermarket, and there's a part where he

Jay-Z (Roc-a-Fella Records/Def Jam)

said all he wanted to do was make it so they wouldn't have to sign it anymore. I also read the Death Row book—*Have Gun Will Travel,* by Ronin Ro. That was crazy. They mad at that writer—guy was saying a lot of things. I'm still trying to figure out where he could get all that from. Did he work there? I don't even know his history. It seemed like a lot of it was hearsay, too. **1998**

coolio *The Autobiography of Malcolm X* made me feel I could make it. He went through drug addiction and prison but came out and became a great leader. **1995**

heavy d.
I read *The Autobiography of Malcolm X* four, five years ago. I was really intrigued by his self-assertedness and his will to overcome a lot of evils prior to being the successful minister that he was. Overcoming the drugs and reeducating himself took a lot of hard work and a great amount of self-discipline. His will was incredible. **1997**

queen latifah
Sanyika Shakur's *Monster* is his life story. He used to be a Crip. He helps you understand how people end up in gangs, the racism involved and the war that's being fought on our city streets. **1994**

jim kerr of SimpleMinds
India always appealed to me—the majesty, the folklore. Salman Rushdie is the last remaining hostage. His life mirrors the absurdity of his books like *Midnight's Children*. **1995**

stevie nicks
Aleister Crowley weaves a story that nearly becomes a film in his *Diary of a Drug Fiend* And you have to figure out why you use drugs. And the reasons that come up are so lame. **1994**

stone gossard of PearlJam
Richard Ford—*Independence Day* was one of the best books I ever read. This middle-aged, divorced guy looks for meaning in life. He just writes beautifully, he's sarcastic and funny. His writing excites me. Martin Amis is the ultimate in cynicism. His English sense of humor and his portrayal of alcoholics are totally right on. Keith from *London Fields*—God, what an incredible character. The way he talks about male jealousy and power struggles is unbelievable. Peter Høeg is a pretty dark author. *Smilla's Sense of Snow* in particular was excellent. It has a strong female hero who is a thirty-five-year-old Greenland superwoman living in Denmark—an amazing, unlikely hero. The book is a mystery. There's always been an adversarial relationship between Greenland and Denmark, so the book is also about that, but it's set in a story about a boy that the woman believes was killed. I also read some political stuff. Cornel West is an amazing author to read about black-white relations in the U.S. He's a professor of African-American studies at Princeton. **1998**

jackson browne
In *Tropic of Cancer*, Henry Miller says the writing that matters is the personal accounts of what it means to be alive and what this life holds for us. That's what's of value. He points out that the letters of Vincent

van Gogh to his brother Theo are of tremendous literary value and that is the kind of writing he would like to do—just discussing life. As for the folk revival that's going on now, it's interesting. Greil Marcus's book *Invisible Republic: Bob Dylan's Basement Tapes* is fascinating. The first few pages—go to the bookstore, open it up and you will have to read it. It's amazing. He's talking about a period of time when—you know what, I won't paraphrase, I just recommend it. You won't be able to put it down. It's the real deal. It's about what music is for. **1997**

mick jones of theClash and BigAudioDynamite

Sometimes when I go to New York, I take Martin Amis's *Money* and read it on the plane. I find it rather inspiring in a mad way. It's a crazy world, and I get off on that. **1995**

noel gallagher of Oasis

I was too young for punk, so I felt I missed that era. It was interesting to read the story of John Lydon's life in *Rotten: No Irish, No Blacks, No Dogs* and how the Sex Pistols were really manipulated by the record companies and Malcolm McLaren. **1995**

thurston moore of SonicYouth

Emmett Grogan created the Diggers in the Sixties. This hippie communal ideology. To me, *Ringolevio* is one of the best histories you can read of that time. **1994**

adam duritz of CountingCrows

The Civil War, by Shelby Foote. I'm more of a novel reader, but this is a three-thousand-page history of the Civil War. An incredible story. I've gotten revenge on several of my friends by giving them this trilogy for Christmas. **1994**

aphex twin a.k.a. RichardJames

IRCAM is a really nutty institution of sound in Paris that does a little journal of new, complicated stuff. Mainly the people in it tend to be professors or some fucking freaked-out composers. I don't read books; I only read scientific things like this. **1997**

david yow of theJesusLizard

Mostly I read menus and traffic signs and that's about it. **1996**

LIFE'S LITTLE GUILTY PLEASURES

I n the cozy confines of home, with the shades pulled down and the phone unplugged, folks can enjoy the things they wouldn't want their friends to know about: a Smithsonian-size porn library, Streisand records, sappy movies, Tiffany. Schlock is good for the soul when one is feeling less than fresh.

beck I love British humor. It's just so—*surreal*. **1997**

geri halliwell formerly GingerSpice of theSpiceGirls
You know what's the greatest pleasure? When you're dying to go for a pee, when you get there and have that pee. **1997**

sporty spice of theSpiceGirls (a.k.a. MelanieChisholm)
What's even better . . . when it's freezing cold and your wee's dead warm. **1997**

mark eitzel Seeing Barbra Streisand at the San Jose Arena in California. She's a guilty pleasure. I'm embarrassed to admit what I paid for the seats. I bought other people tickets, too. I shouldn't say this. **1993**

elvis costello Tiffany's my heroine. She's godlike. I *love* that record. I was on a review program, on the radio in London, and they played her and Julia Fordham back to back, and I had to say, "Come on, you yuppies out there, 'fess up." I said, "Tiffany sings the *hell* out of this song. Julia Fordham overemotes, she overextends herself at every turn. And Tiffany's giving this one trashy little love ballad everything she's got." **1989**

nina persson of theCardigans
I buy a lot of fashion magazines, for the pictures. I always hate myself afterwards. It's one of my biggest luxuries: I buy a fashion magazine, read it in five minutes, and hate myself for doing it. It's like candy for me. *Vogue* tends to be pretty good—but it really doesn't do you any good at all. **1997**

lenny kravitz [Nipple piercing] doesn't hurt at all—actually, it feels really good. **1995**

David Cassidy (Henry Diltz/Slamajama)

david cassidy The Flowbee—okay, it was a gift . . . but I still kept it! **1998**

joni mitchell   I'm a smoker, for better or for worse. **1997**

tracy bonham   I never wanted a fax machine because I never
thought of myself as a business lady. Upon encouragement from managers,
lawyers, accountants, I bought one. Now I'm keeping in touch with my family and
faraway friends more than I ever have. **1998**

d'arcy of SmashingPumpkins
All right, all right! You really want to know? I don't know if I should admit this.
Well, I'll just say it. Duran Duran. Did you dress up like John Taylor, too? I wasn't
like a groupie, I wanted to *be* him. He had the best bass lines. He was awesome.
Fucking rock solid, man. Uses some stupid guitars, but he's good. **1996**

scott stapp of Creed
I was really into R&B because I was a vocalist and those guys can really sing. I
love Jodeci. I'm embarrassed about it now, but I listened to Boyz II Men. Take 6
was a group I really got into because of how talented they were as singers. **1998**

wayne coyne of theFlamingLips
I went to see John Tesh yesterday in Atlantic City. I did. Our road manager,
Darryl, is a real local promoter guy, does cool shit in clubs, lots of little shows. He
was working stage for a promoter there who had done the John Tesh show about a
year ago, and he really liked him. Six months later they give him a call asking if
he wanted to stage-manage John Tesh. A thousand bucks a week. So he said,
"Shit, I'm there." He's still our road manager, but he's also stage manager for
John Tesh. John Tesh only plays, like, once every other weekend, so he can go do
that *and* do us. The Flaming Lips and John Tesh—worlds collide. I like that. I
think you can like the situation without liking John Tesh. **1995**

jay-z   *Pretty Woman*—I don't want to tell nobody I like that one. I ain't telling
nobody that. But yeah, that was hot, yo. I was rootin' for that girl. Any movie
that's people winning against the odds. People don't really understand, they be
like, "Rappers want to be mobsters and gangsters and glorify all that." It's really
not that, it's that they relate to someone who's been placed in the position where
they gotta do whatever they gotta do to rise up and get on top. We can relate to
that and that's why we're drawn to it. We feel like we the underdog, and any type
of underdog, like a Scarface, is gonna appeal to us. He was a refugee, came over
here with nothing and just came to money. Who can't relate to that? **1998**

art alexakis of Everclear

Man, I love Ben & Jerry's Coconut Almond Fudge Chip. It's better than dope. It walks all over your mouth, it's such a beautiful thing. But I just found out that I'm hypoglycemic, so I can't eat it. Sometimes I cheat and take one bite and I just feel like hell. This was my last vice! I've been clean twelve years now; I'm happily married. A man can't have some ice cream? It's just not right. **1996**

busta rhymes

I like a lot of clothes, I like a lot of cars, and I like a lot of homes. I love home. I love to have a beautiful home to go to. I love that shit. I have a wonderful home and I have a nice apartment somewhere else. So my family's company and the environment is in one place. And I have the other place for when I want to bring my homeboys over and smoke weed all day. **1998**

stephan jenkins of ThirdEyeBlind

I'm not a big drinker because, to me, you have a choice. If you want to really throw down every night, really go out there and hit it, you can't do that and party on the road. You can't have both. Like, I can't smoke cigarettes and sing well. So which is it gonna be? Make a bunch of excuses and light up, or quit. Last May, I quit. I love cigarettes, man. I love cocktails, I love martinis, I love the paraphernalia, the conviviality, the intoxication is great, but you just can't do both. I still drink, I just don't indulge. **1997**

mike ness of SocialDistortion

Done it all, more than once. Mainly sex without love. That can be damaging. But sometimes you don't have that option. Sex was really my first drug of choice. It can be addicting. **1998**

moby

Pornography and the sex trade in general interest me on one level—obviously I find it sexually stimulating—but I'm really fascinated by the cohesive subculture aspect of it. It's the same thing that attracted me to the different countercultures I've been involved in, from punk rock and hardcore to hip-hop and dancehall reggae and rave culture. It was subversive and had its own distinct mores and aesthetic. The sex trade is similar to that. It's multi-faceted: On one level, there are the human beings involved, then there is the mythic level of it, and all the social stigma attached to it, then the fact that it is so aesthetically cohesive, and there's also an honesty about it that's weird. **1997**

prince be of PMDawn

I'm, like, obsessed with pornography. Period. Hard-core, anything. Except for child pornography. It would have to be adults. More than two adults. Ed Power has this series called *Dirty Debutantes*. He finds normal-looking girls to have sex with. Not like made-up girls with big boobs and all that. He finds really normal women to have a really normal sexual relationship on camera, and it is just hysterical. The women know what's going on, he has conversations with them, he talks to them. He's like, "How do you feel about masturbation?" It is *so* funny. When he actually does have sex with them, he's like, "Be realistic with me, don't lie about anything." There are a thousand of them. I own volumes one to nine hundred. **1998**

"weird al" yankovic I call it Phenorkling. Krazy Glueing

small furry animals to the wall and watching them wriggle. It's a relaxing moment during the day. Better than listening to Yanni records. It helps me become one with the universe. **1996**

melissa auf der maur of Hole

I would rather be living in Victorian times. In my living room I have turn-of-the-century wall hangings from French castles and a mannequin with a turn-of-the-century hoop skirt on it. All of my paintings are of Victorian towns or houses, and I gaze into them and pretend I'm there. I also collect grand-piano shawls; they're kind of like bedspreads, but they're incredible velvet, intricate things. The best way to hang them on the wall is with a thin piece of wood and a really delicate tack on each end. I have all of this in my house, and meanwhile I play in a really big, modern rock band. **1999**

LASTCALL

**D**on't count on these recollections—more than a few are pretty hazy. Lord knows, musicians have seen the insides of more bars than a guy who delivers Bud. But hey, let's hoist a few for Billie Joe Armstrong—he actually phoned in for his *Raves* interview from a bar.

dave pirner, dan murphy, karl mueller of
SoulAsylum

Dave Pirner: How many Irish bars do you think there are in Manhattan?

Karl Mueller: I don't know, four thousand?

Dave Pirner: Four thousand?!

Karl Mueller: It's gotta be somewhere around there.

Dan Murphy: More. I've been to every single one they've got.

Dave Pirner: There's a Molly Malone's in every city in America, just about. Found a great one in Paris, too.

Dan Murphy: Locals won't even give you directions, it's so cool.

Dave Pirner: It was so funny, I walk in there and hear this band playing and they were just great. These French guys doing Pogues covers and stuff. And my road manager's already there. I'm like, guess I found it. We got those guys to come and open for us. I traded them my shamrock underwear for a tambourine. **1998**

mark mcgrath of SugarRay

I throw a hissy *Spinal Tap* fit if there's no Bud backstage. There's always a club that goes, "You've got to try the local microbrew, you're gonna love it!" Then I fucking freak out. I'm just a white trash guy drinking Budweiser, living this fantasy life. I feel like the Make-a-Wish Foundation granted us this rock & roll fantasy and we're living it. We're fucking terminally drunk. **1997**

billie joe armstrong of GreenDay

I'm having a beer right now. Fuck, yeah, I'm in a bar down the street from my house. I'm on my third Budweiser. You know, Americana. Budweiser's the standard, but I like Red Nectar on tap. It's a Humboldt County microbrew that's sweet and satisfying, but at the same time not too sweet. You can taste the alcohol, so you feel like you're being good and bad at the same time—plus there's no aftertaste and it doesn't give you headaches. My favorite bar doesn't have it anymore, so I'm a little bit irritated with them right now. A good cheap beer is Shaefer, made in Olympia. So is Blatz. It's my favorite—I've even been to the brewery. I started drinking it for this band called Blatz. And I used to drink it with my friend Eggplant when we were sixteen. Some bum named him that. Some drunk fool. **1998**

chris ballew of thePresidentsoftheUnitedStatesofAmerica

I've kinda taken up drinking beer as a hobby lately. And it's gotta be Rainier beer, though it's only available in Seattle. Since we haven't been working as intensely, I can afford to drink a couple of beers every day. It's the best beer in the land. It's a total mass-produced pilsner. I am personally not into any of those, like, bitters or lagers or ales or anything. I used to do Guinness all the time, but then I realized it was giving me raging headaches. You can drink five cheap beers in rapid succession. You can really party. **1996**

jay-z Cristal is so smooth. Moët is disgusting. I almost can't drink Moët & Chandon. And Dom, sometimes Dom Perignon tastes better than Cristal—it's right there with it. The 1997 *Robb Report* voted it over Cristal. Cristal was number two, Dom, number one. Hennessy Richard and Louis XIII were voted the best cognacs. **1998**

dean wareham of Luna

I like a good martini. But I have to watch out for them. The last few times I've had martinis I've wound up in trouble. I just become ill from too many of them. At the Temple Bar in New York City, those martinis are like triples. They're gigantic, they're delicious. I only go there when someone else is paying, the drinks are so expensive. I *have* paid myself, but I figure if I'm going to have a drink there, then it includes the glass and I'm allowed to take it home with me. I have a collection of them now. The shot glasses are also really nice—solid. **1996**

simon le bon of DuranDuran

My favorite restaurant in New York is a Japanese restaurant called Omen. They do sake in the wooden boxes. They always pour too much so some of it drips off, it's the tradition. If you get a couple of those, you end up with a whole new cupful of it in the saucer, but that's when you're so pissed you don't want anymore anyway. But you *do*, which is always the way with sake. You *think* you're not pissed, but you *are*. **1997**

rufus wainwright
I love Akbar in L.A. I like bars that attract very different types of people that clash with each other. But everyone's definitely there to drink, which makes the best bars. This is definitely a unisexual establishment.

Those are also always the best bars, by the way. And the icing on the cake is the great jukebox. It's got everything from my record to, uh, my record, the full circle. No, it's got everything. I find California bars have great jukeboxes because so many types of people end up in California in the end. **1998**

cia soro of Whale

Roda Rummet is an old bar in Stockholm where the waitresses had blue eye shadow and walked like ducks and they decided what you should drink. It was impossible for a girl to order a straight whiskey—they said we couldn't take it and served it with soda. **1998**

les claypool of Primus

I've gotten some of the worst hangovers from single-malt whiskeys—contrary to what a good friend who is a Scotsman with a nice, thick accent told me: "Thisis luvely, and it woun't give you a hanghover." So I just drink Absolut and orange juice. Don't want no Smirnoff. You also can't beat Guinness in a can. Abbot Ale has a similar depth charger in it—it's also really good. **1996**

shirley manson of Garbage

Take a tall glass; add ice, a generous shot of Myers's Dark Rum and a touch of tonic. Pop in lime and raise this concoction to your lips. Sit back and enjoy! Simply sublime. **1996**

gwen stefani of NoDoubt

I'm a terrible drinker—meaning I have a terrible time getting alcohol down my throat. I'm trying to learn how to drink beer and to become an alcoholic so I can fit into the whole rock & roll scene! I think my favorite beer is Corona. I like it a *little* bit. I do like Shirley Temples. Some people think they have alcohol but they don't. Just 7UP with that red stuff in it. And cherries. I have to admit I'm totally a goody-goody. I don't do drugs as of yet. But who knows, I might become some huge heroin addict! **1996**

emmylou harris Scrumpy Jack is a hard cider from the west of England for those few souls who refuse to develop a taste for beer. It's great stuff. You can't get hard cider in this country. Canada makes it and maybe Vermont, but the real dry hard stuff I've never been able to get here. **1996**

aphex twin a.k.a. RichardJames

The last good strawberry daiquiris I had were with Bushwick Bill [of the Geto Boys] in L.A. I'd never heard of him until afterwards. I was playing pool at this hotel, and he came down with his mates. He got shot [in 1991] in the face by his girlfriend. Anyway, that was the last time I had a good cocktail. **1997**

Aphex Twin, a.k.a. Richard James (W. Mustain/Warp)

81

gibby haynes of theButtholeSurfers

Cedar Door in Austin has the best margaritas in town—and they've got dancing trees. **1995**

king coffey of theButtholeSurfers

Carousel Lounge [in Austin] features this guy Jay Clark, who's blind and plays the Wurlitzer. He's been there since the Fifties. It's like walking into a David Lynch film. **1995**

bryan "dexter" holland of theOffspring

I like to go down to bars on Main Street [in Orange County, California], especially this place Taxi—it's more run down, down to earth. Club Mesa's kind of a cool place, and 8½ [now called 369] and Electric Circus are pretty good. **1994**

Noodles and Dexter of the Offspring (Self-portraits by Noodles and Dexter, courtesy of Russell A. Trunk/ Chrisam Enterprises, Inc.)

willie nelson Charley's Bar and Grill is a little restaurant about two minutes from where I live in Hawaii and the owner and I are big buddies—we play golf and chess together a lot. I enjoy going over there and picking out a few songs now and again. Kris Kristofferson lives over there, too, so I'll call him up and he'll play with me sometimes. We'll do that for a couple of nights every year around Christmas. **1999**

alec empire of AtariTeenageRiot

Noise Bar in Osaka, I had such a great time there. They can fit, I think, nine people in that bar. It's next to a sex shop. I got a tape there for free, with electronic music on it, that is still my favorite tape or recording. It doesn't say any name or anything, so I don't know who did this. I made a copy of it onto a CD because I fear that I will lose it. That was an interesting night. I hear Sonic Youth is into that bar—they sometimes like it, or talk about it on some record or whatever. **1997**

gaz coombes of Supergrass

They're Beatles crazy in Japan. So we went to this really mad Beatles club. It was crazy, there were all these little Japanese kids dancing to "A Hard Day's Night." It was weird, man. Danny Goffey and I walked in there on my birthday. We had had far too much to drink by the time we wandered in. Everyone started screaming. The DJ went mental. "Oh! Oh! Danny, Gaz! Supergrass! Oh! Ahhh, hey! Hey!" So we had a little dance to the Beatles. It was quite funny. There's nowhere else you could do that. They made a little circle around Danny when he was dancing. I didn't really have control of my limbs at that point, so I wasn't sure what I was doing. There was this Japanese guy who looked just like John Lennon. Bizarre. He had the little round glasses and his haircut. I was going to ask for an autograph. **1997**

WHAT'S COOKIN'?

Whether you live to eat or eat to live, your taste in food says so much about you. To some, food is just a necessity—if it's easy, it's good. To others, culinary delights are divine ecstasies akin to unbelievable sex. Some require a bit of atmosphere with their vittles; others need only tried-and-true recipes and the privacy of their own kitchens. That might not seem rockin', but after long months on the road, can you blame them?

joan jett

Joan Jett's Falafel Recipe

½ pound (or 1 ¼ cup) dry chickpeas
1 teaspoon finely chopped garlic
¾ cup finely chopped onion
1 teaspoon ground cumin
1 teaspoon salt
4 tablespoons chopped cilantro (or parsley)
Pinch of cayenne pepper
2 tablespoons lemon juice
½ teaspoon baking powder
½ cup flour
Oil for frying
Cucumbers
Tomatoes
Lettuce
Pocket pita bread

Serves six to eight

1. Soak chickpeas overnight. Cook in boiling salted water until tender, 1 ½ hours. Drain and mash to a paste in food processor.
2. Mix paste with garlic, onion, cumin, salt, cilantro, cayenne pepper, lemon juice, baking powder and flour. Form into balls or squish flat, like pancakes.
3. Heat two inches of oil in a heavy iron skillet and throw one in. If it doesn't hold together (would you?) add more flour to the mix. Fry until brown.
4. Serve inside pocket pita bread with festively arranged cucumbers, tomatoes and lettuce. Douse with Tahini Sauce (see recipe below).

Tahini Sauce

½ cup sesame paste
¾ teaspoon finely chopped garlic
3 tablespoons lemon juice
1 cup plain yogurt
Blend ingredients until smooth; add seasoning if needed.

1998

erykah badu

I call it Badu's Love Tea; some of it's on the stove right now. The ingredients are, of course, water, your favorite tea bag—I enjoy Country Peach Passion by Celestial Seasonings. Squeeze in the juice of one lime and one lemon and then drop the whole fruit in the water, add fresh, cut-up ginger root, some grade-B maple syrup—it's better for you than honey—cinnamon sticks and a drop of pure peppermint. It's very very very good; it just makes you feel so *good*. Fix it in the morning for your lover, child or whoever you love. **1998**

melissa auf der maur of Hole

Café Santropol in Montreal is the most incredible health-food and fancy fruit ice cream–cake place. It's right around the corner from the house I grew up in. It's an incredible, total hippie commune restaurant that I've gone to for soy sundaes since I was two. It's run by crazy hippies in an old house decorated like a tea room—a wacky place. **1999**

busta rhymes

Right now? I'd probably make some macaroni and cheese and some fried chicken, or, like, a steamed snapper and some bananas and yams, probably some pancakes and eggs. Yeah, I love pancakes. I could eat that now. **1997**

chris robinson of theBlackCrowes

I have four boxes of Kraft macaroni and cheese in my house now. I really live a glamorous lifestyle. When I had an apartment with our drummer years ago, once in a while we'd chop up a kosher hot dog and throw it in there—when we were really living on the town. **1995**

jeff buckley

Hot dogs—the clean, New York variety. You've got your crappy hot dog, fragile bun, watery sauerkraut, ketchup and mustard, and it's only a dollar. It's like eating the city for a dollar. **1995**

justine frischmann of Elastica

I was a vegetarian until the last American tour, but I fell off the wagon. I still can't eat steak, but I love hot dogs. You can't really get them in England. The first thing I did when I got home was go straight to the deli, but they're not the same there.

They're the best things to eat when you have a hangover, and they're the only choice in airports. **1996**

paula cole
We are very industrious about finding good food—finding the one natural-food store in the entire city. Sometimes there are surprises. For instance in Birmingham, Alabama, they have a wonderful health-food store where I had the best mussamen curry I've ever had. I've been vegetarian since I was fourteen. With the odd exception like birthday cake on a birthday, I avoid eggs and dairy. And my body thankfully feels much cleaner and healthier this way. **1998**

ian thornley of BigWreck
I was the whole-wheat kid who wasn't allowed to drink Coca-Cola. We could have brown sugar and stuff. What sucked was that white sugar was around but I wasn't supposed to put it on anything. There were times when I would just stick a spoonful of it in my mouth straight. If someone had a little tin of Nestlé Quik, I was in that stuff first thing. **1998**

isaac hayes
I've got some secret weapons I pull out for my omelettes. You see, some people have a bag of tricks, but I have a bag of bags. I would love to cook Salma Hayek an omelette. I just love her, she's a beautiful lady. I'd put everything in that omelette if it was for her. Aphrodisiacs in there, some herbs from South America, some Chinese herbs, everything I got. I'd dig into my Kama Sutra bag. **1998**

prince be of PMDawn
My wife makes Ice Blue Raspberry Lemonade Kool-Aid with Nutrasweet. Me and my friends just kill it all the time. She also makes an awesome potato salad with potatoes, mayonnaise, and because potato salad needs to have a sweet and sour taste, she uses Nutrasweet instead of sugar. She puts relish, really fine onions, almost like a paste. I go to the Red Lobster every Monday religiously for the Alaska snow crab legs. It is the greatest. If you like seafood, they have this crab-stuffed mushroom that is really awesome. They put mozzarella all over it and bake it. They have a bottomless bucket on Mondays. It's like fifteen bucks—you get as many crab legs as you can consume. **1998**

glen phillips of ToadtheWetSprocket

I make homemade pasta—I crank it through one of those nice little Italian deals. Linguine or angel hair. There's something good about taking a long time to make a meal. **1994**

gaz coombes of Supergrass

I like food mainly, but pasta—that's my food. My great uncle and his whole family are Italian and they moved over to England. Every time I go over to his place, he cooks the most amazing pasta and pizzas. I don't know what he puts in it, but it's superb. I like the red sauces. If I can get the right bolognese, that will do me fine. But a lot of the time in England, they don't do it right, so I have to go for something more interesting. Arrabbiata is quite nice—it's sort of a chili tomato sauce, and carbonara is always a good sauce. And Peroni is one of my favorite beers. It's kind of an all-around good night for me when I go to an Italian restaurant. I have my favorite beer and my favorite food. **1997**

gary numan

At Ed's Easy Diner on King's Road everyone speaks with an American accent for a bit, until they forget. Then it becomes an Australian accent. It's a proper American diner, and you get the best burgers in London, but they're very expensive. It's a bit of a tourist attraction. **1997**

henry rollins

Versailles in Los Angeles is the best Cuban food I've had outside Miami. Versailles is rocking. And at Gaucho Grill you can get a really rocking piece of beef, which is not very politically correct, but I like it anyway. **1994**

coolio

Pica Pica is a little burrito spot in Los Angeles, on Sunset Boulevard and La Brea. The burritos are so good, I can't even drive past that motherfucker without getting one. And they deliver! **1995**

jackson browne

La Super-Rica on North Milpas Street, Santa Barbara, California, is a beacon for people interested in beautiful, fresh Mexican food. The secret to the whole place is the tortillas. You get a little pot of cheese and these tortillas, and you mix it with salsa fresca and really great Mexican beer. **1994**

edwyn collins Khas Tandoori, on Chamberlayne Road in London—it's my neighborhood Indian restaurant and my favorite. The guy who runs it is named Ali, and at Christmastime, he gives all his regular customers a free bottle of wine and a really chintzy calendar. **1995**

Edwyn Collins (Self-portrait by Edwyn Collins, courtesy of Russell A. Trunk/Chrisam Enterprises, Inc.)

RAVES

mark eitzel There's a restaurant I like in San Francisco, but I'm not going to say where. I don't want it packed with goddamn music-industry people. **1993**

lucinda williams Everything on the menu is good at Guero's in Austin, Texas, including tamales made fresh every day, tortillas made by hand, the best salsas and pollo achiote tacos, excellent flan and Ruta Maya coffee. **1998**

mix master mike of InvisibleSkratchPiklz and theBeastieBoys

I went to this restaurant in Tokyo and had beef sashimi—*the bomb*. They give three thin strips at a time; they have small portions in Japan, so definitely I had to keep tellin' 'em to bring more. **1998**

rick nielsen of CheapTrick

Go eat at Momma'Zu in Richmond, Virginia. It's in a lousy neighborhood, there's a cross-dressing person that sits out front who weighs three hundred plus, and the food's unbelievable. All kinds of people eat there—those with spikes through their eyelids to doctors. People just line up. It'd probably cost you two million dollars to make a place look this bad if you started from scratch. **1996**

leann rimes Chicken Alfredo with fettuccini noodles at Grady's American Grill in Dallas is probably my favorite food, along with bacon baked potatoes. When I'm in Dallas, I go eat there all the time. I don't have my own table yet, but when I go in there everybody knows me. **1997**

art alexakis of Everclear

Kansas City, Missouri, rocks. It has the best barbecue—Gates and Sons. It's just killer. They treat us like rock stars and they have for years. **1996**

fred schneider of theB-52's

Pedro Paramo on Fourteenth Street in Manhattan is my favorite undiscovered restaurant for really good Mexican food. I'd like to see them do more business. It's traditional Mexican, which I like. **1996**

bo diddley In New York there's the Waverly Restaurant, on Sixth Avenue and Waverly. It's in the Village, near Washington Square. They've got good food there; the cooks are very good. Also the Second Avenue Deli. They got some pastrami sandwiches down there make you slap your mama and look at your daddy funny. I just discovered them and they got it goin' on. You gotta check them out. **1996**

lou reed   Hot pastrami at the Carnegie Deli. That's a really serious New York experience. We do this, like, once a year. Order a hot pastrami on rye with mustard. That's it. Period. **1989**

jay-z   Oxtail with rice and peas. Wonderful. Great. West Indian is my favorite food, by far. I'm not even from the islands. I just love the shit. My friend from St. Thomas got me into it. Island Spice on West Forty-fourth Street is the best place to get it in New York. When I go in the studio, I try to get a place right by there so they can deliver. I get curried shrimp with white rice from there, too. And they got the island punch. It's crazy. It's this red punch, man—I don't even know what juices are in it. When there's a lot of us, we get this whole big mayonnaise jar full of it. **1998**

lenny kravitz   The best falafel in the world, particularly the special eggplant falafel with hot sauce, is at L'As du Falafel in Paris's Marais quarter. **1993**

yuka honda of CiboMatto
We don't like to answer food questions because we have many favorites and it's unfair for the other ones we didn't name. But we do like to eat falafel with grape leaves on top. There's a way to eat it: First you eat one grape leaf, then you eat half a falafel, then you eat the half of the rest of the grape leaves, then you eat half of the rest of your falafel, then you eat all the rest of it together. **1996**

jewel   I've been on a jelly-bean binge. I guess it should be its own food group—all those flavors and colors. Then you start combining them—cream soda with a cherry on top, or a juicy pear with a strawberry. **1998**

john popper of BluesTraveler
A Jack and Jill's ice-cream sandwich is a normal junk-foody little ice-cream sandwich, but when you bite into one, you're instantly whisked back to being four and

excitedly waiting for the Good Humor man to show up. Oddly, I would pick the Good Humor ice-cream bar, but it's so hard to find them unless you run down one of those trucks. The chocolate wafers and the vanilla ice cream—you can wait until it melts and squeeze the vanilla ice cream out and chew it all off. You can peel off the wafer. Ahhh, it's wonderful. And a big glass of ice water—people underestimate ice water all the time. If you're really thirsty, you can drink Gatorade, you can drink soda—but have a big-ass glass of ice water with, like, a pound of ice in it. I'm talking one of those huge beer steins full of ice water. Nothing like that. **1998**

darius rucker of HootieandtheBlowfish

A good Southern-made sweet-potato pie *is* like sex. Incredible. **1995**

lil' kim Italian is one of my favorite foods. I like to go to Little Italy and go

crazy. I like Jamaican food and soul food. I love snow crab legs, but I can't eat them. I'm allergic to seafood; I get hives, my throat swells, it's hard for me to breathe. But I love them! Scallops, too, but they break me out. Of course, *Chez McDonalde's*—that's McDonald's! The chicken sandwich with cheese and orange drink is *it*. **1997**

adam duritz of CountingCrows

Boiled crawfish is my favorite food. I could eat pounds and pounds. **1994**

bob seger I eat tons of chicken. I just love chicken; it's good for you.

Especially white-meat chicken breast. That's a big one for me. The old low-fat thing. **1996**

steven page of BarenakedLadies

If I can have an omelette with home fries and toast, I'm a happy guy at any meal. With grapefruit juice—that's a delicious juice. Sometimes I try to mislead myself into thinking I want oatmeal, but I know I never do. Coffee is such a varied drink. You can get dishwater, and you can get dark roast. But if I'm gonna go for the Starbucks experience, I'll have a grande skim cappuccino, 'cause I'm a grande guy, and I need less fat in my day. **1998**

lisa loeb Flourless chocolate cake, and it has to be really dense. I also really like the miniature Reese's Peanut Butter Cups. They have good peanut-butter density. I have a dream of having lemon ice cream, but I have to find somebody who can make lemon ice cream where they use lemons, but it doesn't make the cream curdle. And cheese fries—with *real* cheese. **1997**

Lisa Loeb (Self-portrait by Lisa Loeb, courtesy of Russell A. Trunk/Chrisam Enterprises, Inc.)

adam "ad-rock" horovitz of theBeastieBoys

Just straight-up coffee, with cream or milk or whatever and sugar. I have no problems with espresso. I just need coffee fast. I don't want to wait around. **1998**

tracy bonham
A banana with peanut butter and a big glass of milk. I can't cook. **1998**

"weird al" yankovic
I'm famous for my peanut butter, broccoli and Vaseline sandwiches. On whole-wheat bread, of course. If I ever start a health-food restaurant, that'll be the main item. Once you get past the greasiness of the Vaseline, it does satisfy one of the major food groups—petroleum. **1996**

ziggy marley
I recommend trying some vegetarian dish like callaloo. It's like spinach, but it's different. It's authentic Jamaican—steamed. It's a leafy vegetable, so you just steam it. **1997**

gwen stefani of NoDoubt

Pizza is probably my favorite food. You can't go wrong. Frozen, terrible pizza is good pizza. Basically, even bad pizza is good. **1996**

dave pirner of SoulAsylum

Baby corn makes me crazy. Mutant alien corn. You eat the cob. I can't even think about that. Does it grow on stalks? **1998**

billy gibbons of ZZTop

Mopane worms are a peculiar culinary delight. They're some sort of critter that loves the fruit from the Mopane tree. They're a high source of protein and are harvested by the bagful. They're smoked, salted, hit with a little Peri-Peri spice and, brother, stand back. They're crunchy, they have the delightfulness of the peanut, and they look frightful enough to scare your best friend from ever taking a bite of anything edible again. They're legal for importation across the world—go out and get your bag of Mopanes today. I've actually been leaning toward the vegetarian side of things for the last five years. I think I broke the code—Texas guys are a vital part of the meat industry. **1996**

PLAYTHATFUNKYMUSIC

If your toilet needs fixin', call a plumber. If your record collection needs fixin', find a musician. Yup, like the bards of yore, musicians know their stuff, both past and present, and always have a few perennials to recommend.

shaun ryder of HappyMondays and BlackGrape

Oh, God. My favorite album? It would have to be, like, *Shaun Ryder's Twenty Top Hits* or something. Ha! There's so many good ones—everything from the Beatles to Dr. Dre, man, fuck knows, I love it all. **1996**

sean lennon

I don't know when I realized that [Yoko Ono's] *Plastic Ono Band* was the greatest record ever. I don't know if it was because it's my mom or what. But I got it. Why do I like it? I don't know why people *don't* like it. **1998**

luther vandross

I still love David Bowie—he started me out in the business. I still love the record that we made together, *Young Americans*. I loved *Let's Dance*, too. Laura Nyro left some great stuff behind. She did an album where Labelle did all the background vocals called *Gonna Take a Miracle*. It was a sensational diva meeting. I also love Cyndi Lauper—beneath that image is a really good voice. I love, needless to say, Whitney. I mean, I would buy a recording of Whitney Houston reciting the phone book or the alphabet. **1998**

john popper of BluesTraveler

John Coltrane and Miles Davis on Miles's *Kind of Blue* was the best. These two musicians went in different directions, but this is a great example of them at the height of their playing. After that, Coltrane got a little too avant-garde, and Miles started to explore all different kinds of music. **1998**

heavy d.

Bob Marley's *Legend* is probably the only thing that stays in my CD player. It's timeless. **1997**

paula cole

I love everything by Bob Marley. It's so hard to choose one album—*Rastaman Vibration* would be it. His music is eternal. I feel so humbled by it; it's just so profound. I love his band. I love that he was loyal to the same musicians and that they cultivated a sound over many years. And he makes a political statement. He took responsibility with his leadership—he was a visionary for his lifetime. He's a social speaker for his people, and he helped to educate white people a little bit about race. He gave hope. **1998**

beck

The Osmonds have a great song about going back to Utah. They had one really heavy record in '73. It's their Sabbath record. Its called *Crazy Horses*. The song's like pounding drums and heavy guitars and a Moog comin' in. The music's really rocking and legitimate. They were plugging into the stuff that was coming out at the time. **1996**

jay-z Donny Hathaway is crazy the way he draws you into the story of a song. He was like the Donald Goines of music. He's so visual. Me and my cousin would put on Donny Hathaway's "A Song for You" and drive our little cousins around in the car at, like, five miles an hour on a busy street like Myrtle Avenue in Brooklyn and tell them to look out the window. We'd see people in front of the liquor stores. It would seem like everything was moving in slow motion. It would blow their minds. It was a real trip—almost like a video. I had a pearl-white Lexus then with TVs and all that—I gave it to my mom. **1998**

bob seger The Ronettes' "Be My Baby" absolutely killed me the first time I heard it. Phil Spector is a great producer. Kind of a difficult guy, people said, but a great producer for his era. The Spector era from '60 to '62 just prior to the Beatles was a great era for record making. Never heard any music like that before. It was neat. **1996**

montell jordan Without question, the Isley Brothers' "Voyage to Atlantis" was the song I played over and over again, from when I was about five or six. **1998**

lisa loeb It might be cooler to say *Led Zeppelin II,* but I really do like *Houses of the Holy* the best. I love "Over the Hills and Far Away"—which was actually one of the first songs I played in a band. That was the reason I originally got the album. **1997**

chris ballew of **thePresidentsoftheUnitedStatesofAmerica**
Blue Öyster Cult started off with a trilogy of records that have all black-and-white covers with geometric drawings, full of incredibly psychedelic, weird songs. Like, "She's as Beautiful as a Foot" and "I'm on the Lamb but I Ain't No Sheep" and "Cities on Flame with Rock and Roll." And, of course, the classic, "Godzilla," which is basically what all alternative rock is based on. You can't go wrong with a BÖC greatest-hits record, kids. **1996**

terence trent d'arby Believe it or not, until three months ago, I had never heard Pink Floyd's *Dark Side of the Moon.* While on tour, I decided to put it on while I was in the bath. That way, if I wasn't convinced in the first five minutes, I wasn't going to get up and turn it off. And I was truly moved. I totally understood why it happened to fit in the *Zeitgeist* of that particular time. **1994**

axl rose of Gunsn'Roses
The two records I always buy if there's a cassette deck around and I don't have the tapes in my bag are [the Sex Pistols'] *Never Mind the Bollocks* and *Queen II*. I'd be in a bind to figure out which one I'd want if I was stranded on a desert island. I might go with the Pistols, because maybe a boat would hear me if I played it. **1989**

moby
I missed Eighties metal when it was happening. I started the Eighties involved in the hardcore punk scene, then I got into hip-hop, and from 1985 on I was almost exclusively involved in house music and then techno. So I had no idea about most Eighties metal. My ex-girlfriend told me I absolutely had to buy Mötley Crüe, *Shout at the Devil*, because it's one of the best records ever made. I have to agree with her. A week doesn't go by now that I don't listen to it. **1997**

dean wareham of Luna
The Feelies' first record, *Crazy Rhythms*, is so textured and layered, I hear new things every time I listen to it. Most pop records are something that you like immediately—and disposable after, like, five listens. This one shows you can make a really intense rock record without playing through Marshall stacks. It has a sub-urban vibe to it. **1996**

polly jean harvey
Soft Cell singing "Tainted Love" is probably one of my favorite songs of all time. **1995**

carnie wilson
The B-52's are my favorite band ever, ever, ever. No one comes close. The most original band. I even love an album called *Mesopotamia* that a lot of people don't even know. There's a song called "Cake"—they're talking about a cake! What is better than that? It makes me laugh. They should be selling millions and millions. On *Cosmic Thing* I love "Bushfire" and "Junebug." "Bushfire," ha-ha! I think of a big vagina on fire, isn't that weird? **1997**

stevie nicks

When I rock out, I usually play tapes I've made over the years—all the big songs through the Eighties and the beginning of the Nineties. I can't really listen to a whole CD. I'm gonna have two or three favorites and that's all. **1998**

les claypool **of Primus**

We listened to Tom Waits's *Rain Dogs* a lot in our early touring days, cruising around in a '76 Dodge van with six smelly guys in it, listening to Pink Floyd and *Rain Dogs*. It brings back memories. **1996**

rick nielsen **of CheapTrick**

I recommended Patto to Billy Corgan. He bought *Patto* on vinyl for fifty bucks and told me he took it off after one side wondering if I had been pulling his leg. I didn't *think* I was. I guess he didn't get into Patto. I don't care how talented he is, he still has to go to Rick Nielsen School. **1996**

ozzy osbourne

I thought one of the best albums around in a long time was that Peter Gabriel album *So*. I was waiting for the followup, but it was just a watered-down version of *So*. **1995**

nina persson

of theCardigans

I think anything by Black Sabbath, actually. With Ozzy Osbourne. I listen to very little BS without him. I love the song "Black Sabbath." The one that starts with a church bell. I only heard them four years ago when we were thinking of covering "Sabbath Bloody Sabbath." That

Ozzy Osbourne (Guzman/Epic)

101

was the first time that I realized that it was actually good music. I was pretty mellow in my music tastes before that so that was a bigger step to enlarge my spectrum. **1997**

john lennon "Oh Happy Day" [by the Edwin Hawkins Singers] is the biggest mind-blower I've heard since that Procol Harum thing, "A Whiter Shade of Pale." I have had lots of mind-blowers, but "Oh Happy Day" is the biggest one. **1969**

pete townshend I really dug the Beach Boys. Their incredibly architectural control of music is as powerful as the Who anyday. "I Can Hear Music" has one of the most powerful musical backings I've ever heard. . . . They're another group I dig because they aren't afraid of saying what they feel they should, like the Beatles . . . well, John Lennon at least. Or Dylan, though I think he tends to close himself. **1969**

ana da silva of theRaincoats

Billie Holiday's and Kurt Cobain's voices make me cry when I listen to them. They both express such an incredible amount of sadness. I was standing outside a record shop when I heard Nirvana's "All Apologies" for the first time. My tears just jumped out and fell down my face. **1996**

john wozniak of MarcyPlayground

Built to Spill rock—those guys are amazing. *Perfect From Now On* is currently my favorite. Melodically it's an incredibly beautiful record. And for a third record that's pretty impressive. I missed an opportunity to see them in New York last summer and I was just totally miserable. **1998**

chrissie hynde of thePretenders

I'm certainly a born-again rock fan since I saw Urge Overkill. I think their album *Saturation* is my favorite since [Iggy and the Stooges'] *Raw Power*. Musically, the band has sex, style, swagger. Liz Phair's *Exile in Guyville* is excellent, too. She's a very expressive rock singer. Her songs are soulful, moving and punky. She's from Chicago, like Urge Overkill. There must be something in the water. **1994**

wayne coyne of theFlamingLips

Open-mindedness is a good thing 95 percent of the time. Unfortunately, there is that 5 percent of shit that gets in there that isn't any good. Even a band like King Crimson, who've gone on to make a dozen bullshit, prog-rock nothin' records, there's at least four or five of their songs that are just badass. I don't care what a band stands for, if the song's good I'll listen to it. Some records I know so well I can put them on in my head. Like *Pretenders,* I can hear it without it coming out of speakers. **1995**

tanya donelly of ThrowingMuses and Belly

"Whatta Man" by Salt-n-Pepa and En Vogue is probably the sexiest thing I've heard in a long time. They're in control, and it's a great song. It encourages men to figure out where the button is. **1994**

darryl "d.m.c." mcdaniels of Run-D.M.C.

I love Lauryn Hill because she's like, "I'm not gonna forfeit my individuality or my originality just to be dope in someone's eyes." Those are the people that always last. Be unique, be yourself, do what you plan to do and you will get blessed with the money and all that. She blew up. She sang the songs she wanted to sing, did music she wanted make and this and that. She didn't have to run out and get all these producers and she ain't gotta run out there and get twenty or fifty guest rappers on her album. **1998**

stone gossard of PearlJam

Supergrass's *In It for the Money* is one of the best rock records I've heard in so long. They're fucking genius! The harmonies? They rule! I'm also completely sold on Radiohead—ever since *The Bends.* And they've taken it to the next level on *OK Computer.* It's truly genius. They should be on, like, classic rock radio—they're like Pink Floyd. Wouldn't it be great if somebody at classic rock radio was like, "Here's a band that totally fits our format, let's screw waiting for ten years—let's take a chance!" **1998**

rob thomas of Matchbox20

Ani DiFranco floors me—the honesty in her lyrics. I've listened to that *Dilate* record and I get embarrassed for myself sometimes. Her songs are so great, I want to work harder at writing. Her lyrics are so honest, direct and to the point. It makes me think about my life. I end up thinking I'm an asshole because if she's singing a song about a relationship, it's from her point of view and it's such a great, cynical point of view—the way she just tears into somebody in her songs. I think, "Yeah, that's me, I'm such an asshole. Fuck!" I talk shit all the time, I'm a big liarhead, that's me. Her song "Napoleon" makes me sick that I ever got a record deal. **1997**

prince be
of PMDawn

I listen to *Passionfruit,* by Michael Franks, incessantly, just boom, all the time. My brother Jarrett likes Michael Franks's *Sleeping Gypsy.* He likes them both, actually, but we sort of got introduced to Michael Franks's *Passionfruit,* and now we can't get away from it. Every day. Everybody has to hear it. **1998**

jim kerr of SimpleMinds
Portishead's *Dummy* sounds like spy movies you haven't seen but think you have. **1995**

8-23-97
BIG PLANETFEST
Rock show —
drawn sitting
next to the
Better than
Ezra guys.

yes...
This the only face
I know how to draw —
but it could be me. Really.

↑
FRED

Rob Thomas of Matchbox 20 (Self-portrait by Rob Thomas, courtesy of Russell A. Trunk/Chrisam Enterprises, Inc.)

noel gallagher of Oasis

Dummy by Portishead is moody, deep, dark soul music. And I love Beth Gibbons's voice. A really unique, original record, which is hard to come by these days. **1995**

mick jones of theClash and BigAudioDynamite

With *Definitely Maybe*, Oasis has taken over where the Stone Roses left off, even though the Stone Roses have a new album. It's their attitudes and their haircuts. And they've got a great pop sensibility. I like all the singles, especially "Live Forever" and "Cigarettes and Alcohol." **1995**

queen latifah

The first thing I did when I got signed to Motown was order Stevie Wonder's whole catalog. His writing is ridiculously on point. *Songs in the Key of Life* is one of my favorites. I toured with that album—I played it every day. **1994**

billy gibbons of ZZTop

Chemical Brothers—man, I'm tellin' you, track five and track nine on *Dig Your Own Hole*. Those things are slayin' me. Plus there's just enough room for a greasy blues guitar—I think I know who could supply it. These cats, the Chemical Brothers, are definitely funk masters. I was at this little surf shop checkin' out this sound. I said, "Man, what are you playing in here?" It was G. Love and Special Sauce. The guy said, "They're enough, aren't they?" I tip my hat to them in the third verse of our new song "Rhythmeen." I was happy to find they have a few records available. **1997**

busta rhymes

A Tribe Called Quest always came with the bangin' shit. A classic album is Tribe's *Low End Theory*. They got the phenomenal summertime, windows down, leanin' in ya' jeep, system bangin' type-A beats. Word up. I'm loving Wyclef Jean's *The Carnival*. That's incredible to me right now. On a worldly hip-hop representation level, I just think that album captures so many different things, from cultural significance to emotion, all at the same time. **1997**

stephan jenkins of ThirdEyeBlind

When I was in high school, I went through a phase of wanting to be black and regretting that I wasn't. I got over that, but the music was still there. There's a lot of hip-hop I really loved. De La Soul and A Tribe Called Quest and Too $hort are just the greatest. One of the greatest songs ever written is "Mind Playing Tricks on Me," by the Geto Boys. When people ask me what a lyrical influence is, that eventually comes to mind. A song like that, or "Tennessee," by Arrested Development, is what rock music can do at its best: create this whole world, even if it's a nightmare world. You step into it for two minutes and it makes your whole life make a little more sense. **1998**

neil young I love rap! It's speaking to the people on the streets. It's a whole new way of communicating that's so open to saying exactly what the hell's on people's minds in a clever way, a way that you can listen to and move your body to. Similar to, like, "Subterranean Homesick Blues." Bob Dylan is early rap. What the hell's the difference? This is the shit that's going to keep music alive— don't close it off because you don't understand it. **1993**

tina weymouth of TalkingHeads and TomTomClub
Wu-Tang Clan have the best rhythm. My kids bought *Enter the Wu-Tang, 36 Chambers*, and I love it. Occasionally I listen to the lyrics and they're pretty funny— there's so much fuckin' this and fuckin' that, it cancels out in my poor mind. The music goes back to real fundamentals. The grooves aren't dying in America, they've just changed form. **1996**

simon le bon of DuranDuran
I used to lie on the floor at my parents' house in Middlesex and listen to the *Clockwork Orange* score album by Wendy Carlos. I would turn the speakers so they would point at each other and I would put my head in between them and listen to that. Affected my hearing a little bit, actually. Plus, of course, David Bowie's *Aladdin Sane,* Joni Mitchell's *Blue,* Genesis's *The Lamb Lies Down on Broadway,* Deep Purple's *Machine Head,* the Rolling Stones' *Let It Bleed* and the Damned and the Clash—they are all incredible. Patti Smith's *Horses* got me through three months in the desert in Israel in 1978—that and an Israeli soldier girl. I can go on and on and on—Iggy Pop's *The Idiot,* Joy Division's *Unknown Pleasures,* the The's *Infected*— and, for God's sake, where would we be without KC and the Sunshine Band's "Shake Your Booty"? **1997**

LET'SGETITON

Ah, the mating dance, that tangled tango of love. The drive to procreate has always fueled rock & roll; some even say musicians feel the pull of their loins more fiercely than most. Herein, teenage crushes, make-out music, sex, love and the wide-open spaces in between.

eddie izzard
My thoughts on sex are: Yes it's great and it should be compulsory. **1998**

cia soro of Whale
Sex is a great way to blow your mind out for a while. If you quit drinking, quit drugs, quit cigarettes and coffee—that's what's left. **1998**

anthony kiedis of theRedHotChiliPeppers
Sex seems like the perfect material for art, like death and every other fundamental aspect of existence. **1992**

scott weiland of StoneTemplePilots
Sex. See, *sex* is the most important thing in the whole world. And not just for humans, either—for animals, too. I mean, people seem to think that humans are the only ones who approach sex for pleasure—that's what organized religion tries to teach us. But you know what? When I was a kid, my dog used to hump my leg all the time. And obviously, he *knows* he's not gonna get a puppy from doing that. So there's got to be some kind of sexual pleasure that dogs get from humping your leg. Sex is the most important thing in the world. It's the most important thing to *me* when I get off tour. It's better than going to Disneyland, okay. Better than Magic Mountain. **1993**

Stone Temple Pilots: Robert DeLeo, Dean DeLeo, Scott Weiland, and Eric Kretz (from left)
(John Eder/Atlantic)

moby I don't think there's any reason to hesitate to flirt with someone. Flirting without an agenda: sitting in a bar, meeting someone, having a couple of drinks with them, that sort of nice anxiety that comes with subtle romantic contact. It doesn't mean sleeping with anyone, it doesn't even mean kissing. Just flirting. Just unthreatening romantic contact. You can walk away from it and have a nice little warm glow and your ego's been stroked and you also know that you've made someone feel good. Everybody benefits. I also like flirting because I'm pathologically incapable of committed monogamous relationships. I think it's some deep-rooted physiological response. My limbic system or some ancient part of my brain springs up and tells me I'm physically capable of inseminating half the world—why tie yourself to one person? **1997**

babyface I was in love with love. Puppy love hit me hard. Little heartaches lingered with me for a long while. Even in grade school I had a romantic soul. I'd write poems to girls. I'd write love letters for my pals. I did more writing about love than actual lovemaking. I guess you could call me an innocent. I was a virgin until I was nineteen. I enjoyed the emotion of getting lost in love— like nothing else mattered. **1994**

joni mitchell I don't pray that often. [But once] I prayed an embarrassed prayer: "Look, God, I know I don't write. I know I don't call. However, I don't need that much. All I need is a real good kisser who likes to play pinball." **1991**

alanis morissette I had my first kiss when I was in grade one— that was more of a cheek kiss, but he was definitely my boyfriend. His name was Jeffrey, and I'm very curious to see where he is right now and what he's doing. We were both equally into each other. It was great. He's the template by which I measure all men. It lasted many months and we were exclusive. And the one in grade eight; we were both about to go into class, at the bottom of a set of stairs, and he leaned over and kissed me. It was very exciting. I had had a crush on him for a year. **1998**

iggy pop I lost my virginity the summer I was twenty. I was old. People are like, yeah, he probably did it at ten, eleven. No, I was older. It wasn't so great—it wasn't, like, a winner. It was more like, so that's what the deal is. Then I wanted to try it on everybody. I went around practicing for a whole summer. "Let me see. Would you wanna do it? Let's see how it goes with you." Didn't really matter who it was. But the best one was this little girl with a big cast on her leg and she liked me, so that was really cool. The best thing that can happen in the summertime is to make love to a girl that you really want. **1996**

john wozniak of MarcyPlayground

The first time I ever held a girl's hand—it was Sherry—and I was in a hotel room. We were at a prom. I was a sophomore and this senior asked me to go as her date even though I was dating Sherry. I went and Sherry didn't take too kindly to that so she just showed up. We hadn't done anything yet; we were just "going out" like you do in high school. As soon as she showed up, I totally ignored the girl I went with, who started drinking heavily because she knew her night wasn't going to be any fun. She eventually passed out in one of the rooms a few people had rented upstairs. That was wrong of me, but I was going out with Sherry. That's when we held hands. It was magical and special the first time I held Sherry's hand. It was all about love and being in love. It's innocent and powerful and pure and intense. It was the first time it had ever happened to me. We would spend hours and hours holding each other's hands and staring into each other's eyes. And that's not something that's happened to me since. We're still great friends. **1998**

steven tyler of Aerosmith

I've always been sexually active. If "to climax" is what the term means, to *climax*, why don't we do it all the time? We should be doing it three or four times a day. It's not about stupid and nasty. It's what we should *all* be doing. **1994**

colin greenwood of Radiohead

I've never taken advantage of the opportunity of one-night stands. It's like treating sex like sneezing. Sex is a fairly disgusting sort of tufted, smelly-area kind of activity, which is too intimate to engage in with strangers. I'm all for the erotic in terms of imagination, but the physical side is something different. I feel tremendous guilt for any sexual feelings I have, so I end up spending my entire life feeling sorry for fancying somebody. Even in school, I thought girls were so wonderful that I was scared to death of them. I masturbate a lot. That's how I deal with it. **1995**

rupaul   [Porn star] Daryl Brock is incredible. My second favorite is Mike Nichols—not to be confused with the other one—and my other favorite is Eric Stone. He's got a big, hairy ass and I love a hairy ass. You don't see many hairy asses in gay porn. **1996**

axl rose of **Gunsn'Roses**
I can't get enough of women, and I don't see the same thing that other men can see in men. I'm not into gay or bisexual experiences. But that's hypocritical of me, because I'd rather see two women together than just about anything else. That happens to be my personal favorite thing. **1989**

brian wilson   My favorite make-out music is the Erroll Garner classic song "Misty," performed by Johnny Mathis. **1998**

sarah mclachlan   Peter Gabriel's *Passion* is great music to make love to. He inspired me when I was sixteen to step outside of classical music. He was writing music I wanted to write. He's so crafty at blending cultures musically. **1994**

me'shell ndegéocello   I like Snoop Doggy Dogg. He's misogynist as hell, but you can't tell me he doesn't have a flow. Sometimes you just put on music to hear it, and it's rockin'—it makes you want to move, makes you want to dance, makes you want to fuck. **1994**

mark eitzel   *Here's to Life*, by Shirley Horn, is the most romantic album I've ever heard. **1994**

robyn hitchcock   Music and sex both demand complete attention, so I never mix them. **1998**

david bowie   My favorite make-out music is Vaughan Williams or Public Enemy, depending on the time of day. If there's no CD player around, I have no problem *hummmmmmmming*. **1998**

tina weymouth of **TalkingHeads** and **TomTomClub**
Beau Jocque and the Zydeco Hi-Rollers can do it live, really. You wanna fuck to these guys. I saw them in Lafayette, Louisiana, at a black cowboy bar. All the

ladies were dressed for Sunday, and the men changed their shirts between sets. They'd go out to their trailer, just like rodeo studs, and change their outfits—hats and shirts, everything went together. They have this funky, sexy Cajun-zydeco way of dancing. If you're the woman, they grind on you, but they're not trying to dominate you, they're just feeling what they should be—tough men. It makes line dancing look really cracker. **1996**

john popper of BluesTraveler
Peter Luger steak house in Brooklyn has the best steak on earth. It's like really good sex—a rare and much sought-after commodity. Oh, there's good sex. There's even real sex. But there's not really good sex all that often. And that period afterwards when you're cuddling and you're looking in her eyes and she's looking back at you and you both can't tell if you're dreaming or not. *That* is a great moment. **1998**

janet jackson
Sex isn't just fire and heat; it's natural beauty. Doing what comes naturally. It's letting go, giving and getting what you need. In the age of AIDS, it certainly requires being responsible. On a psychological level, though, good sex, satisfying sex, is also linked with losing yourself, releasing, using your body to get out of your body. Well, for the first time, I'm feeling free. I love feeling deeply sexual—and don't mind letting the world know. For me, sex has become a celebration, a joyful part of the creative process. **1993**

michael stipe of R.E.M.
Even in a marriage or love affair, you never reveal everything to the other person in that love. There's always something you return to yourself. I think that's real important. **1984**

tina turner
I like a man who is strong but giving. I like them not too fashion conscious, but they've got to have their look. They don't have to be good looking. . . . I like what I call ugly cute. I like for a man to have pretty hands—and I don't like ugly feet. When I look at a man, first I notice his hands and next his feet. After that [*laughs*], I'll talk. But I've made allowances—I've dated guys who don't have great feet. I don't like him to wear fragrances; I just want him to smell clean. And he has to be extremely masculine . . . the kind of guy who can put me in my place just by looking at me. **1986**

David Bowie (EMI)

david bowie I'd never been out with a model before so I hadn't even bargained on the cliché of the rock star and the model as being part of my life. So I was well surprised to meet one who was devastatingly wonderful and not the

113

usual sort of bubblehead that I'd met in the past. I make no bones about it. I was naming children the night we met. I knew that Iman was for me, it was absolutely immediate. I just fell under her spell. Our romance was conducted in a very gentlemanly fashion, I hope, for quite some time. Lots of being led to doorways and polite kisses on the cheek. Flowers and chocolates and the whole thing. I knew it was precious from the first night, and I just didn't want anything to spoil it. **1993**

john lennon
I can be [alone without Yoko Ono], but I don't wish to be. There is nothing more important than our relationship, nothing. We dig being together all the time, and both of us could survive apart, but what for? I'm not going to sacrifice love, real love, for any fuckin' whore, or any friend, or any business, because in the end, you're alone at night. Neither of us wants to be, and you can't fill the bed with groupies. I don't want to be a swinger. Like I said in the song, I've been through it all, and nothing works better than to have somebody you love hold you. **1971**

art garfunkel
I think Nicole Kidman is hot. So's my wife, but I mean Nicole Kidman is a really watchable actress. *To Die For*—one horny movie, if you ask me. **1997**

shannon hoon of BlindMelon
Jill Cunniff and Gaby Glaser of Luscious Jackson have sexy voices. It sounds like they're sitting in the corner of a room with their hands half over their mouths. It makes me all giddy inside. **1994**

tori amos
I wanted to give my virginity to Robert Plant when I was ten years old. I was bleeding, babe, I was bleeding. When I would listen to [Led Zeppelin's] music, I would feel passionate. I would get wet, and then it all dried up as I got older. It made me feel like a hot girl. "Black Dog." Yummy. Put it on, throw that head back. *Rrrrowww.* But my commitment is to being wet. **1994**

k.d. lang
I like Kate Jackson from *Charlie's Angels*—the smart, butch one. **1997**

rickie lee jones
Anthony Hopkins—any time, any place. **1993**

thurston moore of SonicYouth

Lili Taylor is a really good actress. Beautiful. I want T-shirts that say her name in Magic Marker on the front and to wear them onstage. But I don't want to embarrass her. She's the coolest. **1994**

prince be of PMDawn

I used to have a crush on Christina Applegate. I don't think I have a crush on her anymore. I think if I have a crush on anyone, it would be Jennifer Lopez. My wife hates any time I see that girl. She was really good in *Out of Sight*. Oh, my God, she was so good! I've seen all her movies. **1998**

paula cole

I'm not really a sports person, although I do have to admit I have a crush. I saw Allen Iverson of the Philadelphia 76ers play and I just about died. I have a crush on him now. It's his attitude: He's so fucking badass that it's beautiful. **1998**

shirley manson of Garbage

Brian Laudrup, Danish forward of the Glasgow Rangers of Scotland—a glorious footballer who plays with awe-inspiring finesse and who's in possession of the most gorgeous pair of thighs in tight white shorts I've ever seen in my life. God bless you, sir. **1996**

NIGHTSTOREMEMBER

**E**very performer has good gigs, bad gigs, okay gigs and gigs he or she will never forget. Maybe everything went right, like it did for Gary Numan at the Hammersmith Odeon or Montell Jordan in Houston; maybe it was the venue, as it was for Graham Nash at Woodstock and the Chemical Brothers in San Diego. Sometimes conditions dictate the surreal—especially if the crowd is high on energy sports-fuel drinks (see Beck).

gary numan
I played Hammersmith Odeon in 1994. For some reason I was really on form, the band was absolutely brilliant, and we just had the best crowd I've ever known, they were on fire. It was the last gig of the tour; there was a little bit of sadness that it all was going to be finishing. It was packed full and the crowd was going absolutely ballistic. There was thundering screaming. It just got better and better and by the end we didn't want to come off. The whole band was buzzing afterward. **1997**

shaun ryder of **HappyMondays** and **BlackGrape**
My favorite gig with the Happy Mondays was somewhere like Portugal. We opened for Santana. That was fucking wild, that one! We were on about eight o'clock, did about an hour and a half, then Santana came out. It was like two types of audience: all the youngsters in there for us and the older people there for Santana—but everyone got into it. It was a top vibe, man. Santana had some Scotch dude singing. The guy was fainting and real rowdy. I had seen him earlier backstage and asked, "Are you fucked?" He just kind of nodded. Two hours later, he's the lead singer! But the show was fucking great. **1996**

gaz coombes of **Supergrass**
We went to Brazil for a week, which was quite crazy. It was so hot all the time: At four in the morning, it would still be above 29 or 30 degrees Celsius. We played some really bizarre stadium gigs for like sixty thousand people with the Cure and Smashing Pumpkins. It was really wild. It was such a vast amount of people it doesn't matter anymore—I find it harder playing acoustic guitar in front of ten people. You'll see a small section of them dancing there in the front, but in that crowd, it's probably five thousand people. You see only 1 percent of the crowd dancing, but that 1 percent is bigger than crowds we get back home in England. **1997**

simon le bon of **DuranDuran**
We played a show in 1987, I think it was, in São Paolo, Brazil, in front of one hundred thousand people who all had their arms in the air singing along with "The Reflex." It was *incredible* to be at that vortex of energy. I can't wait until I do it again, and we will do it again. **1997**

michael stipe of **R.E.M.**
Talk about power . . . put your hand up and twenty thousand people scream. **1992**

andrew gonzales of ReelBigFish

Oahu, Hawaii, is the best. Those kids are friggin' great—they just go nuts. **1997**

q-tip of ATribeCalledQuest

Our first show in Europe was in Sweden in 1989 and that was real good. Real, real, real, real good. I'm glowing right now thinking about it. **1996**

les claypool of Primus

I had a blast at Woodstock '94. Primus hadn't played for three months and we just showed up for the gig. We were *on* that night. I still have mud on my bass cabinet from when I said, "My name is Mud!" and big clumps of sod came flying up at me. **1996**

graham nash of Crosby, StillsandNash

Woodstock [August 1969] was only our second gig, but we weren't afraid of the crowd. We were more concerned with our peers. Backstage was totally chaotic. There was so much dope that it's very hard to remember anything. Whenever three or four of us would get together, especially with the Jefferson Airplane and the Grateful Dead and [John] Sebastian, it was just nonsense. I think Stephen [Stills] and I were a little nervous that Jimi Hendrix and the Band and Blood, Sweat and Tears were there. And I think Neil [Young] was nervous about playing with us. Neil's not in control when he's with us—not in the way he likes to be. I don't really know why he didn't choose to be in the movie. To this day, a lot of people think that it was just Crosby, Stills and Nash that did Woodstock, but in fact, it was the four of us. . . . I thought we did a lousy set. When you consider playing acoustic guitars to four hundred thousand people and trying to reach to the back of the crowd with songs like "Guinnevere," it was absurd. **1989**

dave matthews

We opened three shows for the Grateful Dead in Las Vegas. It was a wild trip because I had never seen the Dead before—none of us had, I think. It turned out to be a great experience. **1996**

david yow of theJesusLizard

We played in Portland, Oregon, one time. It was really, really crazy. Lots of nakedness happening. The place was going completely apeshit, out of hand, out of control. That was a lot of fun. Oh, and Hattiesburg, Mississippi, that was a lot of fun. We played there once about six years ago. It was fucked up. The PA wasn't a PA, the people who worked there didn't know what they were doing, the club was not really a club. But the kids were just very excited. The promoter was thrilled. He was like, "This is so great. This is, like, the best thing we've had since, um, since, uh, the Rhythm Pigs three years ago." **1996**

john feldmann of Goldfinger

My favorite gig so far has been Cheyenne, Wyoming, where this high school kid does all the punk rock shows in town. Basically, the dressing room is his parents'

John Feldmann of Goldfinger (Self-portrait by John Feldmann, courtesy of Russell A. Trunk/Chrisam Enterprises, Inc.)

house and his mom cooks for you. She cooked us the best spaghetti that I've ever had. So fucking cool—Adam, that's his name. You kick back, their basement has trampolines and video games—we didn't even want to go do the show. **1996**

beck   We played a gig in the Swiss Alps at a snowboarding convention. Red Bull—this energy sports-fuel drink—sponsored the whole thing. It has some ingredient believed to be bull-testicle extract. We went way off our tour route, had to take two planes and missed a night's sleep. We got up there and there's no snow—it's all mud. You couldn't walk. You'd step and then be up to your knee in mud. So you had several thousand disgruntled snowboarders tanked up to the max on bull-testicle extract. Of course, for some reason, these strapping brutes were made to wait out in the mud and the rain before coming into the tent for the show. When we get up to play, I see this forty-foot gap between us and the audience—they still managed to nail us with empty cans of Red Bull. After a few songs, I wasn't really playing my guitar, I was using it to bat cans back into the crowd of disgruntled sports enthusiasts. It felt like we were A Flock of Seagulls opening for Napalm Death. **1996**

steve miller   I was going to catch a plane the other night and the limo driver said, "Steve Miller, man, I wonder if you remember the one and only Cherry Blossom Festival." I said, "Yes, I do, I remember everything about it." This guy was there; it was in Richmond, Virginia, back in the Sixties. They had a black music day and a white music day. Boz Scaggs and his band were playing, there were about ten bands total. The promoters had been saying for weeks, everything's gonna be mellow, there's not gonna be any trouble, we worked it out with the police, we talked to the mayor. We get to the gig and there are about twenty-five thousand people on the football field, nobody's sitting in the stadium. The first band starts playing, second band plays, third band plays and all of sudden there's some trouble in the audience. There were two hundred plainclothes narcotics agents in the audience who had started busting people. While Boz is playing, a helicopter with a *judge* flys in, like, thirty feet above the audience. It was turning sideways, tilting to show the judge people in the crowd smoking pot. Then up drive some buses full of storm troopers with four-foot shields, big poles and helmets, everything. It gets better. Next door to this stadium a new one is being built, and some kid goes up this dirt ramp between the two and starts up a bulldozer. He drives down the ramp and crushes, like, seven police cars. Kids start smashing in the windows of the cop cars. Meanwhile the promoter is saying to

121

me, "You've gotta play, man. You've gotta go up and play!" We're up next and we're the headliner. Just as I get onstage, the riot police come into the stadium, ready to storm into the crowd. People start throwing cans and bottles at them. So I dedicated the next song to the police and played "The Star-Spangled Banner." They all stopped, took their helmets off and the whole riot ended. We finished the concert. I'm not kidding you, man. My limo driver said, "Man, I had tears in my eyes when you did that." You know, it's always good to have an experienced hand at the tiller. **1996**

Steve Miller (Self-portrait by Steve Miller, courtesy of Russell A. Trunk/Chrisam Enterprises, Inc.)

rob thomas of Matchbox20

I let some punk kids in the front get the better of me when we opened for No Doubt in San Antonio. I wound up leaving in the middle of my set in front of ten thousand people. I had had a bad couple of days. I had been writing a song called "Texas" because some girl had tried to break my heart. I had just had enough of San Antonio. There were, like, fifteen kids in the front to see the Vandals, this punk band that played before us. They were calling me faggot and telling me I suck. I couldn't handle it, but I shouldn't have lost it. I started screaming at this kid, telling him he's a loser redneck sheep-fucker and how he has nothing to do and never leaves his house, but when he finally does he takes his one opportunity to come out and be a fucking asshole. Then I threw him the microphone so people in the back could see what was going on, and he said, "Get off the stage." I said, "All right," and walked off. [Guitarist] Adam Gaynor got the crowd into a frenzy and people started spitting on the kid and screaming. So I came back and we did two more songs out of the four we were going to do. Then I couldn't do it anymore. I'm embarrassed by the whole incident. **1997**

ed simons and tom rowlands of ChemicalBrothers

Ed Simons: We did this party in San Diego. I think we were playing for some sort of cult—it was a techno cult.

Tom Rowlands: It was some club for people who paid a subscription to get into this weird sort of loft.

Ed Simons: It had two recording studios and computers outputting stencil graphics. There was some kind of control thing going on because we were paid to do the gig but no one was interested in us actually playing the gig. I think they wanted to demonstrate that they had the power to get us there. It was a bit weird.

Tom Rowlands: The most poorly organized thing I've ever been to in my life!

Ed Simons: Their sound system was about as good as my stereo at home. Unbelievable.

Tom Rowlands: There were all of these people running around too busy flower arranging to help us get the power sorted out.

Ed Simons: We had very nice food, though. The promoters made up for some of the inadequacy with a Spanish meal.

Tom Rowlands: I suppose they did. **1996**

123

sean lennon

I've played hundreds of gigs. My strings can all break, the show can suck, and I'm like, "Well, the next show's tomorrow." I've played in the weirdest, most fucked-up situations. Literally getting electric shocks. Playing in truck stops where the soundboard is in a Mack truck and there's a stuffed buffalo above the drum set. That was in Vinton, Louisiana. It was bugged out! Cibo Matto was opening for the Butthole Surfers. There was this hugely obese woman with a gun in the dressing room when we arrived. The stage is twenty feet off the ground; for some reason, they put it on stilts. And we saw boars—I swear to God, wild boars—running in the field next to the venue. **1998**

noel gallagher of Oasis

Playing live is a thing you should enjoy. I don't stand there and feel self-conscious. It's like, fuck it. I know what I'm doing. You might as well enjoy it, because every gig might be your last anyway. **1998**

joan jett

My first gig with the Runaways was a keg party in Huntington Beach, California, at [drummer] Sandy West's house, in her rec room. There were tons of people there and tons of beer, and everybody was drunk. I was scared to death, so I think I had quite a few beers that night. **1997**

ian mcculloch
of EchoandtheBunnymen

Playing the Royal Albert Hall was grand back when we knew we were getting somewhere, when we were getting a real fanatical following. Or you think they're fanatical—they are for, like, two years, and then the music becomes less important to them. **1995**

Ian McCulloch of Echo and the Bunny-men (Self-portrait by Ian McCulloch, courtesy of Russell A. Trunk/ Chrisam Enterprises, Inc.)

montell jordan

Master P is a shrewd businessman. It's a real experience to be around P. He's also an incredible artist. I gave up New York Knicks–Chicago Bulls tickets—swear I did—to fly down to Houston to go on a show with the No Limit family at the Summit arena—it holds fifteen thousand people and it was sold out. Destiny's Child opened, it's standing room only and P comes out with, like, fifty people onstage. P performs, Mystikal performs, C-Murder, Silkk, Mia X—the whole group. They call out Snoop Dogg, then he calls me. It was absolute mayhem. The best thing about it was something I heard on the radio while I was in a taxi going to the airport. A sixteen-year-old girl called in to the station to say the No Limit show was her first concert. She was so excited, it made me feel good to hear that. **1998**

meredith brooks

While playing Lilith Fair, Bonnie Raitt came out onstage with me. We jammed on a song of mine called "It Don't Get Better." That is my greatest memory ever onstage. **1998**

stephan jenkins of ThirdEyeBlind

We had a great time with U2. So many things became clear to me. One is, you can't believe what you hear about people. Bono is supposed to be this megalomaniacal asshole. Not true. He's totally funny, generous and genuine and very interested in lots of different subjects, like architecture and philosophy. He's a cut-up too! Those guys are like Hanson—they were huge stars when they were just little, cherubic boys. But they've stayed grounded and real. One time, I'm sitting backstage outside my dressing room all sweaty from playing and the Edge walks up in his biker cowboy outfit—he knows my name—he says, "Hello, Stephan." I was like, "Edge, how are you?" That was just funny to me—a psychedelic moment. Bono showed up with a case of champagne and a case of Guinness and showed us how to make Black Velvets, which is the two of them mixed and which produces an intense, tight, piercing headache right in the front of your forehead. The next day Bono asked me how it was, and I said, "Fucking awful, Bono, and I'm never having it again." I think you have to be fully, deeply Irish to appreciate a drink like that. **1998**

mark mcgrath of SugarRay

On the Warped tour, we became bros with everybody on the tour. Everybody's, like, in it together and you come to a city and you're a fucking team and you take over. Everybody comes over to watch your show, then the fun starts. Fletcher from Pennywise rips out the barbecue—he ran it the whole tour. Sick of It All and Social Distortion get their Vegas gaming action on down by the bus. They got all of my money. I'm still paying off debts. **1997**

tommy lee of MötleyCrüe

The first Mötley Crüe reunion show with Vince [Neil] back in the band was about a month and a half ago in Tampa. It was first time in, like, oh dude, six years or something—Vince said it onstage and I was like, "Fuck, has it been that long?" There was, like, thirty-five thousand fucking drunk, shirtless guys and girls out there going crazy! It was like, "Oh, man, I miss this." **1997**

anthony kiedis of theRedHotChiliPeppers

When we played the Kit Kat strip club, we decided to come out for the encore with the socks. And brother, let me tell you, when we came out of the little dressing room backstage, we were levitating with nervous energy. I could not find my feet on the stage. And somebody filmed it. I don't know if the film still exists, but we saw it, and we just had this look in our eyes like we were from outer space. **1992**

trent reznor of NineInchNails

At huge shows like Lollapalooza, you're up on a pedestal rather than going head-to-head with people. It's hard to know if the energy you send out is even coming back. **1994**

rick nielsen of CheapTrick

Budokan Hall in Tokyo is fine just because everyone knows about us playing there. It's kind of a cold sumo-wrestler room. Nothing glamorous about it. Just a big old room, about ten thousand square feet, about ten thousand people. We made the Budokan famous and the Budokan made us famous. I think we should do another record there. *Cheap Trick, Really Live at Budokan*. With modern technology we could probably improve on it. **1996**

emmylou harris

I've played the Paradiso in Amsterdam twice. It's an old church, about a thousand people fit in there; the bottom floor is standing room only and there's a balcony in a U-shape where people can sit. The sound is wonderful—and you're in Amsterdam. **1996**

fred schneider of the B-52's

All of our early gigs before we signed were so exciting because we had no clue as to what we were doing. Even the first time. *Now* touring gets to be a blur. You think, "Where am I again?" when you wake up on the bus. Every town in America—especially every major city—looks like postwar Germany after they tore down all the great old buildings and put up all this horrible new crap. **1996**

aphex twin a.k.a. Richard James

I played in an old prison—the Klink Prison—in London. At the turn of the century they used to put prostitutes in there at night; it's a museum now. They have all these, like, exhibits showing where they used to torture people. I played inside this little fake cell with a fake bloke being, like, hung next to me. It was really heavy. You couldn't go out there and pump people for more than a few hours. My mates were going on about something weird in the atmosphere. **1997**

YOUTAKETHE**HIGHROAD** AND**I'LLTAKETHE**LOW

he magic formula for good times, good tunes, good tours? Well, everyone has an opinion and more than a few tips to pass the miles. At the very least, probing the mysteries of the deli tray or hoofing it for a few miles will fill some time.

andrew gonzales of ReelBigFish

I sleep on the bus. That passes time pretty good. A lot of guys will sit in the back lounge and indulge themselves in whatever. Like reading poetry and stuff like that. We sit around in our underwear and paint our toenails a lot. We check out the previous day's show on the VCR, or we wait until we go to a truck stop and buy a movie to watch. Scott [Klopfenstein] just said that's usually the time when everybody pulls his pants down and spanks him—I should stay awake more often! **1997**

lisa loeb

It's an exciting thing to go into a 7-Eleven, leaf through a couple of magazines and breeze out without getting caught. *Weekly World News* is the only tabloid that's true. It's a wonderful thing to read while on tour to catch up on the news. **1997**

beck

On tour, we would test our will and our character and do these eight-hour drives listening to one Spyro Gyra tape over and over. And I think this tested us as musicians to endure the Spyro Gyra–ness. Kenny G is sort of somebody you take for granted, but he is a reality. And I'm trying to come to grips with that reality. He's so . . . what he is. He's so "I Can't Believe It's Not Butter!" I think there's some truth to the fact that his music is, in fact, darker than any Danzig record. **1996**

neil young

I like to walk. A lot of times, I'll stop the bus and walk for three or four miles and then let the bus catch up with me on the road. **1993**

tanya donelly of ThrowingMuses and Belly

We listen to Pavement's *Slanted and Enchanted* a lot when we're on the road. I like their looseness. They're so open to any influence that comes along. **1994**

rob thomas of Matchbox20

It's a weird scene on the bus. Right before we head to the stage, we sing [Heatwave's] "Always and Forever" in a group. We run around, get the energy going, dancing. Then our road manager comes on the bus, we kick everyone else out, huddle up and sing the hell out of it, then go onstage. Sometimes we sing it with our pants down. If it's a gig where the promoters have been giving us a hard time and everyone around us are assholes, we'll stand there and drop our pants in a circle. Usually we've got the underwear going, but if we're feeling frisky, Ky [Kyle Cook, the guitarist] will pull down his underwear. It started off as a joke at our first show, but we do it every show now. We're superstitious—if we don't do it, we realize we've had a bad show. I also pee before each show and while I'm peeing, I have to thank the Great Spirit. **1997**

stevie nicks
I love being on the road. I'm going on a bus this time, which I've never done. I realized that since I don't go to sleep until five or six in the morning anyway, it's stupid for me to go home from a concert and sleep, because I can't. And my bus is so comfy. I have eight fabulous feather pillows. And, of course, my king-size quilt completely takes up the entire double bed, and a fishnet hanging from the ceiling completely takes up the entire room. **1994**

Fleetwood Mac: John McVie, Christine McVie, Lindsey Buckingham, Mick Fleetwood and Stevie Nicks (from left) (Warner Bros.)

mark mcgrath of SugarRay
We have a tour bus, it's a whole new reality. There's nothing like getting fucked up, putting *GoodFellas* on in the back lounge and passing out. We've got deli trays, all that shit. I don't want to brag, but yeah. I'm the guy that eats the hot

dogs at 7-Eleven so I don't worry about the deli trays. My stomach destroys *E. coli.* **1997**

john popper of BluesTraveler

I love the aspect of touring that involves the crew breaking the set down. This is something I have very little to do with, but sometimes I go and watch them work. And it's such a well-coordinated effort that you feel like you're part of a massive military maneuver. The first night before the H.O.R.D.E. tour when they're setting up you really feel the energy of anticipation and the anxiety of not having yet ironed out the system. I love that feeling! That slight desperation of people trying to throw it together the first time—not sure what they're building but starting to get the hang of it. When the band is really clicking and when we've gotten into our zone, then I feel like a professional basketball player on the winning team. I'm in my zone and I know where my man is and I know who's got my back and I know whose back I've got—that's when it's electric. And that's the reason we tour. **1998**

tom petty

I look over the set list and decide what we're going to play. And then I'll warm up my voice for a while with my acoustic guitar, go into the shower where the echo is nice and warm up for maybe twenty minutes, just get confident that my voice is working well. Then I'll get dressed for the show; I always get down for the last ten or fifteen minutes before we go on and hang with the band—try to catch a group vibe before we go up. At least it's *collective* nervousness at that point. **1995**

sting

You have to have a certain amount of vanity to get onstage. If I don't think I look good, I don't perform very well. If I'm fit, toned up, don't look tired and I've done some preparation, I perform better. People pay money to *see* you, so if I had to perform tonight, I'd be going through a certain regimen—work out, take a bath, don't eat any rubbish, get a good night's sleep. Stage performance is more athletic than musical. Well, that's not true, but a large percentage of what you do is leap up and down in time to the music. **1988**

art garfunkel

I want everything to be great when I play. Of course, that means the night before, I'll lie on the pillow saying to myself, "You must go to sleep, you must go to sleep." The more you care, the more you get crazy. That's why the artist's role has that duality, to push it away, keep it light, shake it out, otherwise it'll turn on you and bite you in the nose, this self-consciousness. It's tough. How to show up on time, do a show with sensitivity and sincerity for a certain price at an exact time and promise you will have that feeling, it's crazy making. **1997**

mick jagger of theRollingStones

[Being on tour is] the best place to write, because you're totally into it. You get back from a show, have something to eat, a few beers and just go to your room and write. I used to write about twelve songs in two weeks on tour. It gives you a lot of ideas. At home it's very difficult, because you don't really want to do anything, really, but read and things like that. **1968**

d'arcy of SmashingPumpkins

You can't survive if you don't have something in your day besides playing shows. It's terrible. You lose your mind. **1996**

glenn frey of theEagles

Led Zeppelin might argue with us, but I think we might have thrown the greatest traveling party of the Seventies. It was called the Third Encore. Almost every night when we were on the road, we would throw this fabulous mixer. We'd hand out 3E buttons, and we'd invite all the key radio people and as many beautiful girls as we'd meet from the airport to the hotel and whatever. We had our own sound system and we played Motown records and had a party every night. **1990**

billie joe armstrong of GreenDay

I really like the scene in *Meatballs* when they take the guy who's sleeping and snores really loud and they put him in the middle of the woods, up in a tree. I think Mike [Dirnt] and Tré [Cool] have done that to me a couple of times. It's always unpredictable if you fall asleep with your shoes on in the tour bus I travel in. Tabasco sauce on the lips, shaving cream and the tickled nose. If your shoes are off, you're off limits. **1998**

ALLAROUNDTHEWORLD

Life in a successful band offers all the travel and adventure promised by an ad for the army—and allows just as little time off. Nonetheless, musicians do well to escape the tour bus, the hotel and the hordes of groupies to explore the strange lands they visit. Amsterdam felt like home to Tommy Lee, as New York City does to many artists who pass through or stay for good. Herein, a musicians' travelogue.

david crosby of Crosby,StillsandNash

Tahiti. One of the few things on earth as good as you thought it was going to be. Their music is *crazy*. Sexy, wonderful people. All they want to do is get smashed and fuck—that's their whole program. *Ooohhh, let's get drunk! Make schooner, baby! Fuck the white boys, get the bloodlines mixed up! Paradise. Crosby, Stills and who? Whaat ess you name? You are one auf Bing's boys?* 1985

luther vandross
There is a hotel on Oahu, in Hawaii, called the Kahala Mandarin Oriental, and it is the most special place that I have ever been. It is real quiet and it smells good. It makes you want to read, it makes you want to open your balcony door and hear the ocean and hear the palm trees. I love it. **1997**

ozzy osbourne
My favorite place to vacation is Maui, in Hawaii, and also Antigua in the Caribbean. I got married on Maui, so I go back there a lot and that's one of the most beautiful places on the earth, you know. However, what does piss me off is these French, fucking idiots exploding these bombs around there, you know, let one off in fucking Paris. Anyway, it's a tiny island, absolutely beautiful, and I got married just over thirteen years ago on the beach at Maui at sunset. I love the weather, the climate, the ocean. I've been to the Caribbean a few times and I haven't had very good experiences down there, but I went to Antigua for the first time this year and it was fucking wonderful, just, just wonderful. **1995**

busta rhymes
I like to go to Jamaica, man, in the summer. That's when a lot of the carnivals are happening. A lot of the concerts come through because that's mostly when people make time to go out. Make time to really party, you know what I'm sayin'? **1997**

q-tip of ATribeCalledQuest
Montserrat, West Indies, is a beautiful island, man. I like the hot springs, the food is good and the hospitality is good. There's black sand beaches, and it's pretty developed, but still beautiful. **1996**

sarah mclachlan
Tofino is a village on the coast of Vancouver Island and the closest thing to heaven on earth that I've ever found. **1994**

RAVES

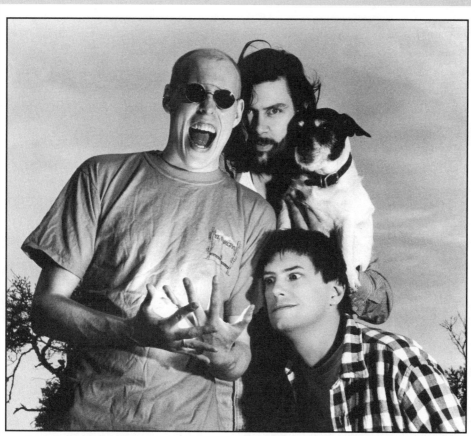

Butthole Surfers: King Coffey, Gibby Haynes and Paul Leary (from left) (Will van Overbeek/Capitol)

paul leary of theButtholeSurfers

Austin's a really cool place. It gets hot as shit, but there's nice lakes and you can always take your clothes off. **1995**

shirley manson of Garbage

The Orkney Islands are the most exquisite place in the world. They are just off the coast of Scotland and house an abundance of tombs and standing stones that date back five thousand years. They're at once terrifying and strangely comforting. This is a sacred place that pulls at my heart. **1996**

stevie nicks I was born in Arizona and there's something about the desert that's very healing for me. You have to slow down and take better care of yourself. **1994**

john popper of BluesTraveler

Colorado in the summer. When you're up in the mountains, there's nothing prettier. But that region of the country when it's summer is some of the most beautiful, lush land I've ever seen. Oh, but I have to say, if I've seen luscious land, it's Alaska. We played a gig up there a couple of years ago and everything was bathed in this really deep and beautiful fog. Everything is in this mist and there's a cool moistness in the air—it comes from the glaciers, I think. The glaciers look like frozen Windex because the ice is so condensed that it turns bright blue. You think you've seen a tree down here in the lower forty-eight? You go to Alaska and it's just . . . bigger. Everything there is huge and wild and lush. Oh! The waves in Hawaii, I love those, too! I jumped in the waves there and almost died. They were so beautiful and so strong. You forget how strong the ocean is until you jump in the waves on the south shore of Hawaii. **1998**

les claypool of Primus

Whenever we book a Primus tour, I always make sure we have time off in Florida so we can spend a couple of days in the Florida Keys and do some scuba diving. I enjoy scuba diving. But I lost a good portion of my hearing in my right ear because of it, so it's probably not the best sport I could have taken up. I couldn't equalize, I went down anyway, and I ruptured my inner ear. The scar tissue cut out some of the high frequencies. So I'm looking for the magic ear surgeon to fix me. Everybody says, "Nope, you're fucked." **1996**

shaun ryder of HappyMondays and BlackGrape

Jajouka, Morocco—it's up in the mountains and is where Brian Jones went in the Sixties. There are no telephones. The way of life ain't changed in hundreds of years. That's where all the musicians are and all the weed. It's all they do. Sift the kif and fucking play tunes. **1996**

john tesh

There's a monastery in San Panfilo, Italy. It's this giant place, a rock edifice carved into the side of the rock. There are six monks there, and if you know somebody, you go in there and they give you some little drink—the kind of little drink where you have no idea what it is and you would normally never drink it, but the monks say you have to, and you don't want to be an ass. So I drank it and I was, like, stoned for the whole day. We stayed there for the whole day and got nailed on grappa, or whatever it was. There's only one restaurant in the whole town. You sit there and you have to eat for four hours. They bring you . . . everything. They probably see otherworldly humans like Americans once every two or three years. **1997**

simon le bon of DuranDuran

Ahhh, Thailand. I take my family to a place called Phuket, which is quite developed. There's an amazing beach, though. A friend of mine just got married there and we went over. It's the rainy season right now, very hot and very humid, and we left there the day the big rains started. You know, they have monsoons—it can rain for ten days without stopping. It can rain for three months without stopping, actually. It can start in August and not stop until September. The food is incredible, really fragrant, with amazing flavors. Spicy and sweet and sour; you get hot and sour, you get sweet and hot. **1997**

Duran Duran: Warren Cuccurullo, Nick Rhodes, John Taylor and Simon Le Bon
(from left) (Ellen Von Unwerth/Capitol)

david cassidy

I flew to Italy alone and took my guitar. I drove for one month through the Alps—spoke no Italian, spoke no German, spoke no French, got very thin. **1998**

mark mcgrath of SugarRay

I can't stand Europe. They don't speak English over there, you know? If you're in Germany, they don't speak any English. I am a total white-trash American kid. I like my conveniences. I like 7-Eleven, I like MTV. I'm a product of a minimall. It's my culture. If there isn't a Starbucks, a 7-Eleven and a fucking pizza joint, I feel out of place. They've gotta unite the currency over there in Europe. When you're touring and you buy something for ten bucks, you get all these coins back and the next day, you're somewhere else, and you can't trade those coins in! I got a list of complaints that could fill up a couple of pages. We're doing so well here that it's hard for me to go play for ten people in Europe. We've flogged ourselves there like the old heavy-metal acts on CMC International. We're here again! The kids there are just like the kids here. If it's not happening, it's not happening. I know it's a line from *Singles,* but we're big in Belgium. **1998**

krs-one

Americans are so rich and fat and uneducated that anybody can come out here and say, "Yo, man, yo, South Africa, that shit is wrong, man, right? Word, that shit's fucked up!" They show a few crimes, a few black people burnin', you got a movement! Yeah, let's fucking kill those motherfuckers! Without really knowin' what the side of the white people in South Africa is. I'm not cynical, just suspicious. I went to see the Dali Lama a month ago at a synagogue in New York. It struck me funny, you know, that he was surrounded by Secret Service. I'll leave it at that. **1998**

mix master mike of InvisiblSkratchPiklz and theBeastieBoys

Me and Q-Bert, from Invisibl Skratch Piklz, were one of the first to bring hip-hop to Beirut, Lebanon. We've thrown DJ battles there for two years; the last time we went, we were, like, huge stars. It's paradise there. We went to these caves in Baalbek—they're perfect holes, built in, like, gladiator days. **1998**

chris whitley

I don't know why I still live in New York, but it's the place I've lived longer than anywhere else. I kind of relate to it. Umm, I would like to have a house in the fucking desert, in the middle of nowhere. I like Belgium—I lived in Ghent for five years—and I like Arizona, and New York City, if I could live in three places. Ghent's flat, and it's one of the oldest cities in Europe. You can get out of university and go into an art academy and study sculpture or photography for, like, ten bucks a year. Art is still valued in a really common way. Theater is common—there's larger productions there. Every single bar has DJs and shit. It's weird. It's a village really, but it's so sophisticated. **1997**

dicky barrett of theMightyMightyBosstones

Boston is by far my favorite town for the history, culture, music. And my friends. I like the way it looks. I like the way owning a car is not a necessity. You can do the whole thing on foot. It's me. It's completely me. I love Boston. **1997**

The Mighty Mighty Bosstones: Ben Carr, Dennis Brockenborough, Tim Burton, Dicky Barrett (seated), Kevin Lenear, Joe Sirois, Nate Albert (seated) and Joe Gittleman (from left) (Danny Clinch/Mercury)

gaz coombes of Supergrass

San Francisco is great. That's been my favorite city in America. I've got quite an affinity with it. I like the vibe there. **1997**

gwen stefani of NoDoubt

Every nook and cranny of New York has some kind of style or weird trippy thing going on. I love it! Everything you see looks like it's been used. I don't know if I could live in New York, but I sure like the energy and the oldness. There's something really neat about the fact that everyone's shared this place over and over and over again. **1996**

rupaul

I like a mixture, so obviously I like New York City. It doesn't attract me when everything is perfect Madison Avenue–type stuff. I grew up with that shoved down my throat! New York is the epitome of a mixture, a tapestry. I love Miami Beach for a lot of the same reasons, and Rio de Janeiro in Brazil. Rio is really, really sexy and sensual. It's just an orgasm for your eyes. **1996**

fred schneider of theB-52's

New York is so open-minded and such a great magnet for all kinds of people and cultures and food and music. It's got character and characters and all that. People say to me, "How can you live in New York?" but then when I travel and go to some of these boondock towns, I go, "How can you live *here*? Like, open your eyes." **1996**

aretha franklin

I like New York. You can see a lot of movies here. Sometimes at four in the morning . . . the kind with Joan Crawford, Barbara Stanwyck, Ingrid Bergman. Those kind. Cicely Tyson. I just saw *Warm December* with Sidney Poitier. It was a good movie. All the black movies are okay. **1974**

matt sharp of Weezer

I like being able to go out at four-thirty in the morning in New York and get good food. Like onion bagels with vegetable cream cheese at Bagels on the Square, in the West Village. **1995**

leann rimes
Chicago is a little bit like New York, but cleaner and you don't hear a lot of horns honking outside your window in the middle of the night. It's a great place. **1997**

bo diddley
I've been all over this land of ours. I could deal with Chicago. That's a beautiful place. I was raised there and the beach is beautiful. The people in Chicago are beautiful. Also the people in Florida are beautiful. L.A. too. I haven't found too many uncool people there, except maybe dudes get a little bit too drunk when it's too hot and they clown and they fall out and they want to fight. I'd tell you to avoid the places where people get mugged and drugged and beat up and all that kind of stuff, until they straighten it out. Know what I'm sayin'? I mean it's enough out here for people to get off their booties and have a good time, work, earn a livin', a good livin', and not be doin' the dirty things to other people, you know. **1998**

dave mustaine of Megadeth
I really like Buenos Aires, but more than any place in South America, I like Scotland, because it is really beautiful there. The grass is blue, it's so green. I went to Tel Aviv, and I thought it was going to be like it is on the news—just all bombs and burning cars and stuff—but it was really neat. I jumped into the River Jordan. I didn't really like Turkey. Somebody made a comment about my wife because she's a beautiful blonde. The guy said something about her body and I was gonna kill him. He had a knife, probably about as big as something we use to cut up Christmas food. I knew I could get the knife away from him, but I didn't know if any of his friends were watching, if any of them had guns—I'm not bulletproof. I just figured I'd get out of there with my dignity and my wife, and although my pride was bruised by not knocking the shit out of him, I figured it would be better licking my wounds alive than being proud and dead. We had gotten off the cruise ship we were on and went to this little grotto. All you could smell was hash and heroin burning. Everybody's eyes were bugging out of their heads and I knew we were in a bad place. You just intuitively know things like that at a certain point. We turned around and boom, there was this freak. We just went back to the boat as quickly as we could. **1997**

aphex twin a.k.a. RichardJames

Glasgow, Scotland: I played there recently for the first time. That was not fun. It's just totally mad—all the people are, like . . . so into it. And they're not passive. There are *mad* people up there. And I like mad people, but it's a different world up there in Scotland. **1997**

carnie wilson

London is fun. There's something about the fashion and people. Copenhagen has some of the cleanest air. They have very little pollution and the water's really clean. It's as bright blue as the people's eyes, it's really a trip. Tokyo—I've never seen people look so much *alike* in my entire life. You walk down the street and you're, like, "Hello? I just passed you one block ago. Hello? What the hell's going on?" It's a trip. And there's no one fat. I felt really out of place. Ha ha! I did not see one overweight person. It's so weird. **1997**

d'arcy of SmashingPumpkins

Venice. I love it. I was just there and I thought, "I could live here." I'm selling the farm and moving there. It's so incredibly beautiful. **1996**

dave matthews

In Cape Town, South Africa, the city wraps around the coast and is surrounded by mountains. There's a sense of comfort there. When I lived in South Africa—even through apartheid—that city was so beautiful that it made things seem . . . hopeful. I love Amsterdam, too, and not only because pot is legal. It's so beautiful, there are great museums and the people are open to conversation. I lived there with a friend for a while when I was traveling around the world before I was playing music. And Montreal is another city I love. It's almost like a European city in North America. It's very foreign territory. **1995**

ziggy marley

Ahhh, Amsterdam. You know, get the good herb. We always have to stop in Holland when we're in Europe. **1997**

tommy lee of MötleyCrüe

The first time I went to Amsterdam, I was, like, "Woah, you mean *everything* here is legal? *Nothing* matters?" People were walking down the street opening their jacket with syringes and fucking heroin. And we were like little kids in a candy store, going, "Aww yeah! Look at all this!" Like a pet shop, instead of puppies in the windows, it was women. You put a fucking rock & roll band in Amsterdam and you have, I don't know, man, you've got a lot of trouble is what you have! It's like we were in an adult Disneyland. The word *no* was just not a part of our vocabulary. It was sometime in '82 or '84 when we toured with Ozzy Osbourne in Europe and did the Monsters of Rock tour with Van Halen and AC/DC. We went all over the place. It was fucking scary, man. I don't know how our security guys and tour managers ever fucking dealt with us and how nobody died or nobody got left behind. **1997**

k.d. lang
I am in Amsterdam right now. I love going and watching the girls in the window, that's for sure. Plus, you can have a beer on the street, and that's loads of fun. Yeah, I'm going to have to go get myself a beer right now, as a matter of fact. I might even have to smoke some hash. I have a little bit of a cold, so I'll see how I feel tomorrow. When in Rome, right? I'll say they made me do it—it was a diplomatic cultural expression. "No, thank you" means "Yes, please" in Dutch. **1997**

dean wareham of Luna
The Spanish know how to have fun. Great food. Interesting sort of music scene. They're sort of obsessed with American garage music and also like the Velvet Underground, Television, Voidoids, that kind of stuff. **1996**

stone gossard of PearlJam
Sydney, Australia, is the ultimate combination of English humor and intellectualism and, like, a Santa Barbara beach community. Twenty minutes out of the city you can be on a deserted beach. There are three million people in the city, but that's it—go north or south and you might as well be nowhere. In land size Australia is almost the same as the United States, yet there's eighteen million people in the country. There's that many people in the Los Angeles basin. **1997**

billy gibbons of ZZTop
We just had our first trip to Africa—ten shows. The band then hung around for three weeks, and after that, I hung around for three months. Every day was new and interesting. I watched their winter change into spring and summer there. Africa is as dramatically progressive as about any other place right now. There aren't lions and spears flying on every corner. Those of us that remember Saturday

morning Tarzan movies remember it differently than it is—it's a romantic thing. It was a surprise to find a society that is trying hard to reorganize itself. **1996**

alanis morissette
I went to Cuba. A whole bunch of us went: artists and actors and people in the political world and investment banking, as sort of a cultural exchange. I was the only Canadian on the trip, so for me, obviously, it wasn't as much of a coup, because I would have been able to go whenever I wanted, but it was amazing to watch the experience through American people's eyes. **1998**

Alanis Morissette (Katrina Dickson/Maverick)

alec empire of AtariTeenageRiot
I recorded a record in Iceland and played there couple of times. The people are great. It's cold, but people live more with nature in a way, because they're dependent on it. They don't pay money for electricity, because it comes off of the waterfalls. And they're really interested in music. **1997**

nina persson of theCardigans
I love Reykjavik, Iceland, very much. I love Scandinavia. I feel Scandinavian myself. The last Vikings must be situated there, because it has the essence of the

Scandinavian spirit. There are totally crazy people. It's a very pretty country and a great town. It's amazing how it's even more up-to-date about what's "in" than any city in Sweden, but also so ancient and raw. **1997**

björk I used to puke in the faces of all the cosmic people who talk about Iceland as one of the energy centers of the world. But it's true. It might just be in my head, but when I go there, I recharge my batteries. I get so overneurotic in cities. Which is good. **1994**

Björk (Nobuyoshi Araki/Elektra)

moby Hotel rooms and other environments that human beings create that are completely lifeless, anaerobic. I don't know why, but I'm completely fascinated with them. Like an airport at 3:00 a.m., when the escalator is still moving, but no one's riding on it. And especially hotel rooms, because on one level they're so anonymous and neutral, but the amount of intimate stuff that goes on in them is incredible. People sleep and they dream and they have sex with prostitutes and they jerk off to pornography and they have screaming fights with their wives or girlfriends. People are beaten up, people cry. And you walk in there and it's just this painfully neutral environment. Nothing's alive, but so much happens there. It's juxtaposition. I see a sterile environment, but part of my brain is saying, "Just think of all the things that went on in here." **1997**

HAVEIGOTASTORYTOTELL

**M**usicians have got them, all right—enough weird tales to beat the band. Unless, of course, the band happens to be Mötley Crüe.

kristin hersh of ThrowingMuses

We were on tour in the Southwest in the summer. I was seven months' pregnant and the air-conditioning in the tour bus broke down. My husband and I were sleeping in the back lounge. My sister had been, like, pouring ice cubes down my dress all day. It was like 120 degrees or something. And I woke up in the back lounge at 4:00 a.m. to see the sheets and rugs and all our clothes flying around the room because the vents were pushing out geysers of hot air. It was like a million degrees. It was like *The Exorcist.* I thought we took a wrong turn into hell. **1996**

rob thomas of Matchbox20

Playing with Jars of Clay was a weird scene. The kids are crazy, but they're not. I thought it was going to be a lot of antiabortion propaganda and a lot of religious brochures being passed out. One time I was trying to talk to this girl, she was really hot, and she says, "Have you given your life to Jesus?" I thought, "Fuck, this isn't my crowd. I am not gettin' laid." Even if I hadn't been concerned about it before, that's all I kept thinking, "I am not getting laid." I told her I wasn't very religious. Everyone kept asking us if we were a Christian band. You don't want to say, "Fuck no." At first, we were worried about cursing around the other guys and all that, but they just let us be what we wanted to be. The last show of the tour, though, there was a rule about not cursing onstage — and I have a potty mouth. We say don't apologize for shit, just turn around and go, "Rock & roll!" and walk away. So right before the last song of the last show, I thanked everybody on tour with us and I thanked the band because they didn't think I could make it through a whole tour without saying fuck onstage. There were six thousand gasps and two stoners in the back screaming, "Matchbox. Yeah!" **1997**

prince be of PMDawn

I love Prince. I met him once. Greatest moment of my life. I have a really ill Prince story. I'd never seen Prince before, and then I went to see him in concert, blew me away and everything. But when we went—we went with Paula Abdul—we were sitting there, and like, there was some sheik, some Arab guy and his wife sitting in front of me, and I'm like, "Damn, I can't see with this guy." So, during intermission, we get up, we go out and chill and I see Joe Jackson and he's like, "How you doin', this is Marlon." And I was like, "Oh, how you doin'?" He's like, "Yeah, Janet and Michael are around here somewhere dressed as sheiks." **1998**

tommy lee of MötleyCrüe

I probably have one of the most fucking disgusting Ozzy Osbourne stories on the planet. I mean, this is fucked up, I don't even know if you could print this, but . . . we were touring with Ozzy—our first real tour. It was in the summer of 1982 or '84—it was Ozzy's Bark at the Moon tour. We were always having way too much fun on the tour. One day, he wanted to ride with us on our bus—to hang with us and see what we were all about. He walks up the stairs into the bus and goes, "Hallo mates. I'm fucking riding with you." He reaches into his jacket and pulls out the biggest fucking bag of cocaine I've ever seen in my life, and says, "I've got fucking bags of this shit!" So, obviously, the bus rolls out and we proceed to drink and party like fucking beasts all the way to the next city, no sleep, we're up all night, just fucking stupid. We pull into the hotel and it's a very nice hotel, kind of a family resort hotel. This was in Dallas. The nice golf course and all the kids and families out by the pool. It's definitely a vacation spot. So Ozzy and Mötley Crüe get out of the bus with sunglasses on at eight in the morning, drunker than shit, up all night on massive drugs. So, what do we do? No one can sleep, we're all wired, everyone goes straight to the bar. We decide to continue this party. Then the bar kicks us out after having a couple of drinks. So we went out to the pool. Remember, there are, like, moms and dads and their kids around. We are definitely in the wrong area. I don't know if you know, but you've got this kind of a thing when you're on tour, bands try to fucking out-gross each other. Someone is always trying to win the title of the sickest motherfucker on the planet. You get a bunch of guys together and that's what happens. So we get out by the pool and Ozzy looks down at the ground. He goes, "No fucking way!" Some kid had dropped a Popsicle stick and it's attracted a big long trail of ants. Ozzy gets on his knees and snorts the line of ants. Snorts them up like cocaine. We're going, "Aww, dude, that guy is fucking gone." So then Nikki Sixx, he says, "That's nothing, watch this." He whips out his dick and starts peeing on the deck of the pool. There's people out by the pool, dude! Little kids and shit. Out of the corner of my eye, I see hotel security losing it. This is going to be a nightmare any second. After Nikki pees on the ground, he shakes his dick, puts it back in his pants, goes to get on his knees to lick up his own piss. But before he can do it, Ozzy pushes him out of the way and licks up Nikki's piss like a dog, lapping it up. Dude, I'm sitting there going,

"God, this is out of control." Ozzy's tour manager at this point comes around the corner and he's losing it because he's been contacted by now and told to get us out of there. For some reason I'm appointed—don't ask me why—to take Ozzy to his room and, like, put him away. They give me the keys, we go up the elevator, we get to the floor, I find his room, I open his door and kinda go, "Okay, Oz, I'll see ya later, bro. Get some rest, whatever." And he goes, "C'mere, mate." I go into his room, he pulls his pants off and then he just takes a big old shit right in the middle of the room. Right on the rug, dude. I'm like, "God, dude, I don't fucking want to see this!" He wanted me to watch. And then he picks it up with his hands and starts smearing it all around the walls of the room. Dude, at that point, I just looked at the door and I fucking peeled out. I did *not* want to be part of that any more. It was me next, I'm sure I was gonna get smeared. I was, like, fuck it, I'm outta here. I bolted. I have no idea where he went or what he did after that. But I got him to his room. It's pretty fucked up. That is one for the books, man. That was one fucking weird-ass, long day. Ozzy probably would embellish the story—I probably forgot a few details. **1997**

steve harwell of SmashMouth

On tour with Sugar Ray we didn't get into too much trouble. I wanted to keep it respectable. There are nights when you want to thrash a little bit, pull the rock star Mötley Crüe thing. You have to do the Aerosmith thing once in a while, throw a few TVs. It's just our way of saying, fuck, man, we're doing it. **1997**

roger clyne of theRefreshments

We just graduated from a van that we've been in since early October, to a bus that just so happens—are you sitting down? This bus was Mötley Crüe's first tour bus. How apropos is that? Fuckin' A is right. That's awesome. We almost called ourselves Motley Clue before we were the Refreshments. The Grand Puppeteer, you can almost see his face sometimes. They actually reupholstered it. We weren't necessarily too happy about that. We wanted it in its pristine condition. Brian's bunk definitely has a pheromone to it, shall we say. And he's fond of thinking that might have been Heather Locklear's place to crash. I personally was happy to give it up to him. **1996**

tina weymouth of TalkingHeads and TomTomClub

It took me a long time to like U2. Until Larry Mullen and Adam Clayton started getting funky and groovy, I couldn't get into it. When it was all that *rat-a-tat-tat,* machine-gun thing, all I was into was Bono and the Edge's thing. Eventually Larry and Adam grew on me as people. I just thought, "Oh, it's *those* guys, yeah." They're so great. I got to liking them through their personalities, and then, surprise, surprise, they got groovy. And that was very cool. Artists do change sometimes, life is full of twists and turns. Adam once told me, "Tina, I think you should really cover your arms onstage because they're too muscular." I thought, Oh, my God. And throughout *Stop Making Sense* I kept them covered. Then some little anarchic devil came over me at this benefit concert U2 had in London. It was fantastic, U2 had an entire show. Gospel singers came onstage, and Keith Richards. They had grown by leaps and bounds; it wasn't just the Edge doing all the work with Bono. Suddenly it was big and magnificent. So Chris [Frantz] and I got a message to them and went backstage to say hello. Adam was wearing a cut-off jean jacket, so I said, "Adam, you were amazing tonight, but really you should cover your arms, they're not muscular enough." He looked at me, totally surprised, and Keith Richards was standing behind him—his arms are totally gnarly, you know. Keith looked at me, then he started looking down at his arms. Then Adam remembered what he told me. He had a sense of humor about it, but I told him he really destroyed me for four years. He said he had no idea he had that kind of effect on me. Keith was looking at the two of us like we were out of our minds, like, "Who gives a fuck about *arms,* man?" **1996**

bob seger
Tom Waits is a funny guy. I met him once in my whole life. I'm driving through Westwood, and I've got my Mercedes out there, I was working on a record, this is 1987 or '88. I've got a Hawaiian shirt on; it's real hot outside. I see Tom Waits, all in black, long-sleeved shirt and cowboy boots—it's 90 degrees—and he's walking through Westwood. So I pull up next to him and I say, "Tom!" I've got these sunglasses on, he probably thought I was with the CIA—car phone and everything—and he says, "Heh?" and looks real startled, so I say, "It's Bob Seger." He says, "Ooh, hi Bob." He jumps in the car and we start talking. I asked him what he was doin' and says, "Uh . . . I'm walkin'." I've loved his stuff down through the years so I started asking him all these dumb questions about his songs. I said, "In 'Cold Cold Ground,' Tom, you say 'The cat will sleep in the mailbox.' Yesterday I went and bought my

cat one of these fuzzy mailboxes. Is that what you're talking about?" He looked at me like I was from Mars—"No, no. My cats sleep under the house." So it goes on, this strange interlude, for about fifteen minutes. Finally, I asked if I could drop him somewhere and he says, "Tell you what, take me back to right where you picked me up." So I drove around a bunch of blocks, dropped him exactly where I picked him up and he says, "And, uh, I'll just keep on walkin'."
1996

rick nielsen of CheapTrick

When I was in high school, I would go to Cleveland to see a band. Once I went to see Jeff Beck with Rod Stewart and Ten Years After. At the end of the show, Jeff Beck put his guitar on top of his amp. His roadie picked it up by the body and dropped it and broke the head off. Back then, there was really no backstage kinda stuff. There wasn't hardly any people there. So I went backstage and told him I collect guitars. I think I told him before he even knew it was broken. Two days later, I got a call from someone who was like, "Hold on for Jeff Beck." He's like, "If you have some guitars, I could use something." So I took a friend and flew down to Philadelphia, and stayed and played guitar with Jeff, and Ronnie Wood was there. He came in at one point and was like, "Look what I got, Rick." He knew my name because I had been introduced, and he had been out shopping and had bought a drink set. He came over with a towel over his arm and was like, "Can I freshen up your drink?" So I sold Jeff a guitar and then stayed at the Holiday Inn. I ended up staying up all night playing guitar with Jeff Beck in the room.
1996

gaz coombes of Supergrass

I hung out with Robert Smith of the Cure on the plane on the way over to Brazil, he came and sat next to me. That was the first thing about him I thought was great. He was in first class and we were in business, and he came over for the whole flight. He's not one of these rock-star guys. "Business class? It's for paupers." It was a great moment for me. I've always been fascinated by Robert Smith. I thought he was a really twisted, fucked-up guy. Robert and I talked about when you're younger and stuff. He was saying about how he really liked our gigs and stuff. I thought about it after and was like, "Fucking hell, that was Robert Smith!" I've met a lot of people before. People like Ron Wood and Van Morrison, and it's not the same. Meeting Robert Smith was very different. We

RAVES

just talked about normal shit, as well, not just music. A lot of the time I'd rather not meet musicians, because unfortunately, your perception is often ruined. Van Morrison was really horrible. We went up to him and were like, "Hey, hey, Van! All right, man!" And he just sort of went, "Urrrch, ehhhh." He's quite weird sometimes. **1997**

ANOTHERROADSIDEATTRACTION

he road is home to many wonders: balls of twine bigger than ten men, covered wagons that peddle gas and enough schlocky belt buckles to hold up all the world's pants.

d'arcy of SmashingPumpkins

They have a lot of nice cemeteries in Chattanooga, Tennessee. They have a lot of nice cemeteries in New Orleans, too. And then there's the cemetery, Père-Lachaise, in Paris, where Jim Morrison's buried, supposedly. I don't know. There are wonderful cemeteries the world over. There's this one, this tiny, tiny, tiny—I live way out in the country, and there's this tiny, old, old cemetery that we always ride to on our horses. It's really fun to ride through cemeteries because the grounds are so nicely kept. You don't have to worry, most of the time, about holes in the way. **1996**

neil diamond

I have traveled a good part of the world, visited hundreds of cities. My favorite roadside attraction remains only a few minutes' drive from my home in L.A., in the movie-theater district of UCLA's campus town of Westwood. Located behind a gray cinder-block wall is a postage-stamp-sized cemetery called Pierce Brothers Westwood Village Memorial Park and Mortuary. It would hardly be noticed if it were not the resting place of some of Hollywood's most fabulous names. I am always left speechless by the irony of these extraordinary people being buried in such an ordinary setting. When I first started visiting this tiny cemetery in the early Seventies, it was only Marilyn Monroe's name that caught my eye. I returned a few times over the years to see if Joe DiMaggio really sent flowers for years after her death . . . he did. But since then, the list of famous inhabitants has increased: Natalie Wood, Truman Capote, Irving "Swifty" Lazar—all of whom I had met in their lifetime—and all of whom I would like to ask, "Why in God's name would you be buried in such a cemetery?" Those two elements, famous names and the irony of their interment alongside a movie-theater parking lot, have always fascinated me. **1998**

"weird al" yankovic

The Biggest Ball of Twine, in Darwin, Minnesota. It's 21,140 pounds. Made by one man, Francis A. Johnson. I wrote a song about it, "The Biggest Ball of Twine in Minnesota." It's one of my more popular songs in concert. He wrapped up this ball of twine and had it basically in his backyard. When he passed away, they rolled it onto a flatbed truck and drove it across the city and put it in the middle of a park and put a gazebo over it. It's a shrine to this huge ball of twine. It's great. You can get close enough to touch it, get your photo ops and all that. Life doesn't get much better than that. **1996**

billy idol
I never saw the giant ball of twine, but the scariest thing I saw was the never-ending roadside world of fast food. It was nonstop junk food and McDonald's. **1998**

les claypool of Primus
The World's Largest Covered Wagon in Milford, Nebraska—I got to see it on our last tour. We have a book of roadside attractions on our bus. A giant Paul Bunyan, in Akeley, Minnesota; and the Biggest Ball of Twine, in Darwin, Minnesota; and the Hamburger Museum, in Daytona Beach, Florida—all these things. We can never stop for any of them because the road manager for Primus is very schedule oriented. [The Covered Wagon] was along the side of the road, so I saw it as we were driving by. It was actually a gas station with big wheels and it's covered. It's a building built to look like a covered wagon. So I saw that. **1996**

steve harwell of SmashMouth
I've been picking up Elvis stuff on tour; I'm into Elvis Presley big time. I just got a Young Elvis phone. He has a guitar on and when it rings he sings "Jailhouse Rock" and dances. It's rad, dude. Our keyboard player bought it at a Flying J truck stop for me. I woke up and it was in my bunk lying next to me. It's, like, a foot high. So, yeah, I slept with Elvis, we spooned. **1997**

dicky barrett of theMightyMightyBosstones
Roadside stops really suck. They were amusing when we first started touring, but now it's just belt buckles and all the nonsense. **1997**

andy partridge of XTC
You get to these hotels in the American Midwest and all the furniture has fake woodworms sprayed on it. They try to make it look old, so they spray these little black dots everywhere to look like woodworms have eaten at it. All these chain hotels had used this spray. What kind of worms would eat plastic laminated material? **1998**

tracy bonham
There's a place down South where you can get a tank of gas, see a tiger in a cage, play a hand of blackjack or sit at the slot machine, and eat an order of hash browns. **1998**

james hetfield of Metallica

America is a fucking good place. I definitely think that. And that feeling came about from touring a lot. You find out what you like about certain places and you find out why you live in America, even with all the bad fucked-up shit. It's still the most happening place to hang out. **1991**

nina persson of theCardigans

We've been traveling through some of those miserable parts of America. I love to be able to go there. I would never spend more time than I have to, though. Such incredible places. We had a day off in a place called Richfield, Utah. I had never

The Cardigans: Peter Svensson, Bengt Lagerberg, Nina Persson, Magnus Sveningsson and Lasse Johansson (from left) (Per-Anders Jörgensen/Mercury)

seen such an incredibly deserted place. Deserted by any style you could find in the world. There's a lot of life conditions and opinions there that scare me. It's the way it becomes when a country is as big as America. As a tourist, you can enjoy it. **1997**

jackson browne
I'm going to the Rodin Crater, which I've been wanting to do for a long time. There's an artist named James Turrell who works with light and spatial perception. He bought the crater, a huge crater out in the Arizona desert, and he's been excavating it and doing stuff that has to do with how you see the night sky. He's got a readout of the next ten thousand years' astronomical movements. So it's a huge monumental work that's going to go into the future for many millenniums or so. There are chambers in the crater, these places to lay down flat and really look—you really have the distinct impression that you can reach up and grab a star, sort of touch the sky. I've always been inspired by this part of the country, ever since I went on a trip out here when I was twelve. **1997**

steven page of BarenakedLadies
I wouldn't pack up and move to Boise, Idaho, but we had a good time there. We tubed down the Boise River and got ridiculously sunburned. There's a little bit of funkiness in the mountains and the dust. **1998**

dan murphy of SoulAsylum
We were touring West Canada once and we passed two twitching elk at the side of the road. We thought it was some mating thing until we saw this car that had just hit them. I went up and knocked on the window—it was these two women in the car—to make sure they were okay. They were more scared of me than the elk they just hit. They seemed okay, but they were terrified I was going to loot their car. Western Canadian vacationers. **1998**

HOMEISWHERETHEHEARTIS

L*ike the animals of the Serengeti, artists have different types of dwelling place, unique to their temperaments and needs. Who knew surfer boy Dick Dale enjoys life in the high desert with his horses and dogs? Or that Dave Matthews retreats to a former mill when he's not on the road? When the sun sets and the tour draws to a close, every creature must return to its natural habitat.*

erykah badu It's wonderful to be from the South. I'm in Brooklyn right now and it's this concrete jungle. The South is so free and auburn and full of trees and land. You can see everything and you wake up to birds. The trees have been there for hundreds of years, and they have so much power and energy. And just your family, man. The South is where my roots are. Wherever you're from, it's just that nostalgia, your family history, your roots. The South feels like home—it's the one place besides inside of me that feels like home. **1997**

dick dale When I am home, the dogs usually wake me up because I live in the high desert, so we get all the desert critters that come out. The dogs let me know that they're out there—the coyotes and mountain lions and all that stuff. I live on about eighty-one acres with a private airport—a twenty-eight-hundred-foot-long dirt strip. When people come out to visit me, they just stand there in awe and go, "Fuck." If you stand and don't speak, you can hear the blood moving in your ears. So I wake up to the dogs sounding off just before daybreak. The first thing I do is push a button and turn on some lights. I look out, check around, see who's out there. And then the horses look at me. I have a black mustang I got from the government to preserve this breed of mustangs. An Arabian mare, so I check them out and make sure they're okay, 'cause the mountain lions will walk through them and say hi or something. I make sure they're still alive, and after that, I go over to my Power Mac and turn that thing on and that starts kicking in and warming up; then I go in and make a cup of coffee, take two sips and never touch it again. Then I go into this blazing regimen of phone calls coming from everywhere, and that's basically it. I build a lot of things on the ranch that I get into and don't finish. My ranch is filled with boxes in every room—I should live in my motor home and use the ranch as a warehouse. **1996**

ziggy marley I love the climate and the mountains in Jamaica. The nature is very natural. I love that. And the beaches. We'll go a lot to the beaches to exercise. The water's clean. A lot of rivers. Yeah mon, we have a hot spring there, so naturally hot. When we doing sports and I get injured, that's where I go. It's in a place called St. Thomas—healing water. It's hot but cool. In the wintertime, in certain places in the mountainous areas of Jamaica it gets pretty cold. My favorite place is St. Ann's. Up there when you look in the skies, you can touch the stars, you know. In Kingston, they can't touch the stars, but when you get up to St. Ann's, the stars are very close. It's about one hour and a half from Kingston. **1997**

polly jean harvey Where we lived was very remote and cut off from other people. I lived in one of those very, very tiny villages, named Dorset, and we don't have a shop or anything like that. We just have one bar. That's it. And everybody that goes to that bar has been going there for the last seventeen years. So I lived quite a quiet lifestyle and didn't have that many other children in the village when I was young. **1995**

bob seger My cabin is my favorite spot in the whole world. I've had it for nineteen years, since we made it big with *Night Moves*. The first thing I did was buy this cabin in northern Michigan, about twenty-five miles southwest of the Mackinac Bridge, on Lake Michigan. The nearest traffic light is twenty miles away. It's great, although we do have the oldest nuclear plant in the United States about twenty miles downwind. If that ever blows, I'm the first one to go if I'm up there. The cabin is four or five hundred feet down a bluff down to the beach. You never hear a car and you really feel isolated. It's very peaceful and very hilly. It's only a summer place because we can't get down the road in the winter. I bought it for seventy thousand dollars and now it's worth about four hundred thousand dollars because I've got lake frontage. It's a small, two-story, fireplace-type deal. **1996**

ozzy osbourne My favorite place is what I work for—my house. It's not very old, it's only a hundred years old. The house I had before was five hundred years old. That one looked kinda like the White House. Nowhere near as big, but you know, white pillars and white on the outside. My wife's transformed this house into a magnificent, wonderful place with a lovely, homey feel. **1995**

billy joel I love where I live—that's why I put a house there. Why would I go anywhere? This is the greatest place I could be. The East End [of Long Island] in general reminds me of the old Long Island—all the farms and the fishing villages and the open spaces, which they still have some of on the East End. It's more like the Long Island of my childhood. **1999**

dave matthews I love my house. It's in Virginia near a really small town; Charlottesville is about twenty minutes away. It's a converted wheat-flour mill. There's a wheel and a river that runs by it and a nice dam. There's always the sound of thundering water. It's a quiet, hidden little place. It's not shiny. I go there a lot. It's my favorite place to be. I can sit and stare at the water. It's enough out of the way that I can do all sorts of sordid things and not be noticed. I can freely read *Story of the Eye* by, Georges Bataille, in my mill and be unviewed as to my reaction. **1996**

joni mitchell
I have a little cottage up in British Columbia; I've had it since 1970. The last couple of years I had a weekly social event that kinda happened by accident. It was a potluck where people would drop by, and yeah, it was usually outside with candles and two strings of Camel lights. I smoked 150 packages of Camels and sent away for two strings of Camel lights. You wouldn't believe how cheap the plastic on them is. The paint peeled off it, and I'm really pissed off. Because that was a lot of smoking, and why couldn't they have sprung for *real* yellow plastic? **1994**

beck
We lived near Tiny Naylor's [in Los Angeles], which was a monument from the age of the Fifties drive-in coffee shops. It was just a megalopolis of hamburgers and milkshakes— you drive up and the waitress puts the tray on your car. They still had that up into the Seventies. And right next to that was Ali Baba's, a Middle Eastern restaurant with belly dancers, and on top of it was a two-to-three-story statue of Ali Baba. Then in the early Eighties, all that was suddenly gone—there were minimalls everywhere. The Eighties came and conquered. **1997**

Herb Alpert (Raul Vega/Almo Sounds)

herb alpert
When I was growing up, Los Angeles was a different city. In my memories of L.A., you could see the mountains, and the city looked different. Pre-smog, it was another city. In about '50, '51 I started noticing a difference. It's gotten progressively worse. I mean, we lost the mountains. It's still incredibly beautiful on a clear day, which happens maybe once every other year. I'm exaggerating— maybe three or four times a year it's the L.A. of old. **1997**

flea of theRedHotChiliPeppers

L.A. has changed so much since I was a kid—there are freaks and weirdos and unsavory characters and people that mean ill harm everywhere. **1995**

anthony kiedis of theRedHotChiliPeppers

L.A. will always be my filthy, dirty, trashy, disgusting, poisonous home because these streets speak to me, and this is where I grew up—this is me. **1995**

gwen stefani of NoDoubt

I like that Disneyland is right there in my hometown, Anaheim, California. I don't get to go as often as I would like to. It *is* the Happiest Place on Earth. But it's corrupt and there are a lot of bad things about it, too. We got to play the Disneyland graduation party for the new employees once. They only reason we did it was just to say that we did. To be able to say that we played in front of "It's a Small World" is pretty intense. **1996**

king coffey of theButtholeSurfers

In Austin, you have to put yourself into the mind-set of the art of doing nothing. *Slacker* is almost a documentary. **1995**

ian thornley of BigWreck

I grew up in Toronto. It was very urban; Toronto's a big city. I grew up right downtown in the west end. It was great in that way that people say the United States, or New York City, is the melting pot. Toronto is more like a cultural garden salad. There are areas that are completely Jamaican—really, really thick—and there are areas like Chinatown; there are two or three different Chinatowns. There are areas that are heavily Indian, heavily Jewish. Everybody has their areas. It's a safe city as well. Downtown, you're sorta in the mix. I was definitely the odd man out, you know. I was the mangia cake—that's what all the Portuguese and Italian kids called me. It's something like the WASP kid, the kid who likes to eat cake, I guess. The kids who eat Wonder Bread with Velveeta cheese and take the crust off. Even though that wasn't really me. **1998**

roni size

I like the St. Paul's Carnival in Bristol. It's a celebration of black music, theater, food. It's mostly about Jamaican culture. There's an outdoor theater and stuff. It's amazing, man. It happens once a year in the summer and lasts for a week. They have sports and talent shows, it's a massive celebration of black culture and history. It's where I learned about my roots. It's where I learned *everything*. They had five soccer tournaments, chess matches. Everyone in the community would get involved. There was always an entourage of floats, all the kids would get these floats and dress them in different ways. **1998**

darius rucker of HootieandtheBlowfish

Rainbow Row, Charleston, South Carolina, is a historical landmark. It's just a row of old painted houses, but it's a great road to walk down. Charleston is the prettiest city in the country *and* it's my hometown. **1995**

art alexakis of Everclear

My wife's from Portland, Oregon; I bought a house there and my daughter was born there. It rains a lot, but that doesn't bother me. Every now and then I need sunshine. It's the perfect blend of city and environment because you can be out in the woods in, like, fifteen minutes. Southeast Portland, where I live, is just a great place to be. You've got gays and lesbians, black people and white people and rockers. It's very working class. People take care of their houses, everyone knows their neighbors, there's kids on our block. I'm really happy. **1996**

kim thayil of Soundgarden

One of the cool things about Seattle is that it can be sunny for a half hour, then gray, then sunny again. But it rains with the sun out. That's a good effect. **1996**

rob thomas of Matchbox20

There's a good rock scene in Orlando. They're aren't many places to play, but there are a lot of bands and really good songwriters. It's definitely got potential, with Collective Soul breaking out of there and Seven Mary Three, and hell, Marilyn Manson. Check out the Sapphire Supper Club if you're ever there. It's a great little room. Playing there's good, man. The crowds are always superexcited when we play Orlando because we're hometown boys and all. **1997**

dan wilson of Semisonic

I don't think we necessarily sound like a Minneapolis band. The North is so cold and cautious and worried—I don't know if that comes out in our music at all. The South is warm and inviting and mysterious, and I'm really pleased people down there like us. But there are two things Minneapolis did to me personally.

There are so many bands that had great albums, and it continues: Hüsker Dü, the Replacements, Soul Asylum, Jayhawks, now there's Honeydogs, Polara, the Hang Ups. There's so much going on that everybody there feels like, "Oh yeah, we can get a record deal, we can put out CDs. Let's do it!" It's good to feel that these things are possible. There's not a big mystique about it. You just ask around, everybody and their cousin knows how to do it. And the other thing is Prince, you know. He's this amazing mix of rock and R&B ideas. It's an incredible ideal to aim for. We're not an R&B band or a rock band, but I want every song to have that incredible swing. He is the absolute ideal. The way he stands in Minneapolis is, like, there's everybody and two clouds above them there's Prince, or, well, the Artist. **1998**

brian vander ark of theVervePipe

We're from the Midwest, so all this Hollywood, coming out to L.A. is fairly new to us. We come from the land of Fratmosphere—just a lot of fraternities. Our personalities are fairly straightforward and quite geeky. We had Bob Seger and Ted Nugent growing up and not much else. To the kids up there we just want to be bigger than Jesus . . . Jones. **1996**

BABY, I'M A STAR!

h, the sweet smell of success. Doors open, cash flows, fans multiply. It is what every artist wants—even the ones who won't admit it. After all, if they didn't want people to listen, why did they get on a stage in the first place?

david bowie
It's an unbelievably wonderful way to live. The hardest thing is not to feel guilty about it. **1983**

eminem
The respect level that I get now, I never got before. I couldn't even get into a motherfucking club just being Eminem before my video and all this shit happened. Last night I was in New York at a club and it was, like, "Eminem's here, clear this table! We need to get him somewhere to sit! Here, take my chair! Here!" **1999**

dave navarro of Jane'sAddiction and theRedHotChiliPeppers
Sometimes I feel like the luckiest motherfucker in the world because I believe that I have no talent. **1995**

pete townshend
I know what it's like to be a member of a successful group. I know what it's like to be a member of a group that it's difficult to be a member of. It's a great feeling to be in a group that's happening of any kind. **1968**

noel gallagher
of Oasis
I nearly got ripped to pieces in Italy by about two thousand people, so I guess it's bye-bye freedom. This will all pass in about five or six years. We have the rest of our lives to sit around our houses and be inconspicuous. Now is our time. We're in the eye of the hurricane now, and one day it's going to blow out. We'll look back in our late thirties, no worries, and we'll still be able to get together and say, "We were good,

Pete Townshend (Atlantic)

man. In fact, we were the best. And this is what we built." As for now, it's a small price to pay. **1996**

tommy lee of MötleyCrüe

After I had gotten in a few bands and then had gotten in Mötley and quit high school my senior year because we had gotten a recording contract, I remember calling my parents and saying, "Oh, my God! Mom and Dad, you guys gotta come down and check it out! We sold out Friday, Saturday and Sunday at the Whisky-a-Go-Go! I've made it!" Honest to God, man, I thought that was it. To sell out the Whisky for three nights, I thought we were the bomb. That was it, we had made it. Little did I know, we didn't do shit. When you're young, it's like, this is *it*. What a trip. **1997**

busta rhymes Success? As far as trying to accomplish something, you want to be heard, you want to be acknowledged, you want to be popular, you want people worldwide to know what's goin' on wit' what you're doin' creatively. **1998**

darryl "d.m.c." mcdaniels of Run-D.M.C.

I want to go out like Sinatra, I wanna be eighty-five and still doing it. I wanna see Run-D.M.C. in Vegas. That's my next vision. You're driving down the Vegas strip, you look up, see the Palace. JUNE 15–JUNE 30: RUN-D.M.C.—LIVE! **1998**

billy corgan of SmashingPumpkins

I can honestly say that we have not had a serious row in about a year. You have your little tiffs, like, "Who stole my water?" but no full-on screaming. We were playing the last show of Lollapalooza, and I thought, "I am really, really glad we're still together." It was really emotional. **1994**

lil' kim When I first went platinum, I said, "Okay. I'm gonna buy myself a platinum ring." So I got a platinum ring, and I was given a platinum bracelet to match. I also have a gold bracelet from when my single went gold. So I have one hand for the gold singles and one hand for the platinum. And basically that's it, I don't have too much jewelry. I'm more of a diamond person, but right now, I don't have enough money to get all the diamonds I want. I want that one-point-five-million stone. I love diamonds. I love glittering things. Sometimes I wear costume jewelry—sometimes it looks better, like, if I'm getting my picture taken. But

it's not the real thing. Back in the day, I had to fake it until I'd make it. Now I got the *real* stuff. I could deal with makin' it more, though. Then I'd have to get a nose thing or something to go around my head because my arms and my neck would be filled. Maybe I could get a diamond dress like Liberace. **1997**

beck I remember being really shocked after *Mellow Gold* came out and going on tour, and all these kids were there. It totally disturbed me. Who are all these young people? I'd been playing Mississippi John Hurt covers in coffee shops to a bunch of thirty-, forty-, fifty-year-olds. Then all of a sudden there were these teenagers. It was very surreal. **1997**

james hetfield of Metallica
Having money, being part of all this, freaks me out. I like being where most people can't find me, doing things by myself or just being with good friends in the wilderness, camping or drinking or whatever. **1991**

mark mcgrath of SugarRay
I'm doing fantastic! I'm out at the Phoenix hotel. It's in San Francisco, you know? Less Than Jake are here filming a video down by the pool, so everybody's partying. I have to move some of the broads out of here, you know? Dude, I wish you were here, man. I can't take them all by myself. It's so much fun, dude, it's killer. It's a beautiful day, sun's out, it's a fucking rock & roll scene. We just did a show in Union Square for a radio station. There were, like, ten thousand people in the park. For us? It was killer. We just got back, so I've had a few brews and I'm fucked up! Yeah! We brought back a few fans from the show. It sounds really cheesy, and it is totally cheesy, but we're cheesy! I mean, I got into music for chicks and beer, and fortunately it's working out. I've got the only job in the world where every day I show up to work and there are three cases of beer and they encourage me to drink them. I don't want to hurt anybody's feelings, so I make sure they're all drunk. I've got a little bit of class. **1997**

ben gillies of Silverchair
You always think that if you ever put a record out that it's all fancy hotel rooms and chicks. And we've seen the other side of it. You gotta do all the shit—traveling, interviews, stupid photo shoots. All that other stuff is just a big pull. Playing. It's cool, too, because me and Daniel [Johns] and Chris [Joannou] have been

RAVES

Ben Gillies of Silverchair (Self-portrait by Ben Gillies,
courtesy of Russell A. Trunk/Chrisam Enterprises, Inc.)

good friends since primary school, when we were five and six. It's really cool to be able to do this kind of shit with good mates, isn't it? **1996**

erykah badu Music and the music-business agenda are two totally different things. One is to capitalize off money and one is to inspire and be inspired. Getting in a business like this as a true artist, as a born artist, and when I say that, I know I've been anointed, that the creator has given me this gift, and that I use it as a gift back. I'd like to say "peace" to all of those artists who, whether they have deals or not, are doing what they do, because that's what makes music what music is. I appreciate them very, very much. They inspire me so. **1997**

steve harwell of SmashMouth

We did demos in a big studio where they do *The Simpsons* and Guns n' Roses actually have a private practice studio. The guy there let us check it out. It was this huge, huge studio. They had every toy you could think of in there. Pool tables, pinball machines, blow-up dolls. It was rad. It was really kicked back, but you could tell these guys had ridiculous money. They had a whole concert PA set up—I was like, dude, I could play an arena with this shit. I took a bunch of pictures. They're so huge and at the time, we were unsigned. It was such a cool rock-star thing to see that. It would be like going to Van Halen's place. Fuck, it's everybody's dream. We've had some cool experiences on this little trek we're on. **1997**

flea of theRedHotChiliPeppers

I remember when my biggest dream of fame was being able to play Perkins Palace, this place in L.A. that held two thousand people. I thought, "One day, if I could just be in a band that could play there, that would be the ultimate." I never dreamed the Red Hot Chili Peppers would become a pop band. We've sold a lot of records and made all this money, you know? It's crazy. **1994**

sean "puffy" combs a.k.a. Puff Daddy

The highlight of my year was reading the statistics of *Billboard,* seeing how many weeks I've dominated rap, pop singles and R&B singles charts. Seeing the records I broke, from the Beatles to Elvis Presley—seeing my name in history with names like that make me wake up every morning, sit back and feel blessed to be here. Statistically, it was one of the best years of my life, but, personally, it was one of the worst. I just have to handle it, take the good with the bad. I would give it all—I would turn the hits into negative hits—if I could just be with Biggie [Smalls] again. **1997**

eddie van halen of VanHalen

I'm a normal guy. I'm a bricklayer. Maybe I lay bricks better than other people. I don't know. It's what I do. The star stuff just comes along with the territory. That's the stuff I hate. Some people enter this arena for that. Not me. **1998**

stephan jenkins of ThirdEyeBlind

It's really the simple things I just can't get over, like the guitar techs. I mean, my tech hands me this perfectly maintained, perfectly in-tune guitar with fresh strings, I walk out onstage, I bang it, sweat all over it, and the next night it's perfect again. That's really the good part. **1997**

brian vander ark of theVervePipe

I met Lauren Holly when we played the Troubador, and I laughed at something she said and accidentally farted. I thought, "Nah, I'm never gonna fit in here." Whether she heard it or not, I don't know, but I got the hell out of there before the smell. I didn't talk to her much after the flatulence. When I was a kid, it was the same thing. I farted when I laughed. It was always at the worst times. I thought I'd gotten that under control. This generation is eating plenty of vegetables and broccoli and everything. I'm telling you, it's terrible for you. It's not good for the person next to you, that's for sure. **1996**

dave matthews
The most affected I've been meeting anyone was, strangely enough, Jim Carrey. He's just as he is. He's an incredibly animated man. But he has such a presence, and on top of that, he's just so generous, and he was so kind. And cool. I left thinking that I would like to spend another couple hours drinking with him and getting high. A lot of wisdom popped out of his mouth in the short period of time we had together. That was strange. Here's this guy that I've laughed at but really haven't thought that much about. Never did I expect that I would be so impressed by him. **1996**

gary numan
About a year or so ago, somebody said, "Marilyn Manson's doing one of your songs," and I said, "Really?!" And they said Foo Fighters had done one, and I said, "Aww, get off!" But it just went on and on; it's such a big deal for me to have so many people doing my stuff. I've got to say, I really don't think I deserve a lot of it. I'm being credited as being an influence. Some person has called me the "godfather of electronica." It makes me uncomfortable. It's a nice thing to say and I really should shut up and say, "Yeah, okay, fair enough." I didn't attach that much importance to what I did. I didn't think it was particularly influential or cutting edge. I was just sitting at home, writing stuff and putting it out. Unbeknownst to me it's become a foundation for other people's careers. It is such a brilliant thing to find out, at my stage in my career. It's lovely. **1997**

rza of Wu-TangClan

Basically, I'm a digital orchestra. I play all the strings, keyboards, bells, guitar, everything you hear. And some of this music can be notated. It can be written down, you can take that shit and add a whole fucking orchestra. And that is beautiful. **1998**

aphex twin a.k.a. RichardJames

I'm too busy doing stuff. I haven't been to bed for like three and a half days. It's fucking mad. I've had massive amounts of coffee, just getting all my stuff done. This is the biggest time in my life, these last four days. I've been working on this mix for David Bowie and Philip Glass and Brian Eno. And I'm getting ready to go to Australia, then Japan to do live sets. And I'm buying a bank to live in. I'm trying to get it today. It's been hectic. But I'm enjoying it. So that's the thing, you see—I couldn't sleep. I did this last week, I couldn't sleep for three days, and then when I tried to go to sleep, I'd wake up after, like, twenty minutes, just completely still wired. . . . I have trouble sleeping. **1997**

aaron barrett of ReelBigFish

Nothing's changed except that now people come up to me and ask me to sign my name on little pieces of paper. **1997**

leann rimes

Bonnie Raitt is awesome. I met her at the Grammy Awards because she was in the same dressing room I was. She actually came up to me and said, "I love your music." It was pretty cool. It was one of those things. I really don't get starstruck by anybody anymore, because some of them are really my friends, and I've figured out that they're just like everybody else. **1997**

dave pirner of SoulAsylum

I was coming through customs in America and "Runaway Train" was on the radio in the customs officer's booth. Our road manager goes to him, "That's these guys, they're on the radio." And the officer was like, "Okay, you guys over here." Searched us. **1998**

WITHOUTYOUWE'RENOTHING

Where is a band without an audience? Band practice. Nothing would be possible without the fans or, rather, the Japanese fans. An artist's fans are the people who feel the music the most. They are there for the ups and the downs, bearing gifts and tributes, and causing the infrequent personal injury.

neil diamond

You don't realize the value of fans until something wakes you up. I had surgery in the late Seventies, and I got a bunch of letters and nice things from people. I was down and out, and it was important. And I didn't think it would be important. I learned a lesson from that. I don't take it lightly anymore. **1996**

alanis morissette

The reaction of the audience has been so amazing and open. It's comforting and bittersweet to know that I'm not the only one who's gone through these things. At the same time it's disturbing that apparently there are a lot of people out there who went through such painful things. The reaction has been pretty intense. There was a mosh pit in Minneapolis when we played there. Is it me, or is this music not about moshing? **1995**

kate pierson of theB-52's

We have always appealed to people outside of the mainstream. Constantly we get people coming up to us and saying, "I was just the freakiest one in high school, I was the only one who kept playing the B-52's." I think more people feel like they're outside of the mainstream these days. More people are doing their own thing, feeling that it's not bad to be a weirdo and respecting other people's differences. And all that goes into the big ol' B-52 philosophy. **1990**

nick hexum of 311

When we got on MTV it all changed—our fans got a lot younger. I try to embrace it. A lot of people lament it, but I want to speak to anyone who'll listen. I don't want to be elitist about it. Most people are really cool and want to give real good vibes, and there are, of course, some psychos who are, like, camping out in front of our old house, sitting out there waiting, smoking weed and shit. It's a little unnerving, even though they have good intentions and they love us. It's like, how the hell did they get our fucking address? I turn on my e-mail once a week, I get fifty to a hundred messages that one day, and it takes me the rest of the week to answer them. E-mail is definitely the way to keep up with your fans. You don't have to deal with stamps, addresses, any of that—just hit reply. **1997**

311: Timothy J. Mahoney, Nick Hexum, Chad Sexton, P-Nut and S.A. Martinez (from left)
(Danny Clinch/Capricorn)

wayne coyne of theFlamingLips

We're open about people sending us stuff, and fans call me all the time because I give them my address and phone number, I don't care. If people think it's really important to call me to say they like our records or they hate our records, I don't really care. I don't feel like, "Oh, I can't deal with our public." Most of the people who come to see us are just people like me. A lot of them are in bands themselves. There was this one kid, and I say kid 'cause I think he was like seventeen. He was just obsessed. He would call me up and say, "I'm coming down to Oklahoma City and I want to record with you guys." It seemed silly at first, and I thought, "Well, you know, I appreciate your enthusiasm, but we're not really into that." And before I could reply, he sent me songs he had done and then he sent me tapes and pictures he had drawn, wanting an honest opinion about them. He'd say, "What do you think? A lot of people tell me I'm great." But before I could really reply—because I didn't really know how to—he killed himself. And the day he did, his friend called me and told me. I didn't even know him—he was a guy who sent me stuff—and I didn't know what to do. He knew me, you know, he'd bought the records and stuff, but I didn't know him. His friend called and said, "I just wanted you to know that he killed himself last night. You were a big part of his life." What do you do with that? I didn't know anything about the guy. I didn't know what kind of life he lived, what kind of person he was. All I knew was this stuff he'd sent me. I wasn't involved in his life, know what I mean? It's like anybody, we put records out there; if you want to buy them, that's all that you're involved in. I don't know why people make rock stars more important than themselves. That whole idea—how that whole structure has been set up, and how rock stars make it seem like, "My life: You should pay attention to it"—is everything we're against. I just hate that. When people come to our shows, it's their night; they make it an event. We're just a band, we're the music, and everything else you do that night is what makes it an event for you—who you go with, who you talk to, the things you do, what you do afterwards. We're just a little part of it. Anyway, that was the worst time. I felt obligated to care. I'm sure every band in the world has a couple of fans who are obsessive. Most people we run into are smarter than we are and they're just like, "We like your music. You guys are weirdos. Take care." That's the best that can happen to us: to really play to people who enjoy music instead of fantasize about what rock & roll is all about. We try to come across as just like you. We are basically dressed the same. All you need in the world is an audience who listens to what you're doing—if it's twenty people or a thousand people. Those are the people, God bless 'em all. **1995**

eminem
The weirdest thing is that people come up to me and want me to hear them rhyme, but they don't even have a tape to give me. They'll want me to come to their car or some shit and listen to some tape. It's like, motherfucker, do you even know what I had to do to get where I'm at? **1999**

billy gibbons of ZZTop
Our fans are a rebellious, raucous bunch. But, they're getting different. I'll see a cowboy hat in the first row, purple hair in the second row and some guy in a suit with a laptop and a mobile phone in the third row, e-mailing his requests to the stage. We have kids there today who think *Eliminator* is our old stuff. They don't even know about the Seventies. **1996**

robert smith
of theCure
Smashing Pumpkins came up to me in Paris and said they like what we do. It's really gratifying when bands tell you that. **1996**

leann rimes
I got a plaque from a fan once. It was pretty cool. It was this little mirrored plaque that had my name on it—the kind of thing you'd hang on a wall. It said LEANN RIMES BLUE TOUR '96 and had the album cover in the middle of it. It was really cool—you could see they put a lot of thought into it. It was from a member of my fan club. It was really sweet. **1997**

luther vandross
Mostly letters are left backstage, but I have gotten a lot of people who paint portraits for me. I keep them in a certain place I have for

Robert Smith of the Cure (Fiction)

displaying stuff like that. It is really nice. Some of them look nothing like me, but whatever. **1997**

the donnas
We love it when our fans and friends give us Japanese candy or paraphernalia associated with our favorite bands. **1998**

lil' kim
Oh, I get a lot of gifts from fans. One day I was out in the Bahamas, I think, and this lady was wearing a gold bracelet on her upper arm. It was so different; I loved it. I see a lot of the ones that are squigglies, just tight around your arm. But this one looked like bubbles. So I said, "That is a beautiful bracelet." And she said, "Do you really like it?" I said I loved it, and she took it off her arm and said, "Here, it's yours." I couldn't even believe it, but I took it and no one has one like it. I still have it—in one of my collections. When I was onstage at the Apollo, someone threw a bag onstage and I kinda ducked. I thought they were throwing stuff at me. I was like, "Oh, time to go." But actually, they had thrown me a homemade outfit. That was really nice. It fit—well, it was a little baggy because a lot of people overestimate my size, but I was able to take it in. It was really nice: leopard skin, with a long-sleeved top and a long skirt with a split up the side. **1997**

aaliyah
I toured Japan for a week. They were wonderful. They gave so much love and energy. I got rings, I got mugs, I got jewelry. I was onstage one night and this one guy threw a silver bracelet—I still have it. I wear it every time I'm onstage. I got makeup kits, lip gloss, everything. **1997**

lisa loeb
I love going to Japan. I see a lot of fans wearing glasses, and a lot of people show up at my hotel. A weird thing that they do when I walk out onstage is yell "Kawaii," which means "cute" in Japanese. It's a really big word there. You'll hear kids yell "Kawaii" and then yelling my name, "Lisa! Lisa!" And they sing along to every song. It's wonderful. It's weird but flattering. My dream is to see a Lisa Loeb T-shirt with a weird English slogan on it. It hasn't happened yet. There was a banner in my hotel that said WELCOME LISA LOEB, HONEY HONEY EYELASH. **1997**

stephan jenkins of ThirdEyeBlind
I was talking to this group of girls and one of them put my finger in her mouth. She took my hand sort of lovingly, put my finger in her mouth and bit. That was

weird. I pried her mouth open and went, "Fuck! Jesus Christ!" She didn't break the skin, but I thought she was going to. She just wanted to make an impact. I guess she did—here I am talking about it to Rolling Stone. A complete victory for her. In fact, maybe I should not encourage this kind of behavior. **1998**

fred durst of LimpBizkit

It's killer to affect people. When people would come up to you and say, "Dude that song, those lyrics, man, I felt like that." I understand that a lot of our fans are really young. The status thing, as far as the girl situation, is really cool, like beautiful women liking you when they would never like you in the first place. **1998**

"weird al" yankovic

I love Canada because people don't seem to take themselves very seriously up there. The Midwest in the States is great because the fans just go crazy, but there's also the problem that people don't really treat celebrities like they're human there. If somebody recognizes me in Ohio, even if he's three feet away, he'll point at my face and turn to his wife and say, "Look, honey! It's that guy on TV, it's that 'Eat It' guy." And I'm like, "Hi, nice ta meet ya." "Honey, look! He's talking to us." Also, there's this guy, Karl Dittmar is his name. I had autographed his arm one year, and the next time I saw him, he'd had it tattooed. My autograph. And a caricature of me tattooed above that. So he dedicated an entire limb to me—well, mostly his forearm. I said, "Aren't you aware that these are permanent?" He said, "Oh yeah, man. This is my shrine to you." "Umm . . . o-kay." On a separate occasion, I met a guy who had met his girlfriend because they were fans of mine. There's a part in *UHF* called Spatula City—"What better way to say 'I love you' than with a gift of a spatula?" is their motto. These two had spatulas tattooed on their stomachs. And then they broke up. He showed me his spatula and I was like, "Ooh, I'm sorry." **1996**

k.d. lang

Women send me their eight-by-tens and measurements, but the last thing I want to do is sleep with a fan. Because k.d. lang the performer is so much cooler than I am. As a lover, I'm not as self-assured and cocky and invincible. **1993**

WHOLELOTTALOVE

Everyone needs someone to admire, even at the top. The ridiculously gifted Stevie Wonder, who, from his lofty perch, need not admire anybody, gets positively giddy when he discusses Prince (certainly no slouch in his own right). Lil' Kim is proud to place her Gucci stilettos in the footsteps of no-nonsense blues belter Millie Jackson. Remember, folks, we all want the same thing . . . to be loved. Group hug, everybody.

lou reed I love Dion. He has the most astonishing voice. I felt this way from the first day I heard him on the radio. He was the first white guy I heard on the radio that could do that "Bronx soul." It wasn't rockabilly, and it wasn't like the Penguins or one of the doo-wop groups. It was just this incredible other thing. He just killed me, and he still does. I backed him a couple of times—I sang the bass part, 'cause I grew up on that stuff. He really complimented me once; he said I could go on the road with him. I had it down. But of course, I've been rehearsing for that for years. **1989**

Lou Reed (Timothy Greenfield-Sanders)

shannon hoon of BlindMelon

Lou Reed is brilliant. There's nothing polished about the Velvet Underground. That's all you ever want. **1994**

erykah badu Busta Rhymes is one of the best new things I've heard.

Busta has pure rhythm-making skill. He's a lyricist whose beats back up his flow. **1997**

ziggy marley I like Erykah Badu and Busta Rhymes. Yeah, mon,

Busta our youth, you know? He's our youth—our friend. Yeah, mon, wild. **1997**

liam howlett of theProdigy

Wu-Tang Clan just run it as far as I'm concerned. When you listen to the lyrics, you believe what they're saying. We listen to Wu-Tang every time in the changing room before we go onstage. We've all got our favorite tracks. Other than *Wu-Tang Forever,* I'm not really into hip-hop now, I'm into the old-school stuff. It's mellowed out too much for me now. Rage Against the Machine capture everything. I try to do this in my music—they take hardness to the extreme, but they keep the funk and the groove in the tunes. It must be so difficult to get that and keep it hard. **1997**

dicky barrett of theMightyMightyBosstones

My all-time favorite entertainer is Neil Diamond. He's an unbelievable songwriter and an entertainer in every single sense of the word. I've seen him twice. The sequins, the stage that revolves—walking against it, riding it, spinning around. What can you say about a guy who can hold a whole audience of middle-aged women and *me* mesmerized for two and a half hours? **1997**

neil diamond Sinatra did "Sweet Caroline" with a swing band and

he *killed* the song. I mean, he just did it better than anybody—including me—ever did. I love that. That's probably my favorite cover version. And I loved UB40's "Red Red Wine," which came out of the blue. **1988**

noel gallagher of Oasis

I met Burt Bacharach. He's fuckin' cool. *Super*cool. He's got this wife and she's, like, twenty-four. And he's sixty-nine. It's like, you've got it going on, mate. You're *with* the program. When I'm sixty-nine, I want to be like you—sitting at a piano, singing "This Guy's in Love With You" to a twenty-four-year-old wife. [Bacharach's wife is thirty-six.] **1998**

jay kay of Jamiroquai

I'm a big fan of the Prodigy. I just like the edge they've got, in terms of the way they make hip-hop and mix it up into aggression with punk. I met Keith Flint, he's a really nice chap, he's not stuck up his own ass, which, uh, usually they are. We're at different ends of the spectrum, but we're trying to do the same thing. **1997**

Jay Kay of Jamiroquai (Ellen Von Unwerth/Work)

sean "puffy" combs a.k.a. Puff Daddy

I'm a big fan of Radiohead. I love the way their shit is orchestrated. That shit is just beautiful—there's so much shit going on, it's beautiful. It's so emotional, so real, so right-there-in-your-face. I love that shit. I love it as a producer as well. **1997**

simon le bon of DuranDuran

Beck is great, absolutely; he does James Brown! Any white guy who's got the balls to do James Brown, I take my hat off to. He puts on an incredible show. **1997**

stephan jenkins of ThirdEyeBlind

Sandinista! is one of the great man-made things of our time. Onstage I sometimes have my Clash moment. I get that feeling for a second and it's great. I have my Sarah McLachlan moment, too, when I feel all groovy. I'll be all by myself singing and picking away on my Martin and it's so goddamned tender. What crosses my mind is "God, I feel like Sarah McLachlan." But when I think that, everything becomes ludicrous for a second. She's sung me to sleep many a night. **1998**

john wozniak of MarcyPlayground

The Hanson brothers may be uncool, but they rock! I saw them on *Oprah* and I'm telling you, man, I was blown away. Those kids can fucking sing. If you're that young, you had better be good, because nobody's gonna give you the time of day. **1998**

elvis costello

The Damned was the best punk group because there was no art behind them; they were just enjoying themselves. There was no art behind them that *I* could see. They were just—*nasty*. I loved them from the start. I like the Pistols as well—but you could see the concern behind it. It's dishonest to say, "Oh, yes, we were just *wild*"; they weren't just wild. It was *considered* and calculated. Very art. The Clash as well. **1982**

stephen stills of Crosby, StillsandNash

I really dig Tom Jones. He's got incredible chops. **1971**

stevie wonder

Prince has really been unique with the way he uses words. The lyrics on "Sign o' the Times" are incredible. He's like the Bob Dylan of the Eighties as far as what he is saying. Incredible lyrics. And the song, the melody, the music, is good, too. It's kind of like Prince is an African storyteller, right? It seems like he's passing on what is happening in this time and place that we're living in right now. And he doesn't say specifically, "Oh, this is horrible; this is wrong." Which you know is what he's saying. He says, "Hey, let's get married, have a baby, raise a family. Let's do something." **1987**

q-tip of ATribeCalledQuest

Joni Mitchell is dope. She's fucking awesome. I've been a fan ever since I was little. **1996**

bono of U2

Bruce Springsteen was our guide, not just in the way he described the world but in the way he negotiated it. Words like *dignity* and *integrity*, they can hem you in, but he actually stretched them and inhabited them to the point where they weren't just corny. I remember thinking we could never play arenas. Then I went to see him do it. I felt it all over the stadium. He made a whisper go a long way. And I thought, okay, we can do this. **1999**

roni size

I was sitting in my hotel room the other day watching MTV show all Beastie Boys videos. When I used to hear the Beastie Boys, I had a different picture in my head of what they really were. When I saw the videos, it changed my whole perspective of them. I still love them—"what's the time, it's time to get ill!" *Paul's Boutique* is my all-time favorite though. That backward bass with a fucking hi-hat is wicked. **1998**

stone gossard of PearlJam

I've seen Ben Harper lots of times. We've played shows with him too. I love his new record, *Will to Live,* that song "Faded" is amazing. I've seen it live and it was even better. His bass player, Juan Nelson, is great. I like a lot of rap hits these days, too. I think Lil' Kim—and her video—are great. I haven't been necessarily buying the records, but I've been listening to the radio and definitely watching MTV, checking out the new singles. Rap Top Forty is more interesting than rock Top Forty, which I feel I'm maybe too close to or whatever. But Lil' Kim's just sexy. Great production, good songs. No doubt about it, there's definitely some good rapping being done these days. Although Puff Daddy isn't my favorite rapper. Makes great records, but not my favorite rapper. Biggie Smalls—I haven't lived with that record, but the stuff I've heard off of it, I'm into. The tone of his voice and his delivery are just too good. I saw that video where he says, "You should be havin' my baby." That is the boldest lyric I've ever heard. **1997**

twiggy ramirez of MarilynManson

I would like to see Dave Wyndorf of Monster Magnet and Courtney Love have sex onstage, every night. I would like to see Wyndorf's mustache in Courtney's downstairs. We need to see the Bullgod get some Love. **1999**

gary numan

Gravity Kills is my favorite band at the moment. I spent quite a bit of time with them while they were in Europe. We went to see them three times and they came to my house, three of them. They almost missed their last gig though; I made a bit of a mistake. They were supporting Skunk Anansie at the last gig of their tour, at a big show in London—very important for them. Jeff Scheel and Kurt Kerns were at my house, and we were a bit late leaving. Then I thought I knew where Brixton Academy was and didn't, so we got lost. I was, like, trying to pretend I knew exactly where I was going and it was getting later and later. It was rush hour and traffic was stopped solid. I was shitting my pants, thought they were going to hate me forever. Luckily, everything worked out. **1997**

babyface

There are few geniuses of our time and I'm not among them. Lionel Richie is a genius writer. He combined black and pop in melodies that people will never forget. As a producer, no one has earned the longevity and respect that Quincy Jones has. I also give high praise to Prince. Take away his showbiz image, and Prince is still a master. **1994**

tom petty

Dave Grohl's such a great musician. I've never played with anyone who plays the drums like that. **1995**

"weird al" yankovic

The Presidents of the United States of America are one of the few acts that are cool enough to be labeled alternative and yet strange enough to be on the Dr. Demento show. To paraphrase *Spinal Tap*, they tread that "fine line between clever and stupid." They loved my parody "Gump." They really seemed to get a huge kick out of it. In fact, I had the privilege of playing it for Chris Ballew in his tour bus and actually watch his reaction. It was cool to be there when the original artist heard it for the first time. That never happened before. **1996**

tina weymouth of TalkingHeads and TomTomClub

Lou Reed and drugs and nihilism and Iggy Pop and his pee-pee. **1996**

paula cole
I sat down and listened to the Rolling Stones for the first time a few weeks ago and I loved them. I grew up so incredibly ignorant to the world of pop and rock. I'm literally only now starting to listen to the Rolling Stones! It was *Hot Rocks*, a compilation. I haven't gotten around to Led Zeppelin yet. **1998**

bo diddley
Hootie and the Blowfish. Yeah, they're neat, they're a little different. You'd be surprised, I like a lot of the things being played. I like a lot of the rap music up until it gets dirty, then I don't want any part of it. I think the guys doing rap with the dirty lyrics can write good, clean lyrics and get the same results. They're sending our youngsters in the wrong direction, it needs to be stopped. I say, rap guys, get on the ball. If you've got any respect at all, you don't want your kid listening to that crap, not until he gets old enough to handle it. It's like pornography. Kids, you get to the age where you talkin' 'bout getting married, you old enough to look at anything you want. If somebody put it out there for you to buy, you can go buy it if you want, you old enough to handle it. But not no nine-year-old kid. Let him be a child as long as he can, okay? Because when it's over, it's over, baby. It's over. **1996**

busta rhymes
Dru Hill have a lot of substance and definition. They don't sound like they just singing shit. It has that soulful feeling. I like the fact that they're young motherfuckers. They don't look at singing as being just some shit that you gotta do for the women. Those motherfuckers come out there and perform hard like MCs. They get busy. I love artists that give shit to you—it ain't just the record, they givin' you a package. **1997**

darryl "d.m.c." mcdaniels of Run-D.M.C.

M.C. Hammer was the James Brown of our generation! He was the hardest-working man in show business. Then the whole world got tired of him, you know. **1998**

polly jean harvey
Tom Waits doesn't care and is not interested in making money. He explores all different avenues, like writing film music, acting, doing music for theater. That's what I'm interested in as well, just making the

most of your time here on Earth, seeing how many different ways you can push yourself and explore. **1995**

thurston moore of SonicYouth

Harry Pussy are a group from Miami Beach. I got their record in the mail. Anarchistic noise freak-out stuff that I think is really cool. **1994**

tricky
Lee "Scratch" Perry made some of the best music there is, so who says magic doesn't work? **1996**

Tricky (Barron Claiborne/Island)

fred schneider
of theB-52's

The only people I'll go see when they're in town are Iggy Pop, Hole, the Jon Spencer Blues Explosion, White Zombie, Pretenders and P.J. Harvey—she's my fave. I've seen her three times. The more eye shadow the merrier, I tell ya. **1996**

dave matthews
I'm out of touch with a lot of music, but I'm a big fan of Soul Coughing. I so admire what they do and that they can do it live. I love the words. They paint great pictures for me. As people, they're really nice as well. All I can say is that I'd love to do that. Maybe one day I will. **1996**

duncan sheik
When I was in London I went to Ministry of Sound, and Paul Oakenfold was DJ'ing and I was pretty blown away. It was completely electronic music, but it had this majesty to it that was incredible. **1997**

billie joe armstrong of GreenDay

Jesse Michaels of Operation Ivy had a charisma about him. He would step onstage and take over the entire room—he could just stand there. And what a great sense of melody. Bob Mould wrote great songs, too. I liked all his stuff with Hüsker Dü; I'm only familiar with that one Sugar record that everybody likes—*Copper Blue*. But I think *Warehouse: Songs and Stories* was Hüsker's best record. What a great way to end a band. Of course, Johnny Rotten was beautiful when he was in the Sex Pistols. Now he sucks. He's got those eyes—the one that wanders a little bit. And his voice. And he blatantly knows he's smarter than you, no matter what. **1998**

d'arcy of SmashingPumpkins

I have to plug the Flaming Lips. I love their music so much. We all know about the Flaming Lips, don't we? Well, they're wonderful, their record kept me sane during the Lollapalooza tour and all that crap. And I can't *not* plug my husband's band, Catherine. Their new record is amazing. And also, Full Fledged. They're the real thing; they're on my label, Scratchy. I listened to their album every day last year going back and forth from Chicago, when we were recording. I used to live an hour away—now we're two hours away. **1996**

jerry garcia of theGratefulDead

When I was fifteen, I fell madly in love with rock & roll. Chuck Berry was happening big, Elvis Presley—not *so* much Elvis Presley, but I really liked Gene Vincent, you know, the *other* rock guys, the guys that played guitar good: Eddie Cochran, Buddy Holly, Bo Diddley. And at the time, the R&B stations still were playing stuff like Lightnin' Hopkins and Frankie Lee Sims, these funky blues guys. Jimmy McCracklin, the Chicago-style blues guys, the T-Bone Walker–influenced guys, that older style, pre–B.B. King stuff. Jimmy Reed—Jimmy Reed actually had *hits* back in those days. You listen to that, and it's so funky. It's a beautiful sound, but I had no idea how to go about learning it. **1993**

john popper of BluesTraveler

Oh, boy. When Jimi Hendrix stops concentrating and starts flowing, that's a great moment. Prince's vocal harmonies—whatever the hell he's called, I call him "good." He's managed to keep control of his own life and I really admire that. Annie Lennox has power, and the way she also uses her eyes in her videos is brilliant. And, of course, the way she delivers on vocals. **1998**

steven tyler of Aerosmith

I can tell you one thing, I wouldn't care how she does it or what she looks or smells like, but I would cut this interview off right now if Janis Joplin were playing across the street. I'd be right there. **1994**

RAVES

shirley manson of Garbage

A while ago, I watched *Gimme Shelter* on the tour bus and saw Tina Turner sing "I've Been Loving You Too Long," and it gave me the chills. I was like, "She is fucking rock & roll." She touches you in a way that's beyond words—she just triggers responses in your body. **1997**

bonnie raitt

I loved Joan Baez. I still do. She was Quaker, like I was, and she was a political activist and a folksinger. And I thought she was so beautiful, and she was part Scottish, and I'm Scottish. She was my hero. **1990**

patti smith

When I heard Hole, I was amazed to hear a girl sing like that. Janis Joplin was her own thing; she was into Big Mama Thornton and Bessie Smith. But what Courtney Love does—I'd never heard a girl do that. **1996**

björk

The Breeders girls, they are so great—their attitude is so fresh and so modern. And I really admire Courtney Love as well. And with Madonna, I'm not going to go into the things she's done for women. You'd fall asleep, there are so many. . . . Just the fact that she made it look good to control your own life when that was something that was not supposed to be very sexy for a woman. She's one of the few women who has remained true to herself and been a character. **1994**

rosanne cash

I'd pay to see Judy Garland right now, if she were alive. I love her. She's my hero. She was an absolute clear channel of emotion through her singing. On the album recorded at Carnegie Hall, her voice cracks, breaks, she misses notes, and nobody gives a shit because the emotion is so strong. Patsy Cline was the same way. I think she had greater technical ability than Garland did, but the same emotional quality. What a voice. Unencumbered emotion. **1981**

lil' kim

I've always loved Sade, Patti LaBelle, Whitney Houston and Millie Jackson—we talked recently. We've had a really common life. Her aunt and my mother have the same name, we have the same last name, my mom is from the same place as her family And our music is basically the same. I am her in my era. We had a good time, she said she was gonna cook me a dinner. I told her I wouldn't forget about that. Mary J. Blige is my best friend, Biggie introduced us. I've known her for about three or four years now. At Biggie's funeral, she gave me a gold cross with diamonds down the middle, and she told me that it would always shelter and protect me. I wear it every day—I never take it off. During that whole funeral scene, I spent the week with her. She definitely was there for me. **1997**

k.d. lang
I love Loretta Lynn because she's such a kook. When I did *Shadowland,* she came in to do a song with me. I was there waiting for this legend to walk in. She comes in with this huge piece of bologna and white bread to make sandwiches. I am not kidding. One of those bologna rolls! I loved it. I thought, "Okay, if there's a moment when I should eat meat, it should be right now, because Loretta Lynn brought me a bologna sandwich." But I couldn't. I think I took one and politely misplaced it. Minnie Pearl was there—who I love. I love that Dead Milkmen song "Punk Rock Girl"—"and you're dressed like Minnie Pearl." I told her about that song, actually. I think she was into it, but I don't think she really got how cool it was. But Minnie Pearl is really smart and really open. **1997**

art alexakis of Everclear
Ted Hawkins was this older black man I first heard on Venice Beach. He was fifty-eight when he died in 1994. He would play with gloves on, and he would tune everything to Nashville tuning, which is where you use one finger to play the chord. He was like Sam Cooke meets Otis Redding. His last album was on Geffen. One on Rounder is called *Happy Hour*—the title track is amazing, so heartfelt. I used to go see him play when I was in my early twenties, when I was still drinking and stuff. I would sit on the beach behind all the tourists, and throw my tips from working as a waiter into his guitar case. I'd ask him to play "Happy Hour"— he was a pro, he would do it. He never got too close to anyone down at the beach, but he was always polite. **1996**

john lee hooker
Stevie Ray Vaughan really had it: his singing, his playing—good boy. Good group with him, too. Really hot stuff. Chopped it up. He really meant it. Albert King had the hard blues—raw. Bobby Bland had the thunder, too. They'd make a good bill. Yeah, but I'd have to be up there with them. We could all duke it out. Buddy Guy's funny. We've been friends for a long time. We did a song long ago called "The Motor City Is Burning." We tore it up. We did an interview together once. He was cracking me up the whole time, I had to tell him to stop. He's always doing that, though. I enjoy it. Yeah, all of those guys can put it down. They tell it like it is. Those are the guys I like to get with when I'm on the outside looking in. Oh yeah, I can't leave Howlin' Wolf out. Oh, that *singing.* That guy could sing, mmm-mmm. He was always

friendly to me. He was a big guy, though. I remember looking up at him, he was so tall. **1997**

herb alpert
I admire Wynton Marsalis, not only as a musician, but what he's brought to jazz, and how he's playing the gospel. He's a good educator. He's revving kids up to really appreciate one of the great art forms that this country has developed. Tom Harrell is an extraordinarily gifted trumpet player who happens to be schizophrenic. He lives and plays in New York. He's been touched by a higher source; when he picks up the horn and plays, it's like he's been anointed. With the horn in his hand, he's more than functional, but when he's not, he has to be cared for. He's a must. Music is supposed to be from the spirit. Most great artists will claim their art is coming through them—he has a direct link. He's out to the other planet. I'm not crazy about music that plays on the weakness of society and hangs there for a long time. Like some rap music to me—I mean, I understand why rap is successful, but there comes a point when music and art should elevate people's spirits, and not just try to grind us down. **1997**

johnny cash
I like the old traditional country music. I like George Jones, Jimmie Rodgers, the Carter Family, early Gene Autry, Hank Snow. That, to me, was the seminal country music, and to me, it's still the best. Whereas now country has gotten to, I think, the age of electronic, push-button, TV, video, special effects and all that. **1994**

billy gibbons of ZZTop
Long John Hunter was the famous Texas bluesman that played on the Texas-American border, just across from El Paso for *years*. Now he's out on the road doin' his thang, which is definitely low down and right where it needs to be. **1996**

tom rowlands and ed simons of theChemicalBrothers

ROLLING STONE: Are there any artists you want to work with in the future?

Tom Rowlands: Someone came up and did a rap.

Ed Simons: Yeah. After a gig in Boston, but we have no real way of tracking him down. I guess if he reads this . . . ?

Tom Rowlands: He was a white guy with dreads and he just came up after our set and did this mad, mad rap about traveling to Jupiter and stuff.

Ed Simons: If he reads this, we think we can track him down.

Tom Rowlands: I'd like to get hold of him. He was cool.

ROLLING STONE: The Unidentified Rapper . . .

Ed Simons: Last seen in Boston. We want *you* to be on our record! **1996**

The Chemical Brothers: Ed Simons and Tom Rowlands (from left)
(Hamish Brown/Astralwerks)

EVERYPICTURE**T**ELLSASTORY

ouring bands slap a lot of movies into the bus VCR and certainly know the ins and outs of Spectravision—so they're bound to have a few favorites. Who knew so many people from different walks of music liked Al Pacino's Cubano machismo in Scarface? Blood, guts and freakiness is a theme with many musicians; same goes with richly visual and deeply emotional films. Okay, roll 'em.

greg dulli of AfghanWhigs

Jaws is the best movie ever made. It has everything: great dialogue, great acting, great directing. I can quotably say that I think *Jaws* is the most important film. I've seen it over fifty times. Even my friend Phil—we used to do videos together, actually Afghan Whigs videos—gave in to *Jaws*. Phil really liked obscure, stark Russian cinema. He'd always tell me about some great Czechoslovakian movie he had seen. I would watch it, it'd be pretty good, but it wasn't the greatest movie ever made. So I was like, "Now I'll show you the greatest movie ever made." And I put in *Jaws* and he was like, "I'm not watching this, this is an insult to me." I was like, "Insult to you? You better fucking watch it. You might learn something, buddy. You might start making a little more money on those videos. Show you how to create suspense, pal. Fucking shark coming out of the water. You're gonna be scared there in about five minutes." Yeah, everyone who's seen it at least thinks of sharks when they go swimming. It's implanted in their minds. Would they if they hadn't seen it? Probably not. It's Shakespearean, it really is, man. Steven Spielberg's finest moment. He did everything perfectly. **1996**

gaz coombes of Supergrass

Close Encounters of the Third Kind is one of my favorites. It's an amazing film. I'm a bit of a sci-fi fanatic. *2001: A Space Odyssey* is a great film as well. I remember *Star Wars* from when I was really young. It's kind of great. I quite like hectic sort of thrillers, too. *GoodFellas* is a great film—tense and hectic. It's that crazy, wild approach. **1997**

nick hexum of 311

My most influential movie is *The Abyss*—it's an unusual movie to like. I mean, of course, I love *Taxi Driver* and *The Godfather* and all that, but *The Abyss* is something that is an alien movie but it also was really powerfully acted as well. **1997**

gary numan

Seven would be my favorite film of all time. The music is so corny, just lyrics, but it's such a great story anyway. *Seven* was so brilliantly done that though it's such a horrible subject, it's fascinating. I can watch it again and again. *Reservoir Dogs* is a film I found really upsetting, it chilled me to the bone. I really didn't like it. The violent part with the ear just turned my stomach in a way that I didn't enjoy. When I was younger I was stabbed, so I have sympathies for cut-type injuries. I could almost feel it. **1997**

ROLLING STONE

shaun ryder of **HappyMondays** and **BlackGrape**

I am your fucking ultimate violent-head when it comes to films. I like the fucking blasting. *Scarface, Pulp Fiction, Reservoir Dogs*, all those sort of films, man. *Mean Streets*. There's some groovy tackle in that—some great clothes. I watched *The Exorcist* and *A Clockwork Orange* when I was, like, fucking eleven years old. And none of that shit made me violent. Just disturbed. **1996**

dave matthews

A Clockwork Orange is fantastic. There's no flaw in that movie. I've watched it so many times and I'm still not sick of it. It's sick but it's cool. **1996**

dj homicide

of **SugarRay**

GoodFellas, Braveheart and *Scarface* we watched a lot on the road. We watched *Tommy Boy* a lot, too. We'll get movies and we'll watch them, and watch them, and watch them. **1997**

art alexakis

of **Everclear**

The classic band movies that we'll quote, over and over again, are *Raising Arizona* and *Scarface*, with Al Pacino. **1996**

mick jones of **theClash** and **BigAudioDynamite**

I like the gratuitous violence in *Scarface*. **1995**

DJ Homicide of Sugar Ray (Self-portrait by DJ Homicide, courtesy of Russell A. Trunk/Chrisam Enterprises, Inc.)

busta rhymes I like more of the less obvious shit about *Scarface*. The "This world is mine" shit is pretty much what everybody is feeling. Al Pacino has other lines in there that I was fucking going crazy over. Like in the scene when he goes back to the first guy he worked for and he decides not to work for him anymore because he realized he was a dickhead, and he goes to meet the guy with his hand in a cast, and the guy was sitting behind his desk with the gun on the table, that shit was intense. What he was saying in that scene was my favorite shit. The expressions on his face and the raw accent, the whole emotion that was captured, it just felt like he wasn't playing. It wasn't a movie anymore, it felt like he was really starving and he's not fucking going back. Regardless of who you think you is, he will bust your shit, because now he got these bricks, and he ain't giving it up. Because you sent him to get 'em and bring 'em back to you, but you didn't put him onto the shit that he had to go through. And he lost two of his homeboys behind that. And when he was saying to Sosa, when he couldn't kill the fucking governor because the kids were in the car. "You ready to fucking fight with me? You gonna fucking fight with me?" That shit was hot to me, too. His going crazy, fucking throwing the phone all over the place, put his head in the big hill of cocaine. That was so crazy. You can't even imagine some motherfucker really getting down like that today. He was, like, one of those one-time-in-a-lifetime superheroes as far as the underworld is concerned. Crazy shit right there. **1997**

shannon hoon of **BlindMelon**

Bad Lieutenant, the uncensored version, of course. It doesn't get any better. Harvey Keitel's life goes downhill. I like the truthfulness of the movie. I don't believe that all police officers are as honest as we would like to think they are. **1994**

q-tip of **ATribeCalledQuest**

I like a whole lot of shit about a whole lot of different things, so I'm just gonna name a couple of movies that I really like. *Serpico*—Al Pacino's clothes. *Mean Streets*—minimal but intense, very filling. *The Five Heartbeats*—the music is great. It was based loosely on the Temptations. Robert Townsend did it. You can see a whole lot of R&B groups going through what they went through. I can relate to that. **1996**

coolio *The Five Heartbeats* hit close to home and made me feel like I could make it. It's about singers in the Sixties and what they had to go through. I've applied it to the way I've grown in rap. **1995**

jay-z I like gangster movies, like *The Godfather*—I've got *I* and *II,* I haven't seen *III.* "I know you did it, Fredo"—that's my favorite part. *GoodFellas* and *Scarface,* of course. Robert De Niro, Al Pacino and Joe Pesci are my favorite actors. My cousin and I used to watch *Cooley High* a lot when I was young. I got to find this movie, *Cornbread, Earl and Me.* It had Laurence Fishburne in it. He was the little boy and a basketball star or whatever. The epic part is when he's running home and the garbage truck is right there throwing garbage and the cops are there and they ask him why he's running, and why he has a basketball in his hand. They tell him to freeze, but he can't hear them because of the truck, so he keeps running and they shoot him. That was traumatic; my cousin and I used to play that scene out in the street all the time, it was ridiculous. Those are my classics right there: *The Godfather, GoodFellas, Scarface,* side order of *Cooley High* and *Cornbread, Earl and Me.* I would never come outside. And *The Shawshank Redemption* was hot. They was jailing forever, right, and then he came out and he couldn't really adapt. That was the joint. Society was like everything had changed. And he hung himself. He tried to go good, too. That one make you think. I like movies that make you think—little lessons. He couldn't adapt. I got friends like that—that's real. They've been in jail so long that they can't even adapt out here. It's like they want to go back. They institutionalized. It's crazy. Then you see a lot of people come home from jail and it's like the time stopped for them. They can't catch up. They still there and they can't remove from that time period. **1998**

lil' kim *Scarface*—that was my joint! I've always loved Al Pacino. Oh, I love Italians. I wanted to marry him when I was younger. That's my man. I've seen most of his movies. I love when they enter the house and he says, "Okay, you cock-a-roaches." That's the best part. And I love to see women, especially, stickin' together. *Set It Off* with Queen Latifah and Jada Pinkett was one of my most recent best movies I've seen. **1997**

heavy d. *GoodFellas, The Godfather, Scarface*—I love all them. *Stir Crazy,* man, I could just put that in and go to sleep on it every night. I know it so well, I could pick and choose when to nod off at. It's so funny. Richard Pryor and Gene Wilder are one of the best combinations. I like when they first walk into jail and they try to be tough. All that shit, it's funny. *The Bingo Long Traveling All-Stars* is about the Negro National League. With Billy Dee Williams, James Earl Jones, Richard Pryor. It's a real great old movie. Made in the Seventies. It's a period piece. **1997**

foxy brown

I was watching *Foxy Brown* last night. You'd be surprised what an impact Pam Grier has had on me. In person, she's like my second mother, you know, she'll always be there when I need her. I think she's, like, that all-around, ultimate bitch. She's sassy, sexy, will shoot you in a minute, like no bullshit. Crazy. It's like old Foxy meets baby Foxy. We first met over the phone. She was shocked to hear me, and I was surprised to hear her. She was like, "Foxy, this is the O.G. Foxy." I was like, "Ohhh, what's up!" And she's been my industry mother always. We clicked. I'm a Demi Moore fan, too. To the fullest—her and Bruce Willis. *Striptease*, that's my favorite. I can identify with all that open sexuality thing. That's my thing, I feel that totally. Another movie that I really like is *The Nutty Professor*, with Eddie Murphy. Eddie Murphy and his, like, eighty-five personalities. He is the illest. **1997**

leann rimes

We quote lines from *The Nutty Professor* on the road. It's a great movie. Like when they're sitting at the dinner table, the little boy flexes his muscle and the lady says, "Hercules, Hercules." I love Eddie Murphy. He's a great actor and a funny guy. I actually liked *Vampire in Brooklyn*. I did. *The Shawshank Redemption* was my favorite movie when it first came out. I saw *A Time to Kill* on the plane flying to Australia and I think that has become one of my favorites. Morgan Freeman is probably one of my favorite actors, he's great. That's probably why I like those two movies. **1997**

montell jordan

I've got an entire Eddie Murphy collection in my home video library. *Harlem Nights*, *The Nutty Professor* and *Coming to America*—those are my three all-time favorites, my ritualistic movies. He can become somebody else and all of his characters are funny. I love *Full Metal Jacket* because of the sergeant's performance in the entire first hour of that movie in boot camp. It's scary but so funny. He's the roughest. "All they got in Texas is steers and queers, and I don't see no horns, boy!" I could watch *New Jack City* over and over again. *King of New York*—I love Christopher Walken, man. He's such a menacing type of guy. If I saw him on the street and he smacked me, I'd be cool with it. If I was at a restaurant eating and he walked up to me, thumped me on the back of the head and said, "Shut up," and went and sat down, I'd be, like, "Yo, man, that's Christopher Walken, he told me to shut up, did you hear him? I'm gonna shut up now." Anybody else would get their ass kicked in a big, big way. I'm six feet eight inches tall. But Christopher would definitely get away with it. **1998**

rick nielsen of CheapTrick

When ever I feel I've overindulged—I mean, I haven't done this in a long time, not that I haven't overindulged, but watching David Lynch's *Elephant Man*—when I feel lousy and sorry for myself, I turn it on and say, "Okay, quit feeling sorry for yourself, pal. Here's real human drama." *Caddyshack* is probably every musician's favorite movie. The girl Lacy Underall, her real name's Cindy Morgan, she used to be a weather girl in Rockford, Illinois. I used to see her, fully clothed, talking about the weather, and next thing I knew, there she was, naked in *Caddyshack*. All right! I like the weather. I hope the women Ted Turner has on CNN will soon be topless in movies. We had a song in the second Caddyshack. That was the worst movie. **1996**

steven tyler

I took *Spinal Tap* real personal. I was really high at the time and Aerosmith was sinking—we were like a boat going down. And that movie was way too close, way too real. At the time our last album was *Rock in a Hard Place*, which sold, like, maybe ten copies; Spinal Tap did *Stonehenge*, and our album cover looked exactly like that. I freaked. **1990**

adam "mca" yauch of theBeastieBoys

In *The Party*, Peter Sellers plays an Indian actor, and the movie was banned in India because he is playing this bumbling idiot in the middle of all these white people, and some Indian people were insulted by it. But the irony is that he's really the only intelligent person there—all the other people are morons. So it has a cool theme. **1998**

justine frischmann of Elastica

Woody Allen brought the whole concept of Jewish humor to Britain. Last time I was in New York sightseeing, I realized that I had "Rhapsody in Blue" rattling around in my brain. And that's purely Woody Allen's fault. *The Wizard of Oz* is probably my favorite film of all time. It comes from that golden period of Hollywood before World War II, and it has that real American naïveté about it. Very romantic. **1995**

207

nina persson of theCardigans

I love Woody Allen, but who doesn't? *Zelig* was one of the movies that I freak out about. I also really like the British director Peter Greenaway. There's one called *The Cook, the Thief, His Wife and Her Lover.* And there's one whose title I only know in Swedish. I think it means *The Architect's Stomach,* or something like that [it's *The Draughtsman's Contract*]. It's bizarre. **1997**

"weird al" yankovic

Top Secret! is my favorite movie of all time. In a way it's the real sequel to *Airplane!* The special effects are amazing in *Independence Day,* it blows you out of your seat. It's an enjoyable movie as long as you don't stop and think about the plot too much. I don't want to give anything away here, but what a coincidence, the aliens seem to have Windows '95! Gee, it's nice that they're on the same kind of operating system the humans are. That makes things convenient. Well, okay, *UHF* is probably the greatest movie [and it's also directed by "Weird Al" Yankovic]. The real shame is that the Academy members didn't even nominate it for the best picture of the year. *Driving Miss Daisy* won in '89. Is there any justice in the world? Maybe if Jessica Tandy had a gag with a firehose, then it would have been a funny movie. **1996**

stone gossard of PearlJam

Austin Powers—I've been watching it way too much. I got an advance video copy and I watched it literally thirty times. Every time I go in the studio, I put it on. That movie, for some reason, touches something in me—how ridiculous it is. I'm happy to have one of those classic comedies come back where you can actually watch it again and again and get something new out of it. Mike Myers is a comic genius. I watch the movie now just to see what Dr. Evil is doing in the background and see his expressions. The Coen Brothers make exceptional movies. "So I take it that's your friend in the wood chipper?" was classic in *Fargo.* I watched *The Hudsucker Proxy* again; I can't believe it got bad reviews. I don't know what people expected, but that movie was so well put together. Jennifer Jason Leigh and Tim Robbins were so great. The whole theme was so great. It's totally underrated. And totally gorgeous. Paul Newman is hilarious. Someone recently told me there's no music in Martin Scorsese's *After Hours.* I've seen it three or four times, and I never really noticed. But if that's true, that's the reason it just has so much tension in it—there's no sound going on. Maybe it's like minimal music or something like that. That movie so sums up a night where you just want to get home from some bad club or something—taken to the extreme. **1998**

dean wareham of Luna

Michelangelo Antonioni's *Zabriskie Point* has a great soundtrack. The final scene of a house exploding—which is shot from seventeen different cameras and set to the music of Pink Floyd—is like going to see a great band. A thrilling experience. It has to be seen on a big screen. The critics trashed that movie. It was a true story about a guy who steals a plane and when he's returning it, he is shot. The actor who played that guy was involved in some weird commune and they wanted him to take the role so he could help publicize the commune. And he was kicked out of the commune, and he decided to rob a bank to show them that he could do something good for them, and he was caught for armed robbery. And he died in prison, in the weight room. A "bizarre accident" in the weight room. Life mirroring art. *Heavenly Creatures*—that's stunning. Just amazing. It's very funny. The first line: These two little girls come running up a hill, covered in blood, and one of them says, "Come quickly! There's something dreadfully wrong with Mummy!" And the truth is they had just bludgeoned Mummy to death. It's great. *Showgirls*—when Kyle MacLachlan is making love to that woman in the swimming pool it's like something out of one of the *Naked Gun* movies. **1996**

terence trent d'arby

Breakfast at Tiffany's is the first film I can remember seeing. For years, I remembered a couple of scenes vividly—but not the film. I kept walking around like an idiot trying to describe those scenes. Finally, someone said, "Sounds like *Breakfast at Tiffany's*." I watched it, and it was very emotional. Like revisiting the womb, because I knew my last connection to it was as a two-year-old child. **1994**

luther vandross
I loved *Love Story*. I saw it when I was pretty young. The death of Ali MacGraw's character put a big lump in my throat. **1997**

carnie wilson
When I was younger, my favorite was *Arthur*. It was the fantasy of having all that money and doing whatever he wants with it, but realizing he's wasting his life away and the real meaning isn't just having money. But what got me was his laugh. *Forrest Gump* is my all-time favorite. It's the most beautiful film ever made. I've seen it six times. I loved every thing about it. Characters,

the acting, the cinematography, the music. It really got to me —sad, but also so inspiring. Tom Hanks is so wonderful. *Mrs. Doubtfire*—"Heelloo!" I've seen that movie almost twenty times. I have to watch it once every three months. I go through withdrawal. Robin Williams is so genius. The whole thing of this father wanting to be with his kids, oh Christ, it's such the opposite thing for me. Growing up, my dad didn't want to be with us, he was in his own world. So that movie just grabs my heart and twists it around while I'm laughing hysterically. I cry every time at the end. **1997**

björk
The Tin Drum is a film that affected me very much. Especially the boy, the actor. Probably the only person in the world I'd recognize in the street and I'd run up and kiss. **1994**

erykah badu
My favorite movie is *Fresh*. It's about this little kid who played chess with his father in the park. I just watched it again. I love it. And that movie is by—I forgot. [Boaz Yakin.] Anyway, I called him, like, two years ago when the movie came out. I was just a fanatic and found his number in the phone book, so I left a message saying, "I really enjoyed the movie, if you ever do any other films, blah blah blah, keep me in mind." You know, that was back in, like, '95 when I did that. He didn't know me from Adam, man; I was just a fanatic at the time. I still am. My second favorite movie is *Sling Blade*. I thought Billy Bob Thornton was great. All the acting was superb. **1997**

john tesh
Well, I don't want to be predictable, but I really did like *Shine*. Parts of it reminded me of my home life. I had a father who didn't beat me, but he was pretty intense. There's so much buzz about it, but it's great, it's just a tiny film. **1997**

shirley manson of Garbage
I watched *Il Postino* on the tour bus a few weeks ago, and it's absolutely unmissable. It's beautiful and simple, but profound and moving. I hurt inside when I think about it. **1996**

steven page of BarenakedLadies
Wim Wenders's *Wings of Desire* is so rich and full of eye candy. There's a serenity and violence and sensuality and everything wrapped into one movie. The first time I saw it, I thought, "I can watch eighteen hours of this and not be sick of it." **1998**

queen latifah *Faraway, So Close* is one of the best movies I've seen in my life. I lost my brother, so it really made me think about whether he's right here, right next to me. **1994**

alec empire of AtariTeenageRiot

In *Carnival of Souls* the atmosphere and music are great. The story is about this woman who's between life and death. It's real in a way, too. When she walks around in the city and tries to talk to people and no one takes notice of her, it can be like that even if you're not in the state that she is in. It was much more scary than all the high-budget bullshit nowadays, where you think, wow, this is a computer-animated alien. I'm *so* scared. **1997**

lisa loeb *Waiting for Guffman* is amazing. I just loved Corky. He's my hero. I loved the way he dances and when he gets angry with people and calls them "ass-face" and "bastard-people." The dentist was one of my favorite people. He was so endearing to me. I felt like it was a good representation of being an actor—large hopes and dreams. And it's a good parody. I'm a huge fan of Christopher Guest and all those guys. I love the dances that Roger Daltrey does in *The Kids Are Alright* and I love the Who. I love Technicolor films with stories and good music, like *Mary Poppins*. But I also like movies like *David and Lisa*—black-and-white depressing movies—and *Ordinary People*. It's manic. **1997**

gwen stefani of NoDoubt

The Sound of Music—It's one of my classic favorite things that had a big influence on my whole entire life and being. I probably sing "These Are a Few of My Favorite Things" in my head at least twice a week. That whole soundtrack is special to my heart and will always be. I always wanted to live in that world and wear those clothes. There's that song that Julie Andrews sings when she and the dad kiss for the first time, "I must have had a wicked childhood, I must have had a miserable youth. But somewhere in my wicked, miserable life, I must have done something good"—I'm going to sing the rest of it—" 'Cause here you are standing there, loving me, whether or not you should." I can't believe the words to that song. That's probably my favorite song for right this moment. I love all the old Hollywood cheesy pictures that tell the story of a girl who gets discovered and gets to be in the powder room and put her makeup on and have fancy dresses with feathers and stuff like that. They used to go all-out on their productions. And it was all live—all the singing and dancing. I can't believe they used to do all that. It's amazing. I like Alfred Hitchcock films a lot. *Vertigo.* I like the twists that he used. I think my dad influenced me because he's a real big Hitchcock fan so we used to always watch all that. *Rebecca,* I think, is just a brilliant movie. Really scary but good. *Rear Window*—I loved Grace Kelly in that movie. She wears a dress that's a black velvet top with this white skirt. I made my mom make me one exactly like it for my prom dress. I still have it. **1996**

paula cole
I've seen *Who's Afraid of Virginia Woolf* so many times, I love it so much. I probably saw it for the first time when I was in San Francisco in 1992. It was made in the Sixties. It reminds me of Picasso's *Rape of the Sabines,* where, instead of the entire battlefield, he takes just one child and one mother. It's so powerful to take human drama and put it in a singular room, in a single night. Besides, Liz Taylor and Richard Burton were just playing out their own lives, with their alcoholism and their pain. **1998**

adam duritz of CountingCrows
On my eighteenth birthday, I disappeared for the day and sat in a tiny movie house in Berkeley and saw *Baby It's You.* It blew my mind. Who is this guy who makes a movie this beautiful? [John Sayles.] **1994**

tanya donelly of ThrowingMuses and Belly
Like Water for Chocolate is my beauty choice. It's incredibly well filmed. The sister who runs away on the horse is my favorite. And *The Misfits,* with Marilyn Monroe, is amazing. There's a scene where Clark Gable says to her: "You have to be the saddest girl I've ever met. What makes you so sad?" A great moment, because it makes her shine when he says that. Everything in her face relaxes. **1994**

andy partridge of XTC
Great Expectations is one of my all-time favorite films, mostly for the reason that it is incredibly overlooked. I also love an American film that came out in the early Fifties and bombed everywhere on Earth— except in France. What are you gonna say about a country who would make Jerry Lewis president if they could? **1998**

juliana hatfield
Splendor in the Grass, directed by Elia Kazan. I relate to the whole idea of a good girl. Warren Beatty's a guy who needs a bad girl,

but Natalie Wood's a good girl who tries to be bad for him. But he doesn't want that particular girl to be bad. A dilemma that can never be solved. So heartbreaking. Every time I see it, I cry. **1995**

matt sharp of Weezer

One Flew Over the Cuckoo's Nest, directed by Milos Forman. It was before Jack Nicholson started playing himself. An amazingly sad movie. And Ingmar Bergman. Can I get a disclaimer on this? I feel it's such a bad tag to like Bergman. In every movie he has someone in unbelievably extreme pain. I love the way he deals with dialogue and character interaction. *Through a Glass Darkly* is my favorite. **1995**

chris whitley

I find Ingmar Bergman sensitive without being sentimental. Lately I've really liked *The Magician*, *Hour of the Wolf* and *Secrets of Women*. I've been watching those on and off for the last three months. I don't find him depressing at all, just intense and intimate. *Scenes from a Marriage* is over the top. I find Tennessee Williams depressing. **1997**

michael hutchence of INXS

I was just watching *A Streetcar Named Desire*. Brando is weird, though. I tried to be unhyped about it, but he sucked me in. You can hardly understand what he's saying. He was quite slim then, wasn't he? A bit of a bod. **1994**

chrissie hynde of thePretenders

Charley Varrick—that was a Don Siegel film. There's a real depth of characters. Joe Don Baker could give Marlon Brando a run for his money, and Walter Matthau is superb. **1994**

emmylou harris

Atticus Finch, from *To Kill a Mockingbird*, played by Gregory Peck—forget Rambo, this is a real screen hero. **1996**

dave mustaine of Megadeth

I really like Clint Eastwood movies. I could sit there and watch him and John Wayne for days. The do-good strong American, Western white guy who rides off into the sunset, helping all of the oppressed masses, and there's always a squaw or a forsaken Mexican family or something. Clint Eastwood and the Duke, what great role models those guys are. **1997**

john popper of BluesTraveler

The Great Gatsby, with Robert Redford in it. There was a quality about that movie when he was looking off at the green light, across the bay. That really made me think, God, I want to be that guy. That was actually a problem because I think I started trying to become that guy—sort of an enigma rather than an actual person. That screws you up. Black-and-white movies? *Rumblefish* was a good one. I wanted to be Motorcycle Boy so bad. The only time I ever wanted to be Mickey Rourke in a film. *Casablanca*—that movie was a complete accident, in that it wound up standing for so much and being so significant because of the dialogue. And some of the dialogue was terrible, like the Nazi going, "Yes, much too good a time." But when Bogey started to lament over his pain of his love for Ingrid Bergman, everyone understood. And that was for all time. It's a timeless moment. **1998**

d'arcy of SmashingPumpkins

I love old movies, like *The Philadelphia Story,* with Cary Grant and Katharine Hepburn, who is my idol. There's no one I want to meet except her, that's it. I have a lot of respect for her. I feel like I could talk to her or at least sit there and listen to her talk forever. Maybe I should do that. She'd probably be annoyed, though. But at least she'd tell me. If she was annoyed, she wouldn't pretend not to be. She'd say, "Get the hell out of here." Another old film, *Mr. Deeds Goes to Town,* with Gary Cooper, is great. Have you ever seen *The Grass Is Greener?* Cary Grant and Jean Simmons are in it. James Coburn is in a groovy whacked-out spy movie called *The President's Analyst.* You've never seen James Coburn in a role like that. Also, *I Love You, Alice B. Toklas.* Smoke pot, watch that movie, you'll die laughing. Peter Sellers is hysterical. *What's New, Pussycat?* is bizarre; it's pretty amazing. It has everybody. There's one scene with Woody Allen and Peter Sellers in the same room at the same time. For me, that is the most awesome moment. **1996**

roni size

I had to watch *Jacob's Ladder,* like, four times to even work out what the fuck was going on. It was like, "What's this guy? Who's that? Where?" There's also that dream about some acid and shit. It's like, "Fill me in?" He's dying. Brilliant. I didn't get it the first time. To be honest with you, my friend Krust had to tell me what was going on. *No Escape* with Ray Liotta—he is one of the most underrated actors in the world. He's got the eyes, the flair, the look, the voice, the presence. Know what I mean? Ray Liotta, man. He can be a normal guy, a psycho, too. Know what? He's my favorite actor, him and Clint Eastwood and Sean Connery. I'm an old-school man. Some of the Dirty Harrys were rough.

Those chase scenes! Ahhh, my God. Tell me, when was the last time that you've seen a wicked car chase? They crash, then they jump out of the car, run down the railway track for like half an hour, trip up and then they race through buildings, have a fight, rip up their clothes—then Clint gets up, walks away and says one thing that says it all. *And* he keeps walking, he throws his badge on the floor and walks off alone. Yeah, man, Clint Eastwood. Sean Connery, he's brilliant now, but in those early Bond films when Connery was Connery, he was just the bomb. Even Michael Caine back in the day—in *Get Carter*. There's one scene where he's beating up the woman and it's just so cold. Too cold. I don't know how they got away with that on prime-time TV. It's funny what they got away with back then. Clint had a bad temper, too, didn't he? Slapped a few girls, as well, didn't he? **1998**

tina weymouth of TalkingHeads and TomTomClub

Trainspotting is like Salvador Dalí's *Un Chien Andalou*. You don't want to see that eyeball getting slit and the ants crawling out of a hat, but they stay with you. **1996**

john lennon

I admire [Federico] Fellini. . . . Fellini's just like [Salvador] Dalí, I suppose. It's a great meal to go and see Fellini, a great meal for your senses. Like *Citizen Kane*, that's something else, too. Poor old Orson [Welles], he goes on Dick Cavett, and says, "Please love me, now I'm a big fat man, and I've eaten all this food, and I did so well when I was younger, I can act, I can direct, and you're all very kind to me, but at this moment I don't do anything." **1971**

eric clapton

I went to see *Purple Rain*, because I've always liked Prince's records. And when I saw that film, it made me feel that something very powerful was going to happen again in popular music and *was* happening with that man. That gave me a lot of hope for the future of music. **1985**

lucinda williams

Wise Blood, directed by John Huston—a brilliant interpretation of Flannery O'Connor's beautiful, dark, Southern Gothic novel. **1998**

marilyn manson

My favorite movie is *Santa Sangre*, by Alejandro Jodorowsky—he's Spanish. *Santa Sangre* is a very surreal portrayal of a boy who grows up after seeing his mother have her arms cut off by his father. He, much like Norman Bates, imagines his mother still to be alive with no arms. He becomes her arms and he acts out things for her. It has a lot of fine-art references and religious overtones, which are beautifully done. There's one scene in particular that was one of the most original and disturbing things that I have seen. It really won me over. They were taking a field trip of mentally retarded children to a movie theater. As the chaperones left them abandoned at the movie theater, some strange pimp-type character pulls them aside, and he gives them all cocaine and they start dancing around with transvestite hookers. It's a really unforgettable scene. I actually stole the videotape from the store. Another movie that had a great impact on me is *Begotten,* directed by E. Elias Merhige. It appeared to be a documentary by the cover of the case. It turned out to be a film that looks as if it was dug from the earth, from a time that's neither the future nor the past. It's a surreal portrayal of the death of God and the birth of man, and it has strong religious imagery, but very ambiguous. It's really disturbing. It has no music and no

Lucinda Williams (Alan Messer/Mercury)

dialogue and a lot of the scenes are unsettling. Somewhere I read someone describe it as a Rorschach test because of the way it looks. Sometimes the images are abstract and you have to stare at it for a long time to understand what you're looking at. You can watch it many times and see different things in it. Don't watch it unless you're open-minded and you have a lot of patience, there's no flashy one-liners. It's hard for a lot of people to sit through it. I normally would have been too impatient to sit through the whole thing, but I had just tried morphine for the first time, and I was stuck to the couch. I was forced to view it. It's terrifying. It's shocking in its strange beauty. I made contact with him and he did a short film for us for one of our songs that we may use in the future. A song called "Crypt Orchid." It's a lost and hidden film right now, no one's seen it. Other than that, the only thing I've watched recently is *Smokey and the Bandit*. There's a weird underlying sexual theme going on between Burt Reynolds and Jerry Reed that I didn't pick up on as a kid. I think it's his mustache that gives it away. **1997**

billy gibbons of ZZTop

Jim Jarmusch's *Dead Man*—great soundtrack by Neil Young. I liked the cryptic reference to one of Rick Rubin's producers. Johnny Depp sees himself on a WANTED poster, he reads off the other names and one of them is "Big George Drakoulias"—he produced a Black Crowes record and now he's in an odd black-and-white film. **1996**

fred schneider of theB-52's

Rudy Ray Moore in all those *Dolemite* movies, they're the best. It's great to put on a movie and watch people's jaws drop. He is the most outrageous character I've ever seen in a movie. My favorite movie of all time is *Forbidden Planet*. I didn't see it when it first came out. I saw it, like, on *Million Dollar Movie*. Then I bought the video and it turned out to be in color, so that was a revelation. It's a *Mad Mad Mad Mad World*, that has good yin and yang. **1996**

glen phillips of ToadtheWetSprocket

Brazil, directed by Terry Gilliam—phenomenal. A complete vision. **1994**

les claypool of Primus

I love anything Terry Gilliam does. I have yet to see a movie by him that I don't like. I liked the visuals in *Twelve Monkeys*. He's the maestro of interesting visuals. I really liked the device that they used to talk to Bruce Willis when he was strapped into the chair—that big, like, multiple-video-screen eyeball thing. It's total Terry Gilliam. The computer screens that are little magnification membranes. Things like that. Good stuff. *Forrest Gump*—I can quote almost any line from it. An all-time favorite movie: *A Face in a Crowd*, directed by Elia Kazan in the late Fifties. It has Andy Griffith in it. A phenomenal movie. Another all-time fave: *Dr. Strangelove*. I've seen it many, many times. **1996**

john wozniak of MarcyPlayground

Star Wars and *The Empire Strikes Back* are still my favorite movies ever. *Empire* is my favorite of those two. The whole beginning of *Empire* on the snow planet, Han is so amazing. That's why I can't stand *Return of the Jedi*—because of the whole ending sequence with the little Muppets. But *Empire* is incredible. I think Yoda has the exact same voice as Grover. The best part is when Luke tells him, "Hey, I'm not scared." And he says, "You will be." It is a very climactic moment, but it didn't really materialize that he was scared. I mean he did lose his hand or whatever, but still. *The Sunshine Boys* has George Burns and Walter Matthau. Incredible. Walter Matthau is one of the greatest actors of the Twentieth Century. He's just so fucking believable. Did you see *Grumpy Old Men?* Man, is he funny. In *The Decline of Western Civilization II: The Metal Years,* when Ozzy is cooking his eggs for breakfast, is Ozzy's greatest moment. He was this absurd little individual. He had a uniquely definable persona that latched on to you right away. **1998**

jim kerr of SimpleMinds
Against my better judgment, I loved *Natural Born Killers.* A feast for the eyes. I thought it was rock & roll. **1995**

matthew sweet
Most people who are real movieheads got into *Ed Wood.* But I think Middle America thought it was too weird and focused on the cross-dressing aspect. Martin Landau as Bela Lugosi made my skin crawl. **1995**

moby
Mars Attacks! is sorely underrated. I saw it twice, actually. Almost everyone I know hated it. It was so absurd and so well made, and it really made me laugh and laugh. I felt happier leaving the theater than I did going in. The little alien creatures are so gleefully destructive and malevolent. There are wonderful scenes, like when Michael J. Fox is disintegrated and a little Chihuahua runs around with his hand in its mouth. The aliens destroy everything. But in such a wonderful, gleeful way. **1997**

thurston moore of SonicYouth
Sir Drone—a film by Raymond Pettibon, one of the original members of what became Black Flag. Recollections of the beginnings of punk rock in Los Angeles. The thing he remembers is that everyone bickered. And the whole movie is about that kind of bickering. It's hysterical. **1994**

sarah mclachlan
Blade Runner was when Ridley Scott was doing good things. Oh, and I just had a total chubby for Harrison Ford. **1994**

Sonic Youth: Kim Gordon, Thurston Moore, Lee Ranaldo and Steve Shelley (from left)
(Michael Lavine/Geffen)

beck *Beyond the Valley of the Dolls.* That is one I watched with a bunch of people and it was great. Then I watched it alone and it felt wrong. **1996**

david yow of theJesusLizard

The Swap No. 2. It's a pornographic movie that *Screw* magazine gave me a couple of tours ago, when we were in New York. They had let [our label] Touch and Go know they wanted to interview us. And so we went to their offices and they talked to us and we got to peruse through their warehouse. The room with dusty nothings. And they gave us pretty much anything we wanted and it was kinda funny. It was good. Anyway, it's the best hard-core porn film I've ever seen because, you know, the lighting is good, there's actual acting, it's the directing, there's a plot. You know what, I guess the music is good enough that I didn't notice it. It wasn't the kinda, uh, *wuh-wuh, wah-wah.* The plot had its little twists and turns. **1996**

art alexakis of Everclear

I think Disney movies are great. *Pocahontas* was kinda weak, though. When *The Lion King* came out, we were on tour and in New York City. Times Square, right, Forty-second Street, our whole band is watching *The Lion King*. We're these punk rockers—colored hair, tattoos, piercings—in there with the kids watching *The Lion King*. That's our idea of a good time. We're shouting, "No! Watch out, Simba!" Going crazy, and we're like, "Aaahh!" We're all bawling. I look over and my drummer is crying into his popcorn when Mufasa died. It's embarrassing, we're not very rock, man. We oughta go to Rock School so we can learn how to be more rock. **1996**

simon le bon of DuranDuran

The last *really* good film I saw was Roger Vadim's *Barbarella*. It is an absolute classic. It is so funny and sexy, and the thing about Jane Fonda is the funnier she is, the sexier she gets. Oh, and of course, it's relevant to us, isn't it? Because we're Duran Duran and we got the name from it! There's one magnificent moment where she's naked in front of this guy from the world, from the Federation of the Universe or whatever, and he says, "I want you to find Duran Duran from Planet Earth." Yeah! **1997**

BUT BOY, COULD (S)HE PLAY GUITAR!

**S**ix strings, twelve strings, four strings; acoustic or amped to the rafters, no instrument is more evocative than a guitar. It can wail, weep, make a hell of a lot of noise and, in the hands of a master, tell a thousand stories.

lou reed

[Prior to *Zuma*,] I couldn't stand [Neil Young]. I couldn't be bothered. His lyrics can be so stupid, so West Coast dumb. But *listen* to this. The guy's been *working* on this. It made me cry. It's probably the best I've ever heard in my life. The guy's a bitch of a guitarist. He's got everything in there and he's got it right. **1976**

tom morello of RageAgainsttheMachine

The guitar player who was most instrumental to me developing the eccentric side of my playing was Andy Gill of Gang of Four. When I first heard him play, it sounded so horrible. It was as if he was playing a different song with a different band. But the more I listened, the more I realized how brilliant the guy is. By deconstructing the guitar parts, playing the unexpected and playing off the funk of the rhythm section with almost atonal drill noises, he made the band so much more powerful. **1999**

joe perry of Aerosmith

I must've been sixteen or seventeen when "Purple Haze" came out. I remember thinking, "Now we're getting radio from Mars." The guitar sounded like a monster coming out of the speakers. Once in a while, somebody comes along and moves the instrument ahead, but not in the way Hendrix did. Jimi took it from black and white to multicolor. **1990**

keith richards of theRollingStones

Chuck Berry always was the epitome of rhythm & blues playing, rock & roll playing. It was beautiful, effortless, and his timing was perfection. He plays that lovely double-string stuff, which I got down a long time ago, but I'm still getting the hang of. Later I realized why he played that way—the sheer physical size of the guy. I mean, he makes one of those Gibsons look like a ukulele! **1999**

melissa etheridge

Keith Richards was really my largest influence because he plays with such a rhythm style. Especially in things like "Start Me Up." It's rhythm, it's all those notes, it's five strings. And they're real open and easy, but man, we never forget 'em. **1999**

chrissie hynde of thePretenders

I don't know any guitar player, any of the real greats, who doesn't rate Joni Mitchell up there with the best of them. Hell, she's a fuckin' excellent guitar player, excellent. And I hope to God you talk to her and encourage her to do some shows. Because we *want* her. We want you, Joni. Get out there. Put down your paintbrush for five minutes, please. **1994**

carrie brownstein of Sleater-Kinney

Ricky Wilson of the B-52's is an underrated guitar player with an endless supply of good riffs. He wrote deceptively simple guitar lines; they were full of so many angles and chord changes. **1999**

robbie robertson

Roy Buchanan's attitude was like a gunslinger coming to town: The Axeman Cometh. He had a command over the guitar I couldn't comprehend. He bent the neck, he bent the strings behind the bridge. He played with both hands on the fingerboard. He used every ornament on it to get a noise out of it. It was like the guitar came to life. It started speaking. **1999**

ziggy marley

The acoustic guitar is what I playin'. It's what I first started writing with. That's my instrument, although I can play other things. I started playing a long time ago—early Eighties. The first time I got the guitar, I started. But the first time I wrote a song was probably in the Seventies. It was, like, some girl song. **1997**

pete townshend

I am one of those characters who, like a teenager, sits at home with a guitar in front of a full-length mirror, and I do it. And I can do it now just as well as I did it then. It gives me just as much pleasure as it did then. I'd come forward a few years and maybe chuck the key away—once you're in, you're in—but I'd never chuck the mirror away. **1987**

billy gibbons of ZZTop

We're a simple band: We know three beats, three chords, we do good with guitars with one volume knob. **1996**

jackson browne

Shawn Colvin's acoustic shows are really about being transported through a whole universe of sound. I was a big fan of her records before I even saw her play live—and it killed me that she was just as great. Her guitar playing is so strong. **1994**

bootsy collins You should check out my new Gadgitmon bass. He's star-shaped, too, with lights on the neck and pick guards that flicker on and off. He's got a built-in mike and tape deck. When he says, "I'm smokin'," he actually smokes. He stands by the mike and introduces me—he's a heck of an entertainer. Hamer built it. I wanted it to take off, too, but they said they didn't have time to make it do that. **1980**

Bootsy Collins (Warner Bros.)

liam howlett of theProdigy

Women respond to bass, let me tell you. Well, everyone's into bass. It's a primal thing. It goes back to the womb. **1997**

paula cole

Bob Marley's bass player, "Family Man" Barrett, along with Tony Levin are my favorite bass players in the world. I love the concept of the bottom—the whole bass, fat bottom as the anchor of the music. Apparently at those concerts in Jamaica, they just have stacks and stacks of woofers. It makes you connected with the root, with the earth, and you can totally feel it in your crotch, you know. **1998**

bo diddley

If you know how to play, you don't need all that noise! We didn't need all of it. All you gotta do is be able to play. And the loudness—where there's a lot of distortion and stuff like that, you don't need that. I play with one amp and a mike in front of it. **1996**

john wozniak of MarcyPlayground

I see my music as simplistic, song-oriented, with no flashy guitar solos. In fact, I think gratuitous solos are pointless, especially for me. Pretty much every song on the radio has a guitar solo. **1998**

dick dale

My old records, I tell people they suck. They're not powerful, that's why I quit recording. Nobody could capture the sound I get live. I was always fighting with engineers. I'd start playing and they'd be like, "Fuck, it's bleeding through the board, man!" Then they'd put limiters on it and it'd end up sounding tinny. I wanted the thickness and fatness I get onstage. **1996**

eddie van halen of VanHalen

Music, you've got twelve notes, you do what the hell you want with them, if you like it, it's good. It's not a competitive thing, it's a language. There's a reason why the note A rings at 440 hertz cycles. It's just a vibration—there's no denying that, it's a fact. But music is also theory, not just fact. So there are no rules. Rules don't leave room for growth for experimentation. I'm here to make music to the best of my ability. I execute my chops to the best of my ability, I enjoy playing, and I thank God every night for having found my gift. Everyone's born with one, some people don't ever bother to look for it or find it. So I do my best to do my best. **1998**

225

bruce springsteen
My mother [used to think] I should be an author and write books. But I wanted to play guitar. So my mother, she's very Italian, she says, "This is a big thing, you should go see the priest." I went to the rectory and knocked on the door. "Hi, Father Ray, I'm Mr. Springsteen's son. I got this problem. My father thinks I should be a lawyer, and my mother, she wants me to be an author. But I got this guitar." Father Ray says, "This is too big a deal for me. You gotta talk to God," who I didn't know too well at the time. "Tell him about the lawyer and the author," he says, "but don't say *nothin'* about that guitar." **1978**

shirley manson of Garbage
The boys turn to me when they need an exceedingly loose and unprofessional approach to recording, and I dazzle them with such prowess on a spanking-new Fender Strat built to my very own divalike specifications. This really cute little certificate came with it to verify that it was indeed the official "Shirley Manson Model." Ha-ha! How fucking cool is that? **1998**

eric erlandson of Hole
Johnny Thunders was sloppy, but in a cool way. A lot of it was just the rhythm. He had a certain style of rhythm. I saw him several times throughout the Eighties and sometimes he would play just one note. But there would be something about that one note. It was so unschooled. That's probably what I like about it. **1999**

bonnie raitt
Ry Cooder has an unbelievably funky sense of rhythm. His tone, what he leaves out when he plays—he's as ferocious and as heartbreaking a musician as I've ever heard. **1999**

donita sparks of L7
Dick Dale's speed and choice of notes are very tasty. He just rocks me. It's so turbo-charged. And I love Les Paul when he gets really out there and really goofy. He, to me, was just extremely ahead of his time, extremely unconventional. He doesn't look like the hippest cat on the block, you know, and yet he's playing this amazing stuff. **1999**

jakob dylan of theWallflowers
Junior Brown is a great guitar player—the only one I've ever seen who can solo while detuning. **1993**

jeff beck
Cliff Gallup played with Gene Vincent and the Blue Caps for only nine months. He played on *Bluejean Bop!* It's almost barbaric. It's like a barroom brawl or a punch-up in a swimming pool. You can hear this echo going, and it's just amazing. Among all the screaming and the shouting you can hear this guitar. It sounds like someone was being impaled on a spit. Maybe it was Cliff's way of saying, "You barbaric bastards. I'm a jazz player, but if this is what you want, I'm doing it only once." He never did anything like that again. **1999**

david crosby of Crosby, StillsandNash
Have you really considered what kind of a musician Phil Lesh is? I would like to make a record sometime with him playing classical music on an electric bass. He is certainly one of the most virtuoso string-instrument players on the planet. **1970**

the edge of U2
I particularly admire the work that Tom Verlaine and Richard Lloyd produced for Television's first album, *Marquee Moon.* The record is timeless because there's nothing in it—a very simple drum sound, a bass, two guitars and Tom's voice. Subsequently I discovered in some of the works of Country Joe and the Fish connections with Television. **1999**

bob seger
I saw Eric Clapton on the Journeyman tour at the Palace of Auburn Hills near Detroit and Stevie Ray Vaughan sat in for about twenty minutes. It was six weeks before he died. It's hard to remember greater guitar playing that I ever heard in one fifteen-minute period in my life. I love B.B. King and I love Albert Collins and all those guys, but these guys were wailing. **1996**

jerry garcia of theGratefulDead
I would describe my own guitar playing as descended from barroom rock & roll, country guitar. Just 'cause that's where all my stuff comes from. It's like that blues instrumental stuff that was happening in the late Fifties and early Sixties, like Freddie King. . . . I think Freddie King is the guy that I learned the most volume of stuff from. When I started playing electric guitar the second time, with the Warlocks, it was a Freddie King album that I got almost all my ideas off of. **1972**

eric clapton
I always like the wilder guys. I liked Buddy Guy, Freddie King and Otis Rush because they sounded like they were *really on the edge,* like they were barely in control and at any time they could hit a really bad note and the

whole thing would fall apart—but, of course, they didn't. I liked that a lot more than B.B. King. I got into B.B. later, when I realized that polish was something, too. **1985**

trey anastasio of Phish

I love Kevin Shields of My Bloody Valentine. He's the absolute best. *Loveless* is the defining album of the Nineties as far as sound goes. Oh, my God, I've never heard anything like that before. **1999**

kevin shields of MyBloodyValentine

Johnny Ramone was the first guitarist who blew me away—he showed me that maybe I could do something with the guitar. People like Hendrix also blew me away, but I felt like that was something I could never do. After getting into the Ramones, my attitude became one of using that guitar as simply a noise generator. On the surface, his playing seemed really simple, but there was a never-ending depth to it, especially on *Ramones Leave Home*, which is my favorite record. It's somewhere between stupid and genius. **1999**

johnny ramone of theRamones

Leslie West of Mountain never gets any recognition. I've always been a fan of his, since back when he was a fat kid dropping out of high school in Forest Hills. He was, to me, one of the top five guitar players of his era. His playing was so soulful and tasteful. His break in "Theme for an Imaginary Western" is the best thing I've ever heard. **1999**

jimi hendrix
The first guitarist I was aware of was Muddy Waters. I heard one of his old records when I was a little boy and it scared me to death, because I heard all of those sounds. Wow, what is that all about? *It* was great. And I like Albert King. He plays completely and strictly in one way, just straight funk blues. It's new blues guitar, a very young, funky sound, which is great. One of the funkiest I've heard. **1968**

rick nielsen of CheapTrick

Les Paul is a great guitar. I paid sixty-five dollars for the first Les Paul I ever got, at place called A Book Store, in Rockford, Illinois. I got it because Jeff Beck had one, I didn't even know what it was. Came with a round hard-shell case. It was a 1955.

I still have it. Don't play it very often. I love the Gibson Explorer. I have two of the originals. They only made nineteen, so I have, like, 10 percent of the market. Those are *cool*. They're valued between fifty and a hundred thousand. No musician can afford it. Just rich doctors, who probably put it in a case where no one will ever see it again. *I don't think so*. Fender Telecaster and Stratocaster—classics. Everything I have is a classic or . . . classless. **1996**

dave pirner of SoulAsylum

The M.O. of the four-piece rock band is something you have to embrace —a limitation you have to exceed, a thing to try and stretch as far as you can. What it comes down to is that hunk of wood with six strings on it, that's your paintbrush and your canvas. **1998**

THESHOWTHATROCKEDMYWORLD

L ive music has changed the course of more than a few lives. Billy Idol saw his future at London's 100 Club in 1975, and a decade later a teenage Gwen Stefani saw hers from the nosebleeds in Anaheim, California. A starstruck young Eddie Van Halen swore Eric Clapton had picked him out of the crowd. Others found the audience as memorable as the performance—just see what happened to Billy Joe Armstrong at his first concert.

eric clapton
I remember the first rock & roll I ever saw on TV was Jerry Lee Lewis doing "Great Balls of Fire." That threw me; it was like seeing someone from outer space. **1985**

eddie van halen of VanHalen
The first concert I went to was Derek and the Dominos in the Pasadena Civic Auditorium, when I was fifteen or sixteen. A friend of mine won the tickets on the radio and knew what an Eric Clapton freak I was, so he gave them to me. Clapton played "Bell-Bottom Blues" and he pointed at me! He kinda did a thumbs-up and pointed. Mighta been to somebody else, but of course I thought it was me. **1998**

david bowie
I saw Little Richard at Brixton Odeon; it must have been 1963, because the Rolling Stones opened for him. Oh, it was wonderful, listen: The Stones opened, then there was Bo Diddley and, if I remember rightly, Duane Eddy, and it closed with Sam Cooke. That was the first half. Then the second half . . . somebody else unbelievable was on, and *then* Little Richard. And Little Richard was *just unreal.* Unreal. Man, we'd never seen *anything* like that. It was still mohair suits then—I mean, just *great* suits—baggy trousers and all that. And he was workin' with a British band called Sounds Incorporated—our only horn band, the only band that knew anything about saxophones. The show was unreal. And the Stones were so funny. They had, like, four fans at that time who *rushed* down the aisles to the front. These four chicks in the front there—it was so funny. Keith [Richards] was dynamite, because he did that aeroplane stuff in those days, whizzing round and round—he really made an entrance. And Brian [Jones] was kind of dominant in the band then; he really was. And some bloke—I'll never forget this—some bloke in the audience looked at [Mick] Jagger and said, "Get your hair cut!" And Mick said, "What—and look like *you*?" It was *so funny!* We just collapsed in our seats. Years later, Jagger and I went to see Prince at his Madison Square Garden debut. We both thought he was pretty sensational. Other incredible shows I've seen were Bruce Springsteen in the back room at Max's Kansas City in '73, I think, and Philip Glass in London in 1970. **1987** and **1998**

david yow of theJesusLizard
The most thrilling show I've seen was probably my first one, which was Led Zeppelin, nineteen years and ten days ago at the Summit in Houston [May 23, 1977].

I was seventeen. I remember walking in, all the lights were on and the stage was all lit up. There was no opening band, and I could see John Bonham's drum set and Jimmy Page's cabinet that said ZOSO on it, and I was thinking, "Goddamn, man, they're here. I can't fuckin' believe this!" They played just shy of four hours, just great. **1996**

henry rollins
I've never seen harder rock and more out-and-out scary talent than Led Zeppelin on their U.S. tour just before John Bonham died. Me and Ian MacKaye from Fugazi were there; they opened up with white light and "Kashmir." It was a powerful moment. I'll never forget it. **1994**

darryl "d.m.c." mcdaniels of Run-D.M.C.
I like Method Man a lot. When he gives a show, he gives a show. A lot of rappers today bring 150 people on stage and you can't even see who's rappin' and it's just ridiculous. I went to the Palladium to see Method Man, Wu-Tang, Mobb Deep and Redman—everybody was there, and everybody who came on stage came with, like, fifty people. When Method Man got up there the fifty people came, but he jumped off the stage and a crowd of people circled around him and he stood there just, like, rapping to the people and for the people instead of standing up there, like, "Let me do this and get out of here." No drinking champagne and smokin' blunts up on the stage, no, he was like, "I came here to *rap*." **1998**

billy idol
The best concert I saw was the Sex Pistols at the 100 Club, Oxford Street, London, in February 1975. Johnny Rotten had a red sweater split up the side, spiky orange hair and those small square sunglasses he wore then. Glen Matlock had the Jackson Pollock paint-splash gear on, and Steve Jones was thin as a rake. They were doing mainly covers—Small Faces, Dave Berry, the Monkees' "(I'm Not Your) Steppin' Stone"—but their attitude and stripped-down three-chord bash was firmly established. Johnny loved to harangue the audience for having long hair and flares. I think they were doing "Seventeen"—"We don't wear flares, we don't have long hair" and between numbers he would tell the audience to go home to their Melanie records. He called Malcolm McLaren a cunt and said, "Get us a beer!" and Malcolm shouted back, "Fuck off!" Then they belted through "Submission." My friends and I were from Bromley in Kent (twelve miles from central London), and we loved it, not having seen anything as stripped down and to the point since the mid-Sixties. I was about seventeen years

old. "You fucking hippies," he would snarl. Soon we started groups of our own: Chelsea (which became Generation X) and Siouxsie and the Banshees. **1998**

jim kerr of SimpleMinds

Iggy Pop at Glasgow City Hall in 1977 was like a Tasmanian devil. I've never seen energy like that. He was Napoleonic, as well, and at the end of the show, of course, he pulled out his penis. He'd been singing about it the whole night, and I was just thinking, "Let's just see it." And there it was! **1995**

andy partridge of XTC

I saw the first Ramones tour, and there was a band called Talking Heads that opened up for them. They bored the shit out of me. I just got incredibly drunk and took my shirt off and went down in the front and had to be carried home. I'm not really a show person. **1998**

dean wareham of Luna

I saw Pere Ubu in about 1981 at the Paradise in Boston. I was on mushrooms. That mighta had something to do with it. They had this long song, a story about sort of walking around underwater. It really spoke to me at that moment. **1996**

cia soro of Whale

Lydia Lunch in Stockholm in '81 or '82 did one song, forty minutes long and then feedback. Bravissimo! **1998**

gwen stefani of NoDoubt

I'll never forget the David Bowie, Go-Go's and Madness concert at Anaheim Stadium in 1983. It was the summer before ninth grade. My brother got to go, but my dad said I was too young—I cried myself to sleep on the couch. The next thing I know, my mom puts the phone on my ear and it was my dad, saying, "Are you too tired to go to the concert? I got tickets and I'm coming to get you—be ready in ten minutes." When we were in line, we saw my brother and his friends going in, so we all hooked up. It was perfect. I cried the whole time during the concert because it was *so* intense. I couldn't believe I was seeing Madness, even though I was really far away and it was a really big place. It was awesome! I don't even think I watched the other bands. I was mesmerized by Madness. **1996**

billie joe armstrong of GreenDay

Bloodrage and Transgressor at the On-Broadway in San Francisco was my first show—and the first time I saw people slam-dance. I was about fourteen, and I remember being nervous. There weren't that many people there—speed metal was happening then in the Bay Area. I was with my friends, and since none of us had been to a show before, we sat on the side. Then this group of skinhead guys ran by and dove on us. **1998**

john wozniak of MarcyPlayground

I used to see a lot of good shows in Olympia. I saw Fugazi. Ian MacKaye personally escorted some skinheads from Portland to the door to give them their money back. They were *Sieg Heil*ing right up in front of the stage, so they stopped the show and him and Guy were, like, rolling up their sleeves, ready for a fight. It was wild. He started debating with them. He was like, "What the fuck are you doing? What are you doing *Sieg Heil*ing? What is that?" One of the guys said, "Oh, it's an ancient Roman symbol." Ian was like, "Ancient Roman symbol? Why don't you go to a library. You're an idiot. I will personally give you your money back to leave." Everybody started cheering and cleared a path and Ian jumped offstage and went outside and apparently gave them their money back. **1998**

alec empire of AtariTeenageRiot

One of the most important things I've seen in electronic music was Underground Resistance playing in Berlin. Jeff Mills, the DJ, was changing records every twenty seconds or something. Another guy standing behind him was pulling out these records, then Jeff would throw them in the back because he didn't have time to hand them over. There were, like, thirty DJs from Berlin standing around just watching that. It was really cool. **1997**

juliana hatfield

One of the best concerts I have ever seen was Prince at the Avalon in Boston in 1988—it was a secret show during the *Lovesexy* tour. Prince is a total master of the stage—totally in control. And he's so fucking funky. **1995**

paula cole

Bill Frisell played "Somewhere Over the Rainbow" when I saw him at the Village Vanguard, and it was completely impromptu. The band had stopped playing while he was improvising and then he went into "Somewhere

Over the Rainbow." He played it like such a frustrated genius Charlie Brown. And it was incredibly poignant, so truly in the moment that he started crying and I was crying. Then the band members started crying, too. It was a profound moment that stirred my soul. **1998**

rickie lee jones
Seeing Luka Bloom at the Troubadour in Los Angeles was really inspirational. He reminded me of what it's like to go play by yourself. When you can't do that anymore, you're in trouble. **1993**

matt sharp of Weezer
Oh, that tour where Electric Light Orchestra had a spaceship land at Anaheim Stadium, in California, with the band in it. **1995**

shaun ryder of HappyMondays and BlackGrape
Something that isn't really my style that I enjoyed in Brazil was watching George Michael. To be hip and cool, I should say, "Cypress Hill at the Brixton Academy, man," or something like that, but George Michael in Brazil was fucking brilliant. Maybe I was just pissed on capsules or something. **1996**

tracy bonham
I've never laughed as much during a concert as I did at Beck's in 1997 at the Universal Amphitheatre in Los Angeles. **1998**

adam duritz of CountingCrows
The best thing I've ever done was go to the New Orleans Jazz and Heritage Festival. It was pouring rain so I ended up ankle deep in water and mud while I stood in the gospel tent, but I stayed there all day long. **1994**

dave matthews
Tom Waits, on the tour that he did before he put out the film *Big Time*. It was in the Warner Theatre in D.C. He's an incredible performer, so rounded. He's someone to admire. He has had a monumental effect on music. Bands come and go, as we may or may not, but he's an example of the few people who are endlessly fresh. **1996**

john popper of BluesTraveler
A Phish show is a joy forever. When they're on, they transcend their compositions. They become an utter experiment and everyone gets to contribute, everyone in

the audience gets to contribute to that experiment, and it really transcends even improvisations. They become one converging, reshaping unit. **1998**

herb alpert
Miles Davis was *the* seminal jazz musician. I really resonated to how he approached music. He had the whole tool kit: He was lyrical, he was funky, he knew space, he was up on the tightrope all the time—always anxious to be himself—and he earned every note he played. It's a matter of giving up trying to be right and just letting it happen. If you play for someone else's attention or adulation, I think you've got a problem. You'll be too concerned with not making a mistake, which is the first step in the wrong direction. I saw Miles with the dream group: John Coltrane, Red Garland, Philly Joe Jones, Paul Chambers, Cannonball Adderley. They played a two-night concert in L.A. I was there on the Friday night and it was the most spectacular experience I ever had watching and listening to jazz. So I called all of my friends who I thought would appreciate the music and brought them on Saturday only to hear the worst fucking sound I've ever heard in my life. Miles was off, nobody was into playing. I'm not kidding, man, in twenty-four hours it went from the greatest experience in jazz to, like, I couldn't believe I was listening to the same group. Miles played a couple of notes, went in the kitchen and got stoned or whatever he was doing—I don't know. But that's how volatile jazz is, it is what it is when it's happening. They could probably do the same thing several nights in a row, you just can't count on it. You can bring all the great musicians together, but you never know when it's really gonna hit. But I thought with a group like that—these were, like, *the* musicians of our time— they couldn't miss. But man, they missed. It was embarrassing. All of my friends were wondering where I was at. **1997**

LONGLIVEROCK!

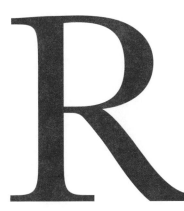ock & roll has died, gone to hell and come back to talk about it. It's like the cockroach—capable of surviving a nuclear holocaust, and as enduring as Rod Stewart's hairdo. Like muttonchop sideburns, it resurfaces in a new form for a whole new generation, just when you thought it was gone forever. Want to get a rise out of a musician, any musician? Ask about the state of rock & roll.

beck

To me, *rock star* conjures up something like a mystic: someone who has the key to the secret that people want to know. The cliché of what a rock star is—there's something elitist about it. I never related to that. I'm an entertainer. I think of it as, you're performing for people. It's not a self-glorification thing. **1997**

john lennon

[Rock & roll means so much to people] because the best stuff is primitive enough and has no bullshit. It gets through to you, it's beat, go to the jungle and they have the rhythm. It goes throughout the world and it's as simple as that, you get the rhythm going because everybody goes into it. I read that Eldridge Cleaver said that blacks gave the middle-class white back their bodies, and put their minds and bodies together. Something like that. It gets through; it got through to me, the only thing to get through to me of all the things that were happening when I was fifteen. Rock & roll then was real, everything else was unreal. The thing about rock & roll, good rock & roll—whatever good means and all that shit—is that it's *real*, and realism gets through to you despite yourself. You recognize something in it which is true, like all true art. Whatever art is, readers. Okay. If it's real, it's simple usually, and if it's simple, it's true. Something like that. **1971**

lou reed

I was in love with rock—because rock does this thing to you. You get directly to somebody, unfiltered. This person doesn't have to go to the movie theater. This person will be listening, alone, maybe at five in the morning. **1987**

joni mitchell

Music is like sex. It's difficult to give instructions to a man. **1998**

david bowie

Rock & roll is a very accessible medium for any young artist. Don't you think so? I like music, but it's not my life by any stretch of the imagination. I mean, I was a painter before, but as a painter, I couldn't make enough money to live on. **1976**

noel gallagher of Oasis

Without music, there would be no point in being around. I'm not saying I'd kill meself, but if I got my hand chopped off in a car crash, I'd have to have music. It's everything. It's the be-all and end-all of my life. Fuck art. Drawing pictures—big deal. And I don't read. I sometimes read books about groups, but I can't read fictional books. Somebody telling a story—how boring. **1996**

pete townshend
If anything exemplifies Sixties pop, particularly '67 through '69, it was its strong connection with the roots of spiritual theosophy and the language that rang with it—the idea that pop music was about spiritual uplift, human potential, solidarity, unification. And that is very difficult to re-create. When you look back at the flower-power era, it all looks daft. I feel particularly cynical, because I thought it was daft at the time. I didn't like Haight-Ashbury; I didn't like Abbie Hoffman. I didn't like Timothy Leary, and I didn't like Woodstock. **1987**

jerry garcia of theGratefulDead
Music is a thing that has optimism built into it. Optimism is another way of saying "space." Music has infinite space. You can go as far into music as you can fill millions of lifetimes. Music is an infinite cylinder, it's open-ended, it's space. The form of music has infinite space as a part of it, and that, in itself, means that its momentum is essentially in that open place. **1972**

elvis costello
It's all a consequence of making rock & roll really important. America's the only country that thinks this way about rock & roll. Everywhere else it's just pop music. Over here it's culture—because it's the only damn culture you've got. So you make it more important than it is. **1989**

david crosby of Crosby,StillsandNash
I [play music] because it gets me off, every time, man, and somebody points me at a microphone, I have—I can't say every time—ninety-nine times out of a hundred, I have as good a time as most people do balling. And wouldn't you want to do that? And wouldn't anybody want to do all they could? I want to do it all I can, because it gets me off. I love it. **1970**

don henley of theEagles
The beginning is when it's great. Money and girls were the two big motivations— that's what it was for everybody. Then you become a serious artist and set out to change the world. **1990**

DRUGS, DRUGSANDROCK&ROLL

Yeah, yeah, drugs are really bad, they affect your judgment and they're illegal most places (except in certain parts of Morocco, South America and Holland). Fine, but musicians go with drugs like peanut butter goes with jelly. Understand, we're not saying all musicians do drugs, but the topic sure pops up a lot.

steven tyler of Aerosmith

Even in the old days, we'd make an effort. When I'd go out to score on Eighth Avenue, I'd get my junk and a chocolate doughnut. But I'd always also pick up one of those pita-pocket health-food sandwiches. You know, something really good for me. **1990**

bonnie raitt By the mid-Seventies, I started running and stopped drinking bourbon. I was drinking wine and beer. And then eventually I drank tequila—I was part of the Seventies tequila circuit in L.A. We were proud to drink tequila and stay up all night. That was a lifestyle we all espoused and loved. Nobody that was around the Eagles, Little Feat or me or Jackson Browne's band is going to say we got a lot of sleep when we were in our twenties. **1990**

ian mcculloch and will sergeant
of EchoandtheBunnymen

Ian McCulloch: It wasn't so much psychedelic drugs. A lot of bevy. A lot of drink. When we made the records it was all pretty straight, wasn't it?
Will Sergeant: Yeah. You can't make records when you're tripping.
Ian McCulloch: The Rolling Stones did it.
Will Sergeant: Yeah, the Stones did when they did *Their Satanic Majesties Request,* but the Beatles were all pretty much all right when they did *Sgt. Pepper's Lonely Hearts Club Band*—they must've been. It plays too well. If you listen to the Stones one it's a bit all over the place, isn't it? It's a bit like you think it's a good idea and you play it later and it's a bit fucked. So we followed the Beatles' example and didn't while we recorded. **1995**

jarvis cocker of Pulp

In my experiences in the rave scene in the U.K. at the end of the Eighties, it always seemed that there must be something deeper about it. And you know, dancing is a deepness thing if you dance hard enough, but I was always convinced that it would bring about a different frame of mind for people because everyone was friendly to each other and stuff like that. Then I realized that everyone was just off their head on E. I hoped once people realized that it would be better to be friendly and nice to each other, they would do that in everyday life. Unfortunately they didn't. **1998**

greg dulli of theAfghanWhigs

[While we were recording *Black Love*] we had a lot of mushrooms. I tripped for, like, the first ten days. Just while we were playing, not while I was singing. But the playing was remarkable. We would never try to play right at first, when it first comes on. We were laughing, can't really do anything. It was usually a couple hours after they had settled in, when you're feeling cool and you're hyperaware and extrasensitive. That's when we would play. When we had our faculties back but still felt connected someplace. Like a peyote spirit buzz. That's what we were kind of going for, because it wasn't like we were getting all fucked up on booze on top of mushrooms. **1996**

busta rhymes

I don't smoke before I go onstage. Discipline, the breath control, everything gotta be balanced, focused, and sometimes the stimulation doesn't let you focus on as many things at the same time. The buzz is more effective when you're writing and being creative and shit. **1998**

keith richards of theRollingStones

Obviously, there was drugs in rock & roll, and the sex wasn't too bad. But I don't know anybody who actually *lives* like that all the time. I *used* to know a few guys that did that, but they're not alive anymore, you know? And you get the message after you've been to a few funerals. **1987**

eminem

I like writing songs on ecstasy. My brain thinks differently. I've written two on it that will be on my next album. Off-the-wall shit. I'm talking about bouncing off walls, going straight through 'em and falling down twenty fucking stories. Crazy. That's what we do when I'm in the studio with [Dr.] Dre. **1999**

nick hexum of 311

Weed. Only the high grade. Call it kryp, chronic or Willie's. Potency of marijuana has come a long way in the past ten years and life is too short to trash your lungs on schwag bud. **1997**

shaun ryder of HappyMondays and BlackGrape

It's weed, now, dude, it's weed. I mean, I don't class weed as drug. We should get that out the window, calling marijuana a fucking drug. You see, since I've got straight I've been a bit of a fucking preacher. And I shouldn't preach, I should shut the fuck up. **1996**

john popper of BluesTraveler

Really good weed. Yes, that's excellent. Especially when taken in the right amounts. That's the key. You have to just take a little. **1997**

sting I like to take care of myself, but I'm not a health freak. I do drink. I do have the occasional joint. But I don't do anything to excess. I don't think anyone should take drugs before they're forty years old. I'm talking strictly about casual use. If you're not addicted to drugs by the time you're forty, you're not going to become addicted. **1993**

jonathan davis of Korn

We did a CD signing at Tower Records in L.A. and 2,200 people showed up. It's overwhelming. But that's what Xanax and alcohol are for. **1998**

john tesh I think caffeine is what all the shootings are about in L.A. People are either too jacked or they're coming down from being jacked. My sound engineer is the most mild-mannered guy, and the other day he was totally distraught and was breaking shit—my shit. He was breaking stuff and screaming at people. He thought it was some protein that he ate. Then he remembered he hadn't had coffee in two days. Let that be a lesson. **1997**

NICETHREADS

usicians are a lot like everybody else—they're just not supposed to dress that way. Face it, even rock's everymen and -women have cooler flannel and T-shirts than the average Joe. Take a peek into these closets: You'll see a few Chanel pumps, a pile of kooky custom Vans and a pair of pants that goes way beyond a snug fit in the can.

"weird al" yankovic

The high point on the tour of Yankland is whenever somebody comes over I have to open this shoe closet and they see, like, hundreds of pairs of these wild shoes. Vans have become kind of a trademark for me. They give them to me pretty much for free. I just go to their warehouse with a wheelbarrow and I'm set for the year. I prefer the slip-on. If it takes more than one step to do anything, I'm not interested. Same thing with cooking. If it requires taking it out of the can and heating it up, forget about it. I strive for simplicity in my life. If I could be any animal, I'd be an amoeba. One-celled, just keep it simple. **1996**

busta rhymes

My closet's real ill: a bunch of different shit, a bunch of flavored shit, a lot of colorful shit, a lot of subtle and conservative shit. Varieties. Pretty much just different moods, do you know what I'm saying? Whatever the call of the function is that's goin' on, you know, I pretty much try to have something that accommodates every situation. **1998**

foxy brown

I love Stephane Kelian for boots and shoes. For clothing, I would say, like, any *designer*. I'm the Gucci *f-reak*. But on my off days, I just have on sweats and sneakers. If you saw me on an off day, you'd be like, "Nah, this ain't Foxy." But right now, I have bags under my eyes. Literally. I just came from shopping—there's no tax in the city today. I was like, "Let me go for it!" I went to Gucci and Fendi and spent about nine thousand dollars. Today, alone. I got four things—pretty much luggage stuff, though. And I went back and I was like, "Wait a minute, why was I charged six hundred dollars in tax?" I found out only purchases under five hundred aren't charged. I was like, "Anything *over* five hundred—that should be no tax!" My accountant really thinks I have a problem with spending money, but I think it's like, I have somewhere to stay, I bought a car, I'm trying to invest some stock, but while I'm young, I want to live to the fullest. That's my heart. **1997**

lil' kim

I wear a lot of Chanel—she caters to petite women. Also Dolce & Gabbana. The most I've ever spent in the Chanel store at one time was about eight thousand dollars—well, really about ten, once you round off the tax. Believe it or not, I only came home with, like, four items. It was, like, an outfit, some shoes, a belt and a bracelet. I can't find a shoe that fits me as well as Gucci and Chanel. There were a couple of days that I went in there and just went crazy. You won't believe. Gianni Versace—I want to shout him out because of the tragic death and give him a Rest in Peace. I wear a *lot* of his clothes. Basically, I wear anything I like, it doesn't have to be name brand, but my favorites are those. **1997**

beck
[When] I come out in a fringe Nudie rhinestone suit, I'm doing it as a tribute to the late-Fifties George Jones or Webb Pierce. I've always loved the Nudie suit. I've always thought of it as one of the greatest clothing styles in any kind of music. But when I come out, people immediately say, "Oh, he's doing an Elvis." I mean, how simple-minded can you be? The reference is a little more interesting than just "doing an Elvis." It's like you pick up a harmonica, and you're "doing a Dylan." **1997**

mike d of theBeastieBoys
Elvis's biggest contribution to our career: He was the first person to sport B-boy gold. **1987**

thurston moore
of SonicYouth
[Fashion designer] Marc Jacobs opened my eyes to people in fashion who had serious and intellectual ideas similar to people in rock & roll. **1994**

cher
I took [wearing Bob Mackie] pretty seriously. We all want to be sexy because it makes us valuable. I always wanted to be valuable, and before I became an entertainer, I was just not valuable to people. **1984**

lady kier kirby
of Deee-Lite
Even before we had a public career, people made assumptions about us because of the way we dressed. They'd

Lady Kier Kirby of Deee-Lite (Self-portrait by Lady Kier Kirby, courtesy of Russell A. Trunk/Chrisam Enterprises, Inc.)

throw rocks at us, or they'd put a ticket on our car because it had a peace sign on it. For a lot of people, stagnation is security. They like to wear the same thing all the time, and that's great for them. But the three of us have always been attracted to change. We've always been in the University of Life. . . . People think that to make a political statement you have to wear a poncho and Birkenstocks and, like, love beads. **1992**

axl rose of Gunsn'Roses

If we're going to do a show, I wear a headband because my hair gets in my face. When we do a photo session, a lot of the time I'll wear a headband because that's how I am onstage. If I feel real dominant and decadent, I'm gonna be wearing my jackboots and stuff like that. I try to express myself through my clothes. It's another form of art. I'm not afraid of what people think about different ways I look. I'm gonna do what I want to. **1989**

joan osborne

A friend of mine works at Armani, and I got a message that he wanted to dress me for the Grammys. I think I'd feel more comfortable being dressed by Urban Outfitters. **1996**

emmylou harris

Ghost clothing, they use great fabrics and have a beautiful feminine line. They're comfortable and travel well. They're English. All rayon, skirts, dresses, pants, tops. Skirts and dresses cut on the bias, they fold up to nothing and they just steam out. They're good for casual and I wear them onstage. All-purpose, all perfect. **1996**

Joan Osborne (Mercury)

jay-z Before I even started talking about platinum jewelry on records and everybody was at it, it was so down low, it's like you wearing something and people don't pay attention because gold was the big thing. To me, platinum was the thing because it was so expensive and so rare. Then me, I opened my big mouth on the record and people don't even buy gold no more. They all buying platinum. You rarely see gold anymore. I got to find something else now. And keep my mouth shut. **1998**

lenny kravitz No, I couldn't just wear a regular suit at graduation— I had to wear ruffles and frills. I mean, in the third grade I had a pair of suede chaps. I had some cool clothes. My mom knew where to shop. I had the big shirts with the sleeves that puff out and come back. Knickers, man. My mom bought the stuff, not me. I remember my fourth-grade or third-grade school picture. I was wearing a pair of jeans with patchwork and cool sneakers and a big ol' Michael Jackson shirt with a peace sign around my neck, and that was just normal. **1995**

polly jean harvey When I was younger, I used to dress up all the time—in Mum's clothes. Then I got serious. And wore black. **1993**

jakob dylan of theWallflowers
Red Wing Shoes—America's oldest work-boot company. They make Doc Martens look like penny loafers. **1993**

pat smear of theGerms and FooFighters
Opera pumps by Gucci or Ferragamo are like little-girl shoes for men, especially in patent leather. Great with fancy socks and Levi's. **1996**

sinéad o'connor Wedges with high heels. They're very easy to stand on, but they're sexy, and it's important to feel sexy. I also always wear something that makes me smell nice. **1997**

shirley manson of Garbage
Guerlain's Nahema perfume—I feel completely unlike myself if I don't wear it. It's a strange scent, but I love it, and I confess it's a luxury I can barely live without. **1996**

ani difranco

I'm into crazy, clunky platforms, just so the guys don't tower over me too much onstage. Every now and then, they creep up to my mike, and I suddenly look like a midget. **1997**

Ani DiFranco (Albert Sanchez/Righteous Babe)

fred schneider of theB-52's

Whoever came up with the T-shirt is my favorite designer. And the American Cotton Garment Workers' Union. **1996**

stevie nicks

In one of those first shows when Lindsey [Buckingham] and I went on the road, I saw this woman walk by, and she was wearing a mauve chiffon layered midiskirt and high platform cream-colored suede boots. I thought, I want to be her. So when I joined Fleetwood Mac and I had some money, I went to a lady and I said, "I want you to make me a raggy chiffon skirt that looks sort of like an urchin on the wharves of London." **1998**

simon le bon of DuranDuran

Black Fly sunglasses. Very important. Daytime and nighttime. They're great because if you sit on them the lenses pop out, they don't actually break, and you can pop the lenses back in. I'm into completely bending them. I think my summer motorcycle gloves are my favorite thing in my closet. Kushitani makes them and they're lightweight so I can wear them in the summer. When you ride a motorcycle the order of protection goes like this: First, most important thing is your head, second most important thing is your hands because if you fall off a bike, you put your hands down and if you take the skin off your hands at seventy miles per hour you'll never ever be able to feel anything again with your fingertips. It will just take all the nerves away. You have to protect your hands. I see these guys riding around without gloves on and I think, you poor fucking idiot, don't you know what can happen? After that your knees and your hips and then your feet. The last important thing is the jacket, that's the least important really. Your elbows and shoulders can get it, but not nearly as bad as your knees do. **1997**

iggy pop

A good thing to do is get a pair of pants that fits really well, like a good pair of Levi's, and you wanna wear them over and over. Soon *you* become those pants. Your whole being is defined by your butt as it fits into those pants. You're like, "Yeah, these are my pants, man." They get funny, they get fruity, you know? Like if you don't wash them enough. **1996**

john popper of BluesTraveler

Scantily clad fashions for women. The way women dress in the spring is incredible. You know, I go through winter thinking, okay, the scenery around here is kind of bland. But when spring comes out the first warm day, I suddenly find myself noticing pretty much all the women everywhere and it's beautiful. **1996**

rupaul I love fashion, but I've gone off that whole thing. I love beauty, I love art, I love beautiful people but not all the attitude that goes along with all the fashion shit. If you ever have to be around those people—*uck*. They're all frustrated, and they're all projecting. It's a really sick psychological tale, because here are these people that are the tastemakers and obviously they don't look like the supermodels they project in the magazines, so that's all a fantasy for them, but they're all so bitter too, that they're not that. All the fashion press and all that stuff, they're all really nasty people. I don't even go to shows anymore. You get slimed by them. All these people with their sunglasses and shit, it's like, "Fuck you." That shit is over. That shit is o-ver. **1997**

MYFAVORITETHINGS

We can't always tell you why artists like what they like. We certainly try. But sometimes the only answer is: They just do. Stevie Nicks cuddles up to crackling, warm fires—with the air conditioner cranked up to high. "Weird Al" Yankovic prefers the letter P, while Beck delights in the mistranslations of his lyrics.

"weird al" yankovic
Letters of the alphabet that I like: the *P*s and the *K*s. I like percussive sounds. **1996**

noel gallagher of Oasis
We like annoying people. It's a Manchester thing. It's a trait. We just like pissing people off. **1996**

gary numan
Industrial music is my absolute favorite. I love the emotion, the attitude of it, the way they put the sound together. It isn't just electronic, it's mixing guitars, but using them in a relatively unusual way. The guitar is usually quite innovative. Good melodies. You know, the only problem I have with electronica is the lack of vocals and the lack of melody. What little there are is often sampled and replayed. There's a lot more life in it yet. I think it's going to get better. **1997**

stevie nicks
I keep a fireplace burning even when it's 99 degrees. I just turn the air-conditioning up. My mother goes crazy. She says, "Do you know how much money you spend to keep this house cool, and then you burn fires in every single room? You're so weird, Stevie." A fire creates ambience. I need that fire. So back off, Mom. **1994**

jay-z
I like checking out *The Robb Report*, shows you just how far off you are. Every time you accomplish something, you look in there to find out how much further you have to go. Keeps you working. There are mansions in there with little moats and little ten-thousand-dollar duck boats for the kids. It'll say, like, fifty-six acres, fifty-six million dollars—a must-have! **1998**

björk
Milton Nascimento is brilliant. Odd chords, so it brings a bit of an edge. I listen to him when I'm in a shivery mood, kind of like when you haven't got a skin on. And it makes me happy. **1994**

fred schneider of the B-52's
When I was little, I liked dinosaurs, still do. I'm always interested in the latest paleontological discoveries and things like that. **1996**

chrissie hynde of thePretenders

The freedom fighters People for the Ethical Treatment of Animals kick ass. PETA has attacked multinationals across the board, from slaughterhouses to circuses, and have come up trumps every time. **1994**

tanya donelly of ThrowingMuses and Belly

Dr. Jack Kevorkian provides dignity to the dying. I think it makes sense. Tubes hanging out of a dying person—that's cruelty. **1994**

herb alpert
Honesty is the universal language. When somebody does something with love and tender care you notice it. For instance, even when non–jazz fans listen to John Coltrane or Charlie Parker or Miles Davis or Stan Getz, it penetrates them because those guys send out the real goods. They know they're feeling something that's right. **1997**

joni mitchell
I'll tell you what's knocked my socks off: Edith Piaf, Billie Holiday, Miles Davis, Pablo Picasso, Chuck Berry. **1994**

steven tyler of Aerosmith

Playing with Joe Perry really gets me off. I'm not gay, but I love him. **1994**

john popper of BluesTraveler

The feel of the smooth action of a Colt Python is like butter. There is nothing like that feeling. When it's been well taken care of, it has the most seamless and smooth mechanism as ever existed on the face of the earth in any kind of machine. You can take your favorite camera, your favorite recording equipment, and I'll put up a Colt Python .357 Magnum six-inch revolver in a classic blue finish any day of the week. And it shoots! You can hammer nails with it all day. Hit the bullseye, fifty, hundred yards if you're good. That's a lot of punch. They make bigger guns, but very few smoother. Dirty Harry was packing a .44 Magnum, which is bigger, and that is a good gun. I have a Smith and Wesson. That's an excellent weapon but there's something about a Colt Python. **1998**

raekwon of Wu-TangClan

My cell phone [Motorola Nextel il000] is the shit. This is me right here. It's like holding a Magnum in your hand. You always want to be on that shit, know what I mean? We call that walkie-talkie feature life or death. Yo, you always want to know where your people at. When you got this shit, it's, like, push the button, "Where you at? I'm over here. All right, talk to you later." I can know my family is all right by hearing their voices, just like that. That's the illest shit they could have made. You got twenty cats down with you, you got twenty of these shits, it's real. You might be coming through the movie theater, you can let niggas know, "Yo, I'm up at the flicks right now. I'm gonna be up here for two hours. I'll get with y'all when I see y'all, but I'm all right." That's how the Clan niggas like to roll. You might see ten of us together, you might only see one of us, but we're always connected like that. **1998**

carnie wilson

My favorite thing is making crazy messages. You should hear my *Mommie Dearest* ones. "Christina! Christopher! Damn it!" I seriously become Joan Crawford. I'm just nuts. I am obsessed with that movie. "Christina, get out of that bed!" I'm out of hand. "You deliberately embarrassed me!" There's something about Faye Dunaway that trips me out. She's so intense. **1997**

beck

I remember talking to some journalist in Hong Kong and he read me out lyrics to one of my songs that weren't anything close to the lyrics I wrote. They were so much better. I've been kicking myself ever since that I didn't write down what he thought they were. I think I'm gonna try to track him down next time. **1996**

mike simpson of theDustBrothers

I think that we should eliminate the whole Daylight Savings Time change thing. It's very confusing and seems to serve no purpose whatsoever. We all like it better when it stays light later, don't we? **1998**

pat smear of theGerms and FooFighters

Tyson vs. Bruno at the MGM Grand in Las Vegas. The most exciting ten minutes of my life? Maybe. **1996**

rupaul
Mike Campbell is a fabulous model. He's not hunky hunky good-looking, but he's gorgeous. He's in the Dolce & Gabbana ads. He used to have long hair, but he's cut it now. Jason Lewis is this big, hot fucking blond guy. Forget about it. I saw him in a DKNY show, he had on these knit pants and his fucking dick was so big, you can't imagine. It was just bouncing around in his pants. **1997**

john wozniak of MarcyPlayground
I go to the Slap-a-Spice-Girl Web site when I'm not busy. It's got a thing with a bunch of holes in it—it looks like a plate or a table—and the Spice Girls come up and you have a hand that you control with your mouse and you go and you slap them, and their faces get all distorted when you hit them. Every once in a while Margaret Thatcher pops up. My playing's improved and getting better all the time. I hope to win the World Championships. **1998**

jakob dylan of theWallflowers
I love the SST Superstore on Sunset Boulevard in Los Angeles. Hüsker Dü, Minutemen, Black Flag. They sell all the hits from the fabulous 1980s—a time when "grunge" was the sound of your car smashing into the one in front of you. And the Good Guys—it's a twenty-four-hour audio-video store. Where else can you bump into other spaced-out insomniacs looking for speaker wire at 3:00 a.m.? **1993**

shirley manson of Garbage
Jack Russell terriers are my favorite breed of dog, still officially unrecognized by the powers that be! The dogs are smart, brave and notoriously difficult to train. Unthwartable spirit—I admire that. **1996**

david yow of theJesusLizard
I cry at *Miracle on 34th Street.* I sure do. I cry at *E.T.* When they find him and he's all pale in that ravine. Yeah. I cry really easily. There ya go. **1996**

sean "puffy" combs a.k.a. puff daddy
I love being a role model. I really don't have pressure like that. I'm human, but I'm trying to do things positive for kids. I'm trying to represent as a positive figure for kids. I have Daddy's House for underprivileged children; I have a charity

gospel album coming out. Seventy-five cents a ticket on my tour goes to Daddy's House—they're one of the sponsors, and they do a lot of great things in the community. They have computer camps for boys and girls in the summer, and they feed the homeless on Christmas and the holidays. They're doing a trip to Africa to teach a lot of kids about their roots. **1997**

jim morrison of theDoors

Who isn't fascinated with chaos? More than that, though, I am interested in activity that has no meaning, and all I mean by that is free activity. Play. Activity that has nothing in it except just what it is. No repercussions. No motivation. Free . . . activity. I think there should be a national carnival, much the same as Mardi Gras in Rio. There should be a week of national hilarity . . . a cessation of all work, all business, all discrimination, all authority. A week of total freedom. That'd be a start. **1969**

k.d. lang To me, music is like food—there are all these ingredients, but it's how you cook 'em, it's how you *spice* 'em. You can take the same five vegetables and make them taste very different. I see no segregation in music at all. **1997**

alex empire of AtariTeenageRiot

Of course, my favorite video game is from Atari, and it's called Pong. It was the start of everything for me in a way. It's so simple, you can play it with just one player, and you play against the wall, which is sometimes how I feel—you just always try to break through the wall, but it doesn't happen. But you can play with two, and then it's funny because it's so stupid, it sometimes reminds me of personal relationships. You're throwing the ball back and forth and it just makes this sound, "ping-pong, ping-pong." It's the same ball, and the worst thing is, it's pretty much preprogrammed. And you wonder to yourself why after, like, ten minutes you're in a form of trance. You don't really think about anything else. But some people realize this only after a long period of time. There's a lot of philosophy in that game. It's very simple, but it's so true. **1996**

jonathan richman I'm an apprentice to a stonemason here in northern California. About three years ago I told him, "Hey, Pete, I'll carry around a bag of cement if you let me watch you work." The next thing I knew, he was handing me trowels and saying, "Okay, you mix this batch." **1998**

john lennon

If I could be a fuckin' fisherman I would. If I had the capabilities of being something other than I am, I would. It's no fun being an artist. You know what it's like, writing, it's torture. I read about van Gogh, Beethoven, any of the fuckers. If they had psychiatrists, we wouldn't have had Gauguin's great pictures. These bastards are just sucking us to death; that's about all that we can do, is do it like circus animals. I resent being an artist, in that respect, I resent performing for fucking idiots who don't know anything. They can't feel. I'm the one that's feeling, because I'm the one that is expressing. They live vicariously through me and other artists, and we are the ones. . . . I'd sooner be in the audience, really, but I'm not capable of it. **1971**

moby

I'd open a sex store. Pornography is so boring because it's all the same: not-very-attractive men and artificial-looking women doing the same old thing. There's so much room to make interesting pornography—pornography that's funny, pornography that's scary, pornography that's threatening, or really sweet, involving real people, involving fake people, whatever. There's this store in San Francisco called Good Vibrations—it's this really upscale sex store for women. It's very clean, sanitary, safe and nice. I think anyone who started a chain of yuppie-bourgeois sex stores would clean up. Actually, with two friends of mine, we had a business plan ready to go, we were looking for spaces on the Lower East Side, but zoning-wise you can't do it. We even had names ready to go. I envisioned some young, attractive punk-rock kids, with a sense of humor and a relaxed attitude to it. **1997**

dave mustaine of Megadeth

I like golfing. I'm good, but they're not, like, jumping over barrels to put me in *Golf Digest* magazine. Alice Cooper's my godfather, and I won the longest drive contest at his first golf tournament. The first time I'd ever went golfing was [while we were recording] *Youthanasia*. I was really pissed at someone, and I went to the driving range and oddly enough, the golf ball had a name similar to his on it, and I just clobbered the ball as hard as I could and it went about three inches. This game sucks. So I put another up there and I said, you know what? I'm just gonna try and bump it, and I just swung regularly, and the thing went forever. And then I'm playing in Alice's contest, and I win the longest drive and I mean, he had people like Marcus Allen and Jerry Rice there and I'm thinking, shit, these guys are Hall of Famers and I outdrove them. They're probably like, "Who's the long-hair who won? His ball must be loaded." It was fun. **1997**

stevie nicks I love to dance and I can do cartwheels and I can jump down into splits. Yesterday my assistant was dying, because back here they have the ESPN hip-hop aerobics at six in the morning, and I'm doing this. She said, "Nobody would believe this, Stevie. You're forty-six years old!" **1994**

HOTFUNINTHESUMMERTIME

 **L**iberating for some, tedious and TV-filled for others, summer happens every year. The hair comes down, the doors come off, the clothes get skimpy, and the little kid comes out in everyone.

ringo starr I love summertime. It's a big moment in most musicians' lives because you're on tour. The great thing about summer for me is that it's light longer and it seems to go on forever. I love it being light. I get up somewhere between seven and nine. If given my choice, I would spend summer vacation in Anguilla. The most beautiful water and beach, but also Fiji is pretty cool. **1998**

steve miller Best thing that happened to me in the summer is that I met my wife on tour. She was on the entertainment committee at Washington State University and I played there one summer. What was really goofy was that her father was a really good friend of mine, I had known him for five years and I had never met her before. Another thing that happens in summer is that we get to grow as musicians by stretching out and playing. That's the main thing I do all this for is—the music. My dream one-day festival would have T-Bone Walker, Les Paul, Muddy Waters, Otis Redding, the Grateful Dead, Cream, Mountain—they'd be fun for a few numbers—and let's throw Jimi Hendrix in just for the hell of it. Joni Mitchell can open. And then let's go for some new guys, Kenny Neal and Curtis Sallgado and the Stilettos. That would pretty much take care of me. **1996**

john lee hooker I like to see summer. I'm not crazy about winter. Summer is the time where people get together to have a good time, travel. People really let their hair down, as we call it, in summertime and just have a good time. I think the United States of America is the summer place. I've been to other countries and all that kind of stuff, but it's not like home. I mean that in a lot of ways, you know. We're not suppressed here and dictated to in an evil manner, but we are dictated to, you know. You've got to have "yes" and "no" and "don't," and "should I" and "can I" and "no you will not" and all that. We gotta have those, those the rules and regulations that a few people put together and said, "Well, we'll try this and see if it works." A lot of the time summer brings out a lot of uncool people, too. I wish that they would take another look at what summer means and make summer happy all the way through. **1997**

the notorious b.i.g. a.k.a. **BiggieSmalls**
Working shows and working on an album. Sitting in front of the AC or chillin' until the sun goes down. Listening to the first Teddy Riley and Guy albums. Playing in front of a hydrant and watching girls. Hopefully spending summer in California—at the beach with my bitches. Just chillin'. **1996**

dick dale My vacation is coming home, putting my feet in the dirt. But in the summertime what I would love to be doing is going to Hawaii. That was my other life, surfing my brains out. But the water is so polluted it sucks. I'd just go to the areas where I can enjoy the smell of the tropical flowers with my wife and my four-year-old son. I took him out in the ocean the other day, and the water went over him and I had to dive for him. He got his first taste of being sucked under. When I took him back up and squeezed the water out of him, he said, "Come on, we've got to go chase the water again. Daddy, you hold on to me, you saved me." So in the summers, I'd like to show him all the wonderfulness of what's out there. In the high desert where we live I'd fly him in my plane to the dry lakebeds and land out in the middle and just sit there and show him what true meditation is. **1996**

jewel Most summers I spent a lot of time helping out at my aunt's place in Homer [Alaska]. She owned a farm, a youth hostel and a bed-and-breakfast— she'd also give horse rides to tourists. I met tons of kids who were just looking for places to pitch their tents for three or four dollars a night. And there were lots of college kids who came to Homer to work for the summer—we called them spit rats, because they lived in a tent city out on a spit of land. I'd ride my horse down there a lot and sort of meet people along the way. You know, when you're sixteen, hanging out with people in their twenties who have already been through college really opens up your mind. They'd turn me on to books to read, we'd talk about traveling. It really keeps you from being prejudiced at a very young age. Homer was filled with travelers. I'd meet people from all over. I had friends from Chile and Guatemala, Puerto Rico, Australia and New Zealand. Those people turned me on to a lot of different languages, religions and different ways of thinking. Summer was always a good education. **1998**

busta rhymes Summertime? I love summertime. Word up. First of all, summertime is the best time to sell some records, 'cause it's hot, you can be all across the country, the weather is nice, you can relax, you can vacation at the same time that you're working 'cause of the weather. You can do a lot of shows, people could come out and enjoy the weather with you. You can chill. I can drive around with my truck with the sunroof wide open, Landcruiser now, bangin' the system all day with my bangin' album. I love going to the beach during the summer, no question. Seeing all the love from all the people and all the people gettin' the love back from Busta Rhymes. Word up. When I go to the beach, I never forget the blunts, dude. Nah, and I never forget my crew. That way everybody can have a little fun together. You don't want to have fun by yourself 'cause then it ain't no fun for real like. So, I gotta roll with my Flip Mode Squad. Everybody needs to dress appropriately in the summer. Don't be comin' outside tryin' to look hard core just because that's the style. Dress to accommodate yourself in your comfort zone. Then make sure you got loot in your pocket. Gotta have some loot to get your own drinks this year. Women always expect men to buy 'em drinks. We need to be buying each *other* drinks. And be peaceful most of all. No uncivilized ways of being, because then you start destroying the loveliness of summer. Especially being that it only comes once a year. Motherfuckers had better have the best time they can have this summer. And all the rest of the little summers we got left to encounter in our little time frames living and shit. Make the best of life while you can, dude. You know, shit be real hot, but motherfuckers need to understand that either you gonna be civilized or you stay the fuck home. Know what I'm sayin'? **1996**

dmx Beach is where you want to go in the summer. Bring something cold and a lotta ice. Kool-Aid, that's good to drink. And those Fla-Vor-Ices, the long ones in the plastic. Those right there, the piña colada or the blueberry. All else you need is blunts—plenty of smoke. And always the dog. **1998**

coolio Go to the beach, get in one of your homeboys' convertibles, ride around, look at the girls. We have barbecues, picnics. Once in awhile we go up to Bear Mountain, go around Lake Arrowhead. **1995**

iggy pop I like to lick girls' sweaty armpits in the summer. The smell really turns me on, especially if they have hair. I go crazy. Every summer I avoid Beach Boys concerts. I've been going to Europe a lot and playing in these festivals. When I don't, I go to Mexico and just jump in the ocean. I jump in the ocean a lot. Ocean over pool. Pool is bad—bacterial breeding ground. I've got pool bacteria right now. I've been going to the pool here in Los Angeles and I have a weird viral feeling. Body aches and weird chest. I probably got some movie producer's viral germs. It's like, a bummer, you know. So is air-conditioning. I was raised in climate control. My dad was like, "We have complete control over the temperature of this housing unit." Ah! I couldn't open windows—it warped my adolescent psyche. So I never used an air conditioner in my adult life until one year, we had an incredibly hot summer in New York and I got one. I used it twice, and then it sat there. I didn't know you had to remove 'em from the window, so I got sick all winter because the air would come right through. So was it worth it? No. Junior Kimbrough was on tour with me recently. It was cold the whole time. I asked if he hated it. He said, "No, I likes the cold. Then when I'm fuckin', I don't get too hot." **1996**

dave navarro of Jane'sAddiction and theRedHotChiliPeppers

When it comes to summertime, I suppose I enjoy any type of water, whether it's the ocean or a pool. I look forward to much scuba diving, snorkeling, etc. In summer, I most enjoy motorcycling, long walks, picnics, getting up late and the ability to wear the same pair of shorts for a month and have nobody turn an eye to it. I'd imagine losing my virginity was the best thing that ever happened to me in the summer. I don't think going to tennis camp was. **1996**

bob weir of theGratefulDead

I had one summer job when I was growing up that was cowboying, and I hated it thoroughly. I was sixteen or so. The rest of the time I've pretty much been on the road all summer, every summer. I kinda like to see America in the summertime. That's what I get to do every year, so I have no complaints. I've had so many great summers, I don't even know how to shovel my way back through them. The best summer concert ever? I'd include the lineup at the New Orleans Jazz and Heritage Festival, and after that, Duke Ellington, Count Basie and Jimi Hendrix. **1996**

yuka honda of CiboMatto

In Japan, on the beach they play a game where you put a watermelon on the sand, and then blindfold somebody. You turn them around a couple of times so they cannot remember where the watermelon is exactly. The person holds a big stick and tries to guess where it is, and tries to hit it really hard. A lot of times you hit the sand. But really the place to be for the summer is 'burbs. *The* 'burbs, with your friends' parents. That's the way. **1996**

jarvis cocker of Pulp

In the summer, I go fishing. I wear a wide-brimmed hat. If I were stuck in my hometown, I would have to pretend I was somewhere else. I think I would most like to spend this summer in Iceland. The best thing that ever happened to me in the summer was last year at Glastonbury [England]. We played a concert in the shadow of the Tor. It's a castle. On the whole, summer touring is a waste of quality time. It's also too hot. **1996**

Jarvis Cocker of Pulp (Self-portrait by Jarvis Cocker, courtesy of Russell A. Trunk/Chrisam Enterprises, Inc.)

junior brown

I remember one summer I smoked a lot of cigarettes and watched a lot of TV. That's probably the first one that I remember vividly. Somethin' I'll always carry with me, you know. I think I was about eight. Yeah. The main thing is, when you're doing your summer activities, stay inside, don't even leave the house. That way you can enjoy your vacation without suffering the heat. That's what I find. Stay inside a lot, best way. And if you do go to a concert, make sure everyone's good. **1996**

kim thayil of Soundgarden

Each summer I'd get new gym shoes and swear I could jump higher and run faster. I liked playing baseball until it was too dark to see the ball. We'd go to creeks to spot turtles. Most often, we came up with buckets of leeches—half a dozen kids with buckets that they'd have to leave on the porch. By morning they were always mysteriously empty. We found out that at night the leeches crawled into the yard, where they'd dry up or get eaten by birds. The summer I was sixteen, I earned the money to buy my first electric guitar and amp. For some reason, the first Van Halen album represents summer to me. It was released in '78, and when it got around to me, around the end of my senior year of high school, I was very resistant to listening to something that I thought was metal. At that time, I was not at all into stuff like that. But even though I was resistant, it ended up being the soundtrack for the summer, because it was everywhere. That record seems very sunny and warm and stands out by association with that year. A second one is *Meat Puppets II*. It had a very strong effect that way. That's a great summer record. Even though it's a little bit melancholy and isn't overtly summery, the album is very—it's great in the middle of North Dakota. My dream summer concert would have to be outdoors. But not a real huge one, because then I wouldn't go. The first band I'd put in there would have to be the MC5. Then Blue Cheer. And as the sun is setting in the evening, I'd have the Stooges come out and play. I would have loved to have been at the Democratic convention in Chicago in '68 and seen the MC5 playing. You listen to *Kick Out the Jams* and *Vincebus Eruptum* and they sound live. I don't know if they are but it certainly feels that way to me. When I think of "Summertime Blues" by Blue Cheer, I haven't heard it in about a year, but I remember it as being live, very outdoors. **1996**

grant lee phillips of GrantLeeBuffalo

Summer is lemon-limes and daffodils, picnic benches and lobster tails. Summer is bowling shirts and sticky Naugahyde in a hot Toyota Tercel. Summer is yankin' off the AM, slapping down that Nick Gilder song, puttin' on the Pixies tape you found in your trunk at the car wash. Summer is all these things and more. Last summer, we took time off. I mixed mai tais, painted birdhouses, hauled in a piano, wrote operas, crime dramas and eventually an album full of songs called *Copperopolis*. Summer is hot. To beat the heat, you need to keep up enough speed. If you're walking, try a nice fast jog. The idea is to keep the wind moving, and then you can avoid a possible collapse and overheating. You don't want to drink too much water, that'll slow you down. What you want is coffee. See, you want to keep the inside the same temperature as the outside. If it's 120 degrees out, then what you need is a nice cup of joe, warming up that system. And keep the pace up. **1996**

kristin hersh of ThrowingMuses

Once I went camping with my then boyfriend and climbed a waterfall. It was cool—it was fucking freezing. Then the endorphins kicked in. At the top there was a sign: COME HERE AND YOU DIE, and crosses with names of people who died climbing this stupid waterfall. We felt very smart because we weren't dead. On a lighter note, a good summer song is the Meat Puppets' "Up on the Sun." I live in a beach town, so if you're not a surfer, the rule is, you just sit and stare, which is pretty Zen as far as tourist activities go. So I bring nothin' to the beach. It helps with the sitting and staring. It's a fine line between Buddhist and boring. I used to bring my dog, but he'd swallow so much ocean water, he'd puke. He's not very cool. Last summer we bought a Snoopy snow-cone maker. I remember snow cones as being great. They're not. They're sticky and gravelly. Now my kids want them year-round. Don't do it. **1996**

sheryl crow

Where I grew up, summers were always about cruising the strip and going to drive-in movies. Kennett, Missouri, is a really small town. We had the A&W at one end and Dairy Queen and the Sonic at the other. The Sonic had roller-skating waiters back then, but I guess they've kind of done away with that kind of thing. As soon as it got warm, you'd start cruising back and forth and hanging out in the parking lots—that's what you did as a kid in my hometown: turned the radio up and watched the cars go by. There was one year where *Billy Jack* seemed to be playing at the drive-in for the entire summer. I remember sitting in lawn chairs in the back of pickup trucks, singing "One Tin Soldier" and watching that dumb movie all summer long. I remember congregating in the Dairy Queen parking lot and listening to the Allman Brothers. That, to me, means summer. All of the radio stations around there played nothing but Southern rock. We used to go water-skiing, and I'd hear them out on the boat. Every time I hear the Allmans, it takes me back. **1998**

Sheryl Crow (Self-portrait by Sheryl Crow, courtesy of Russell A. Trunk/Chrisam Enterprises, Inc.)

jim "the reverend" heath of ReverendHortonHeat

Well, I play horseshoes, have barbecues, hire a mariachi band. I take the dog for a Go-ped ride—aw, man, it's a skateboard with a motor. And my dog, on his leash, he stays right with me and we just go cruisin' down the street. He loves it, man, he gets a chance to really stretch out and run. He's part Rottweiler. Summertime, everybody gets into fights, and shit gets broken. For sure, I stay out of fights while I'm playing horseshoes. Somebody could hit you with one of those things. There are just not enough days in the summer. Once I lived in a warehouse in the summer. It was about 120 degrees in there—life threatening, it was so hot. Big ol' huge rats walking around. But it was a place where bands played. I worked, and I played gigs, too. That was the summer that Reverend Horton Heat really started. It seemed like hell back then, but it sure was a lot of fun. **1996**

Reverend Horton Heat: Scott, the Rev. and Jimbo (from left) (Marina Chavez/Interscope)

bo diddley

When I was a kid in Chicago, in the summertime we'd shoot marbles, roller-skate in the street, stuff like that. I'm sixty-nine years old, and I still got a pair of skates, man. I got a pair from way back, Daddy—you know the ones with the iron wheels that hooked on the side of your shoes? Shoes were hard to get back then, and the skates would rip 'em up. You'd get your booty whupped if you couldn't get the skates off your shoes. They'd buy you the skates, but how the hell were you supposed to ride 'em without your shoes? Summer's when people get together and let their hair down. But it brings out a lot of uncool people—though I haven't found too many down here in Florida, 'cept maybe the dudes who get too drunk when it gets hot. I mean, it's enough for people to get off their booties and have a good time and not be doin' dirty things to other people. **1998**

boy george of CultureClub

In 1988, during what we call the Summer of Love, I was on holiday in the south of France, and a friend of mine got involved with a local gangster's girlfriend. We had to leave *tout de suite,* so we went to Ibiza, Spain, on the spur of the moment and stayed a month. It was during the early acid-house scene, and it was just fantastic. I'm not a sun person, per se. Summer is the enemy of drag, so it's not a good time for me. I do love to go on holiday—when I can wear a pair of shorts and a T-shirt, sit on the beach with my feet in the sea. But if I'm working, I dress up and wear makeup, and find myself melting; it's just not good. So the Culture Club tour this summer will be stressful. All of the dates are outdoors. I'm going to have to get a straw hat and some calico pants. **1998**

natalie imbruglia

The first summer I lived in London was amazing—it was hot and sunny. Everyone said it was the first real summer in a long time. When it isn't cloudy and raining, London is the best place on earth. People come out—they're always hanging out, drinking in the streets. I didn't work much that summer. I was really into the whole Portobello vibe. Portobello is a really bohemian section of London. I spent a lot of time at Jimmy Beez Cafe. They had tables outside, and they served this amazing crispy spinach. Occasionally they'd have parties and they'd serve free vodka shots downstairs; we'd dance to different DJs spinning trip-hop or house. It was hot and sweaty and a little drunken, too. It was just one of those places; it really felt like it was ours—but then it closed, and now it's gone forever. **1998**

missy "misdemeanor" elliot
One summer, when I was six years old, I went to my aunt's house in Virginia, and my two cousins were fighting. One was real fat, and the other was real skinny. The skinny one threw the fat one down, and he landed on my arm and broke it. I got ice cream all summer. I had to get a new cast damn near every week, because I'd be running wild outside, playing in the mud. But come Sunday, when it was time to go to church, my mother wasn't having me going to church with a dirty cast, so I had to keep getting new ones. **1998**

steven tyler of Aerosmith
In 1969, I was living in New York, playing in all these different bands. It was so cool. You'd go down to the Village and see the Stones walking around when they were in town; you'd bump into Bob Dylan. There was the Electric Circus, a club that was specifically made for tripping; they actually had a rubber room. There was the Fillmore East and the Salvation at One Sheridan Square—that's where I met Hendrix and Tiny Tim. It moved to Central Park West, then out to Southampton, Long Island, where the band I was in [William Proud] was the house band for the summer of '69. The whole band lived in Southampton, and it was heaven! We lived in a house with four people who were buck gay. It was a big family, and it was cool, 'cause two lesbians were constantly trying to get me in their room. But after a month, I started losing my mind. I wanted to write songs with people, I hadn't really written a song yet. Our band was doing speed and not getting it together. One day I just said, "Fuck you guys, man!" I started screaming and dove over my drums (I was a drummer then) to try to strangle my guitar player. I ran out of there crying, I was fucking so angry, man. I didn't get anything—I grabbed my money and I grabbed a few things. No suitcase. I left all my clothes and started hitching home to New Hampshire. The first ride I got was on a tractor from this guy with no teeth. He kind of scared me, but he was fun, kind of cool. He rolled his own cigarettes and I said, "So do I, but the funny kind," and he didn't like that. He starts telling me this story about how he loves pussy so much, but he never seems to get enough. I'm thinking, "Well, no doubt!" He goes, "You know what? I was thinking, man, you know when I die, I'm gonna be cremated and that way my son can take my ashes and spread them all over the beach and that way, even when I'm dead, I'm gonna still be getting in girls' pants." Somehow, it was an epiphany. I thought, "Man, this could be the beginning chapter of my life." At that moment, I *knew* something was going to happen; it felt like my adventure had begun—like the first time I got laid. It was just one of those moments, something is gonna happen. I thought, either I'm gonna get raped or

RAVES

shot or—but I felt really good about what I was doing, which was *leaving* them and going somewhere else. Anyway, I almost got all the way home to New Hampshire without calling my parents. I was so sad. I thought my dream of being a rock star was over. The next day while mowing the lawn I met Joe Perry. Man, when I hear that song "Summer of '69," I think, "That guy has no idea." **1998**

lars frederiksen of Rancid

Oh, Jesus, when I was eleven, I had this friend who was sixteen. Our girlfriends hung out together in south San Jose [California]. One day we went to his girl-friend's house while they were in summer school. We climbed through her win-dow and, before long, we raided the liquor cabinet and put chewing gum on their dog. My friend had a bag of PCP-laced oregano—that's the way they used to do it—and we started gettin' all fucked up. The next thing I know, the world is spin-nin' and my friend is freaking out, beating the fuck out of me—obviously, he smoked more than I did. Somehow, I got away and got home. And my mom's there. I'm fucking high, I'm drunk, it's hot. I had egg whites in my hair, and I just smelled like shit. I passed out on the floor. Then the police called and told my mom to bring me back to the girl's house. They found my friend tearing up the place, and he ratted me out. I ended up in juvenile hall for two weeks. **1998**

liz phair
For me, summers in Winnetka, Illinois, were about all these long-haired high-school girls riding around in Rabbit convertibles. There were bonfires and new swimsuits to wear, escapades into the city with fake IDs and big, bombas-tic midwestern thunderstorms. And, of course, there was the annual Dead-show event. We'd go up to Alpine Valley [Wisconsin] to get away from our parents. That was where I first tried drugs. There was this bunch of girls, and we'd get into scraps and try to keep each other out of trouble. My girlfriends all had brothers that were about two years older, and the summer before our senior year, everyone in their circle dated one of us. I remember that I felt pretty that summer. My high school was very *Ferris Bueller, The Breakfast Club.* John Hughes went there, so at one point the national perception of the teen experience was somewhat based on our high school. We were so giddy and power-bad, but the attitude changed. One night my friend and I were driving her Rabbit home from a party, and we'd both had too much to drink. I was leaning my head out of the passenger side, resting it there because the metal felt cool and nice. Then I noticed the parkway trees whizzing past my hair. I was like, "Shit! We're driving up on the grass!" That pretty much sobered us up. The whole summer euphoria sort of ended. **1998**

maxwell   When I was eleven, twelve, thirteen and growing up in East New York, Brooklyn, there would be fire-hydrant parties on my block. When it got hot, one of the kids would bust open a hydrant to make the water spray. I started it once, but I was the only one out there for a long while so I learned to stop it. We'd do it at times, like when the pool was closed or at three o'clock in the morning— when it was just one of those special summer nights where everybody just happened to be up really late even though it was a weeknight. The hottest days were when you could see rainbows and stuff. People would come out on their porch. All the kids ended up doing it and then you ended up always grabbin' one of them girls who were, like, completely dressed and throwin' them in. You know, I liked girls but I didn't understand the magnitude of what they totally represented. It was like, "Yeah, I like 'em. They're cute. They feel good." But in reality it was, "Yo, I'm gonna get in this water!" Plus, I wanted to see her T-shirt wet, too—let's be real about the reason why we were trying to get 'em wet. There were many hotties on the block definitely, but they were all older than I was. There wasn't that much traffic—some of the people would get their car all wet on the inside. Then, of course, the fire department would come and close it down. As I got older, there was a water shortage so we couldn't do it as much. **1997**

PUTMEIN, COACH

xercise, or watching others exercise, is a delightful way to free up the mind. America has its balls—base, foot and basket—while the rest of the world loves a good footie match. Other musicians prefer to free their minds (and their asses) with martial arts, yoga or a gory game of racquetball.

emmylou harris
Minor-league baseball is a good night out with friends and family. The parking is painless, the seats are cheap, and it's played on natural grass the way God intended. **1996**

darius rucker of HootieandtheBlowfish
I live and breathe for the Miami Dolphins. I have their emblem tattooed on my body. I don't ever want to meet Dan Marino because I don't think I'd be able to talk. **1995**

jay-z
Michael Jordan is the best, not only physically, but mentally he's light-years ahead of everybody. I think it's that [Chicago Bulls coach] Phil Jackson connection—Phil's over there burning sage in front of his locker and teaching him all of that Zen-master stuff. I read an article where he said he goes into a zone while he's playing a game. He finds this inner peace within himself even while he's exerting himself. He's just calm and mentally strong. I like the L.A. Lakers' youth and energy. Every time they on a fast break, they trying to break the rim. They don't know what they doin' in set play, but when they get open court, they tearin' it down. Shaquille O'Neal's not having it at all. Shaq don't care if nobody like him. He's not running for office. You gotta like that. He's got a tattoo on his arm that says AGAINST THE LAW. **1998**

busta rhymes
[The Seattle Sonics'] Gary Payton, [Minnesota Timberwolves'] Stephon Marbury, [Los Angeles Lakers'] Shaq—they my peeps. I got to respect how they play the sport. **1997**

cia soro of Whale
NHL Hockey. So masculine, so violent, so beautiful. **1998**

jim kerr of SimpleMinds
This is from someone who doesn't even eat meat, but I love boxing—the idea of being that strong and nimble and the fact that it's so corrupt and fucked up, as well. **1995**

eddie izzard
My favorite sport is football (with a round ball). I support England and a team in London called Crystal Palace. Crystal Palace are very good at losing, which pisses me off, but now we have a new owner so maybe our

future will be fantastic and we will conquer the English leagues, but I won't hold my breath for that. **1998**

shaun ryder of HappyMondays and BlackGrape

Football. Well, soccer to you. Manchester United all the way, all that's right. The only sport I really play, or ever really played, is football, soccer. You know, I've never been, like, Mr. Basketball, or Mr. Long Jump, or anything like 'at. **1996**

noel gallagher of Oasis

Soccer—as you people call it. I support the Manchester City football team. I try not to play myself because I'm not all that fit, if you know what I mean. Every time I get persuaded to play a game, I usually run out fast and fall over. **1995**

paul mcguigan of Oasis

Watching football [soccer] is my main hobby. Watching football, watching videos about football, reading about football and talking about football. That's pretty much all I care about. **1996**

ziggy marley Football [soccer] is my favorite sport. It's what we use

to get in shape, yeah. On the beach or anywhere we are. We go on the beach and play there, we play on the streets. That's the way Jamaica is—put two stones in the road and start playing. **1997**

coolio Night fishing's goodass fishing. If you get a good spot, you might

catch forty fish. You catch rock cod, perch, bass, all kinds of stuff. **1995**

michael hutchence of INXS

I never thought I would get into a martial art. But kick-boxing keeps you fit to start with, but now I'm possessed and do it every day. **1994**

dave mustaine of Megadeth

I've been particularly fond of martial arts for a while. I started when I was twelve doing Shorin-Ryu. When I was eighteen, I started doing Kung Fu San Soo. I've been doing Ukidokan for about seven years, and I recently started studying Songahm Tae Kwan Do. The last teacher that I taught with, I studied the whole system and learned it in nine months and got a black belt. After you've been doing

279

martial arts for that long, it's not really hard to learn all the fundamentals, you just need to learn the routines. They have a lot of different ranks and a lot of different styles, and the most important thing to me right now is how I parent my child, not how tough I am, it's how gentle I can be. It's a total dichotomy. You surrender to win. I ceased fighting everything and everyone and now my life has been peaceful. Being my teacher's Sensei was one of the highest honors of my life. You go through a lot of training and a lot of stuff, and you get to a period where, I mean, even if you pass all the tests, you still can be beneath the teacher. **1997**

tina weymouth of TalkingHeads and TomTomClub

I do Shao-lin Kenpo with my kids. It's very cool stuff. It makes you not want to fight, really. It's very centering. One of the things about karate and martial arts is that they make you work really hard on the chakra of the will. It's very important not to stop there but to go past, so you spend a lot of time centering on the heart chakra. Martial arts can do that, you can stay blocked at the will, as in willpower, which is right at your sternum, before you get to the heart chakra. Some people can become very mean and bad, powerful martial-arts masters, but they can be stopped from their true spiritual development. Like Rasputin, the mad monk. He had mastered himself clear through to the will chakra, but had no heart. That's not the way. **1996**

paula cole I do yoga. It's something you can do on the road wherever

you are. I do it in the morning or before I go to bed. It keeps me more humble and thankful and grateful. It also keeps my body much more pure. I think it's true that stiffness is death in the body. So you address wherever there is stiffness. You give attention and love to that part of the body that's suffering and you kind of heal wherever it is you need to heal. **1997**

m. doughty of SoulCoughing

Walking is the reason you live in New York. I'll walk from Rivington [Street, on the Lower East Side] all the way to Fifty-seventh Street. You sort of go into this trance and stay there. You wake up and you're on Eighty-eighth Street on the Upper West Side. All these rhythmic and linguistic patterns come up; that's when the best writing happens. **1998**

gwen stefani of NoDoubt

Swimming is the only sport I really like because you don't sweat. I used to be on the swim team in high school. It's neat. If you're in a race, you go up and down, in and out of the water. Every time you go under it's silent, and then your head comes up and people are screaming for you. It's really trippy and you can get in this really cool zone. **1996**

stone gossard of PearlJam

It's amazing to not be able to talk when you're scuba diving. It's totally outer space. Zero Gs, you're floating, you can fly. I've always been fascinated by fish, and in particular sharks. Any chance to see that is great. Plus, you get all puppety down there. You go down sixty or seventy feet and you start to get buzzed. It's a natural way to get high. It's the nitrogen. There's a little bit of nitrogen mixed in with your oxygen, and as you get deeper it gets compressed by the pressure and seeps into your bloodstream. It's like going to the dentist and getting a little shot of gas. It's pretty good. If you go deep enough, it's like getting drunk. You don't want to do that. **1997**

jerry garcia of theGratefulDead

I still have that desire to change my consciousness, and in the last four years, I've gotten real seriously into scuba diving. . . . Scuba diving is like an invisible workout; you're not conscious of the work you're doing. You focus on what's out there, on the life and the beauty of things, and it's incredible. So that's what I do when the Grateful Dead aren't working—I'm in Hawaii, diving. **1991**

bob seger

I've got a forty-five-foot sailboat and I single-hand it on the Great Lakes. I take my family, too, but my wife doesn't like it as much as I do, so I learned well enough so that I can single it myself. I like crossing over to Canada and back and forth. It's very nice. I take friends, too; we have fun. The band goes with me sometimes. I run all the time, too. I ran five hundred miles last year. I'm going for seven hundred this year. I've been runnin' all my life, it's not like a hobby. I run two miles a day. I'm going to try and do two miles a day, average, this year. I even have a treadmill on the road, in my dressing room, so I run two a day on that, and then I run outside on the off day. **1996**

billie joe armstrong of GreenDay

I suck at skateboarding. But it keeps my mind off the music for a while. I've got a real Max Schaaf board and my buddy who's got a ramp is teaching me. I've never done it before in my whole life, and I've literally been doing it for two weeks. So I've been skating a ramp—one of those half pipes that go from side to side. There's a five-foot part, a seven-foot part and an eleven-foot vert part. I can roll back and forth, but that's it. **1998**

chris ballew of thePresidentsoftheUnitedStatesofAmerica

Frisbee is the greatest cooperative aerobic sport that there is. It's not competitive, the point is to connect with the other person, and get the Frisbee to them. It's good low-impact running around. You immediately get your heartbeat up, and there's that great thrill of throwing a huge, long throw or bouncing it along the pavement and making contact. It's got everything that's great about football, which is making a pass, and everything that's great about basketball, which is accuracy. You don't need a lot of equipment and it's not competitive. **1996**

matthew sweet I've been playing racquetball every day. I like it for
the violence. **1995**

DIG IF YOU WILL, A PICTURE

Pictures, paintings, photographs, buildings—musical artists need something to look at, don't they? Some even dare to dream, taking pencils to paper and clicking cameras in their spare time.

luther vandross
I love Cubism and Georges Braque or Pablo Picasso. I recently sold a five-foot oil canvas by David Hockney called *Two Men in a Shower*. I had loaned it to the Los Angeles County Museum of Art and the Metropolitan Museum in New York and also the Tate Gallery in London—Hockney was the first living artist to have an exhibition at the Tate. **1997**

chris robinson of theBlackCrowes
Egon Schiele's nudes are so erotic to me —but sickly. Insanely depressing. **1995**

justine frischmann of Elastica
Notre-Dame-du-Haute, Ronchamp, France, designed by Le Corbusier—I think it's my favorite building. It's basically a modern take on a church. I love concrete when it's used properly, and this combines concrete with stained glass. **1995**

moby
The Empire State Building is the most remarkable building in New York City. It's the linchpin of Manhattan. When you fly in, the World Trade Center's towers are bigger, but they're way down on the end of Manhattan, and they're not that architecturally dramatic—just two big sticks in the air. They're cool, but the Empire State Building even looks like Manhattan, stuck on end. I've been walking around Chelsea at night lately, around Twenty-eighth Street and Sixth Avenue, looking up at it at about eleven at night. It's just so dramatic, actually, before the lights go off. It's just so huge. If it's huge by our standards, imagine how people in 1931 felt about it. Far and away the most remarkable building in Manhattan. With low cloud cover, you'll look up, it'll be obscured, then the wind will blow and it will be revealed for just a second, and all the clouds around it will be glowing. A friend and I had a theory that the hole in the ozone was actually caused by the tip of the Empire State. Whenever I leave Manhattan and go to Brooklyn, I'm always reminded of how looking at Manhattan is sometimes more dramatic than being in it. The Empire State Building is the same: In some ways it's nicer to look at it than be in it. I've been in it and you have no concept of how dramatic it is. It's just a mundane office building. **1997**

lenny kravitz
My favorite style of architecture and furnishings is art nouveau. My world would be designed by Gaudí. **1993**

john lennon
I admire Fluxus, a New York–based group of artists founded by George Macuinas. I really think what they do is beautiful and important. . . . All I ever learned in art school was about van Gogh and stuff; they didn't teach me anything about anybody who is alive now, and they never taught me about Marcel Duchamp, which I despised them for. Yoko has taught me about Duchamp and what he did, which is just out of this world. He would just put a bike wheel on display and he would say, "This is art, you cunts." He wasn't Dalí; Dalí was all right, but he's like Mick [Jagger], you know. I love Dalí, but fuckin' Duchamp was spot on. He was the first one to do that, just take an object from the street and put his name on it, and say this is art because I say it is. . . . I admire Andy Warhol's work . . . because he is an original great and he is in so much pain. He's got his fame, he's got his own cinema and all of that. **1971**

kevin martin of Candlebox
Andy Warhol—a genius. I like his Campbell's Soup cans. He was a warped human being who had everyone so caught up in what he was doing. **1994**

Candlebox: Dave Crusen, Barti Martin, Kevin Martin and Peter Klett (from left)
(Danny Clinch/Maverick)

fred schneider of theB-52's

The Dada period was when all of a sudden everything fell apart and things—sculpture, art, photography—had a sense of humor and took on a strange new direction that was much more shocking than anything before or since. Once I started reading about that, it was hard for me to write serious poetry, and Dada was just so out there and amazing. I tried to apply that to my writing. You let whatever come out, you know—might be good, might be trash. It helped me get through a final thing for a creative-writing class. I decided to do a book of poetry and I just wrote anything that came into my mind, and the teacher said, "This is so different, and I don't really know what to say, but I know you're serious." I got an A. I had to read it in class, though. One person laughed and everyone else just sort of sat there looking at me, like, "What on earth?" They all wrote short stories and like serious poems about, you know, horses running through the desert and junk like that. **1996**

m. doughty of SoulCoughing

Sekou Sundiata is a poet who teaches at the New School in New York. I was in a class of his with Ani DiFranco. He really squeezed some amazingly good, honest stuff from people who were kind of, like, whatever. I remember his saying, "You're trying to make this poem a house, but the poem is saying, 'I'm not a house, I'm a bird.'" Maybe that sounds pretentious, but it meant something to me at the time. **1998**

graham nash of Crosby, StillsandNash

[Photographer] Richard Throssel excites me. A Cree Indian adopted into the Crow tribe, Throssel's gotten much closer to the Indian spirit than a white man could. **1979**

tanya donelly of ThrowingMuses and Belly

Frida Kahlo's paintings are very spiritual, rich and full. Kahlo had a real sense of herself from the second she was born. **1994**

ana da silva of theRaincoats

I bought a calendar of Jean-Michel Basquiat's paintings, which have inspired me to write. I love the sense of freedom and joy in the way he painted—the hard-edged issues he expressed, the humanity of it all. **1996**

herb alpert
I paint professionally and sculpt, as well. I've been painting for twenty-five years and had shows in different parts of the world. I'm an abstract expressionist—I do everything from four- or five-inch paintings to twelve- and fifteen-footers. As for sculpting, I was a great fan of Henry Moore—I guess he was representational—and the pieces I work on have soft edges, as opposed to ones it looks like you could get impaled on. Mine you can touch. They're friendly. Most of them are bronze, but right now I'm experimenting with cement and plaster. My sculptures are objects, they're forms, and there's a story in them. Part of the attraction is that the viewer gets to participate in that story. But there are definite suggestions as to what it's about. And sometimes they're not too subtle. I've got one that's an obvious cock and a half. My wife calls him Richard. **1997**

andy partridge of XTC
The Rijksmuseum in Amsterdam has something I like just completely for the wrong reason. There's a big glass case and this beautiful Seventeenth-Century fort that's being besieged. They have the little men besieging it and the cannons and the ladders and the hooks and all of that sort of stuff, and I happened to notice that all of the little figures are converted U.S. Confederate figurines. **1998**

ozzy osbourne
I do a lot of abstract artwork. I like doing kind of crazy, very brightly colored artwork, though not on canvas. Abstract stuff on a sketch pad and very brightly colored freaky pictures. It's just personal, you know. I've only given about four or five away. I've got so many unfinished; I'll start one and I'll leave it and I'll start another one. I find it very relaxing, you know. It's better than watching CNN and this fucking Bosnian bullshit on television all day long. **1995**

art garfunkel
Lately I've been doing this thing that is very unlike me: I have fallen in love with a certain painter and I want to buy this guy. Do you know who Adolphe Willliam Bouguereau is? He's a Nineteenth-Century realistic painter, very romantic, loves to paint angels, and I have fallen in love with one of his paintings, *L'Amour au Papillon*, in the Sotheby's catalog. It's one angel, he's fairly large. I call him an angel but he's actually a cherubic boy, kind of like my son, but he has wings. He's sitting on a stone fence, picking a butterfly off of his arm. The painting technique is great. Bouguereau is, to me, like finding the Beatles before they happened—something about this group is really good. **1997**

chris whitley

William L. Hawkins is this outsider painter from the South I've really dug. He died in '90 at ninety-four. He's a dude who started painting when he was like eighty. He used paint that he'd find in Dumpsters and he put his name and birthdate on every painting. After he was "discovered" in the Eighties he started using real paints on masonite. His work is rough and fucked up, but inspired. It's pragmatic, but I like it. He probably started making money toward the end of his life, but probably never valued it. There are quite a few books on him, too. He's one of the most-known untrained artists in the last couple of years. He's really art, not just some curio thing. It's cool stuff. **1997**

emmylou harris

Henri Cartier-Bresson's photographs—in black and white, he captures all the shades of the human condition. A few years ago when he was still alive, there was an article about him in *The New Yorker*. I first came across him when I was in college at a collection called "The Family of Man"; it was all black and white and really extraordinary. Pictures of life, of the world, from all around the world. **1996**

lisa loeb

René Magritte combines elements of realism that play with your mind, like having a daytime house with a nighttime sky. It doesn't really mean anything, but it's fun to look at. **1997**

nina persson of theCardigans

I've been photographing for about a year, so I'm just setting up the darkroom. I enjoy it, but people steal my stuff all the time. My favorite camera just got stolen in Mexico City and customs officers picked it up. But now I have a new one, so that's all right. There have to be people in the pictures somehow, either intentional portraits or candid. I like photography and film. I like new art—do you call it abstract installation?—and video art. There's this American artist Cindy Sherman. She had an exhibition here, in our hometown actually. I went to see it a lot of times, I just couldn't stop looking at the pictures, they were so good. **1997**

michael stipe of R.E.M.

I love photography. I photographed children for a long time. And buildings . . .
I'm beginning to sound like David Byrne. **1992**

R.E .M.: Mike Mills, Peter Buck and Michael Stipe (from left) (Anton Corbijn)

I'VEGOTATVEYE

elevision has it all: *pointed satire, bizarro entertainment, educational tidbits and plenty of mindless garbage. Whether it's* The Simpsons, The X-Files, *Carl Sagan's* Cosmos *or infomercials, there is something for everyone.*

stevie nicks
One of my favorite shows is *Star Trek: The Next Generation*. I don't usually like science fiction. But I particularly like Jean-Luc Picard. When everything's closing in on me, I can go to my living room at home, put on my surround sound, and the whole room sounds like we're flying. I have the *Enterprise* at my fingertips. **1994**

d'arcy of SmashingPumpkins
I'm a big *Star Trek* fan, but I'm not into the conventions or the ears or anything like that, I just like it. That and *The X-Files*. You know what, I'm surprised they put that on the air, because all the theories that they have on there are so close, almost exactly like all these theories that people have anyway about aliens and the government and stuff. I think it's gonna get people really freaked out. It's so well done and a lot of the stuff that's in there is based on real cases and it's really freaky. It's gonna push a lot of people right over the edge, let me tell you. But I enjoy it. I can't watch it before I go to sleep sometimes. The cinematography is awesome and Fox Mulder is just great. The only thing that's dumb about it is what's-her-face, Dana Scully. Episode after episode of freaky things that she sees and she's still skeptical. You want to slap her. Not her, but the writers anyway. C'mon! It's getting ridiculous. She's not that stupid. **1996**

fred schneider of theB-52's
The Invaders was a sci-fi show about emotionless aliens who come to take over human beings. I like it better than *Star Trek*. It was really popular in the Sixties. They showed it again on the Sci-Fi Channel and it held up just as well. It ran in color. There's only one guy who knows about them, he gets people to, you know, fight them and then eventually I guess they had to throw in a few nice aliens, because these people didn't care who they zapped, women, men, grannies, grandpas. Then if they got caught, they'd take some sort of pill and they left no trace when they died. They just disintegrated. They had a minimovie, showed it two nights in a row on the Sci-Fi Channel. It was *Invaders* updated. It wasn't bad. I must say they had some good writers. Really great creepy music by Dominic Frontiere, who did a lot of soundtracks. I think it was a Quinn Martin production. They stopped showing it on the Sci-Fi Channel; I'm so pissed. You know, I'd gladly let them have the Family Channel, because Pat Robertson's on it. We should get everybody to say, "We don't want this." Everybody's bitchin' about censorship, well, let's censor them! **1996**

john curley of theAfghanWhigs

I have cable TV and there's, like, sixty channels. At night, it's just crap. The best thing on a lot of times is the Christian channel. It's the most entertaining, outrageous thing on TV after two in the morning. **1996**

david yow of theJesusLizard

I like some public television. Things like black gospel shows are pretty amazing. Like where they really, really get down and there's, like, a piano and a drummer and a preacher and they're just really fuckin' lettin' loose. I like that. **1996**

noel gallagher of Oasis

John Cleese is just hilarious. The Monty Python stuff is a big favorite of mine. Especially the killer-nuns skit and the Ministry of Silly Walks. **1995**

pat smear of theGerms and FooFighters

I love HBO. Chris Rock's comedy special was the funniest thing I've ever seen. *Paradise Lost: The Child Murders at Robin Hood Hills* was a disturbing documentary, and the Bowe vs. Golota postfight fight . . . whatever! **1996**

jakob dylan of theWallflowers

Flowbee Infomercial—fascinating late-night entertainment. A do-it-yourself haircut kit for those of us who don't qualify for admittance into beauty parlors. **1993**

tanya donelly of ThrowingMuses and Belly

Kids in the Hall—because they keep me laughing, and that helps prevent cancer—I think! **1994**

chris robinson of theBlackCrowes

I love *The Larry Sanders Show*. Rip Torn warms my heart being the manipulative, evil show producer. If I didn't have Torn and *Larry Sanders*, it would be ugly around here. **1995**

mix master mike of InvisiblSkratchPiklz and theBeastieBoys

Ultraman, a Sixties Japanese TV show, where this guy holds up a capsule that turns him into Ultraman. Monsters come out of the water, tearin' shit up, so they call

Ultraman to save the day. The light on his chest would blink when his energy got low, so he'd only have so much time to save the day and fly back to space. It's a trip. **1998**

billie joe armstrong of GreenDay

Cartoons have gotten so good lately, but Bugs Bunny—those are classic. *The Ren and Stimpy Show* has definitely set the standard of the new raunchy cartoons out now. *Beavis and Butt-Head* is like my childhood passing in front of my eyes. **1998**

les claypool of Primus

They've just colorized the old black-and-white cartoons of *Popeye*. They were great and now they're completely ruined. On the Cartoon Network that's all they'll show. The old ones had all this depth to them, but the colorized ones are all flat and boring. I damn Ted Turner for doing that. It's like taking a '57 Chevy and putting air bags in it. **1996**

moby
The Simpsons is like the *Economist* of animation. Except for that show, we don't have any passionate, politically engaged satire anymore. It's easy to poke cheap shots, but to actually do aware, socially active satire is a rarity. **1997**

jay-z
Seinfeld, that's number one. *The Simpsons*, crazy—that is *not* made for kids. *SportsCenter* on ESPN. If I'm not watching basketball games, I watch *Seinfeld*, *The Simpsons* and I always catch *SportsCenter* at two in the morning. Puts me right to sleep. **1998**

ozzy osbourne
Thank God the fucking O.J. Simpson thing ended. You know, at one point, I said to myself, "I hope I don't die before the verdict, because I'll be really pissed off." **1996**

stephan jenkins of ThirdEyeBlind

If you had Daft Punk's "Around the World" mixed with the Weather Channel and shots of the invasion of Normandy going on a tape loop, I'd never turn my TV off. In fact, I want to start a TV channel that's that. It would go over really well. Just show weather, floating through as a background, and that grainy footage of bombers overhead, which is kind of a guy thing, but that's what guys want to see. And then "Around the World" would go on every couple of hours. **1998**

rupaul *Style With Elsa Klensch* on CNN, as always, top of the list. She is the best. I speak fluent television—grew up on it, and regular TV bores me. I like public-access shows. They're so raw and unslick. I think I've just gotten too old for MTV. I can't watch it. There's no music and it's all these shows and all these fast cuts of things. It gives me a headache to watch it. But, you know, it must appeal to some fourteen-year-old white kid in Missouri. **1997**

carnie wilson *Ellen*—she's just so fucking funny. And VH1's *Pop-Up Video*—they did one on Wilson Phillips for "Hold On." It was so funny. They were talking about, like, condoms holding on, and all the different names for Carnie: Carrie, Carly, Corny, Carniasada. I kind of dug that. **1997**

gwen stefani of **NoDoubt**

We used to be religious watchers of *Melrose Place* and *Beverly Hills 90210*. But since we went on tour, I gave it up because I figured if I was going to miss any of them I would be really depressed. We were offered a chance to be on *Beverly Hills*, to be the band on it. To be able to do it, to hang out with those *Beverly Hills* kids would be so fun. We're not gonna do it—that's so cheesy. But I've gotta have the fax of the offer to put it in my scrapbook. It was gonna be us playing for the—what's the buff guy's name with the blond hair? Steve Sanders, fraternity guy—it's his twenty-first birthday—yeah right, he's, like, probably thirty-five. It's a bunch of sorority and fraternity blah, blah, blah. I was laughing so hard when I read it. **1996**

grant lee phillips of **GrantLeeBuffalo**

If I were the Unabomber, Ed McMahon's home would be number one on my list. For wasting trees, wasting my time. He's actually probably a fine gentleman. Him and Dick Clark. I like the part of *American Bandstand* when he sits up there with the audience. I don't think he would get away with that today. Not with today's youth being so pierced and aggressive. Actually, it's pretty cool how he makes a point of introducing everyone in the band. **1996**

chris ballew of **thePresidentsoftheUnitedStatesofAmerica**

Cosmos, Carl Sagan—that TV series kinda ruined and enriched my life when I was fourteen. It completely shattered a lot of preconceptions I had about the universe. **1997**

"weird al" yankovic

My all-time favorite is *Police Squad*. They only made six episodes, but they're classic. In fact, that was the reason I was in the *Naked Gun* series. Robert K. Weiss produced both, and he's an old friend of mine. When I heard about the movie, I grovelled and said, "You've got to put me in the movie someplace. I'll get coffee for the crew. I'll be in the crowd scenes. I have to be somewhere in this movie." He told the guys and they wrote me in. The scene in the airport, I come off the plane. **1996**

PLEASEDTOMEETME

Musicians often say things about themselves that average people just can't get away with. In fact, a lot of these things, if uttered by a stranger at a cocktail party, would cause everyone to run screaming from the room. Then again, who can refute Paul McCartney's claim that the Beatles were the greatest? Anyone?

stephen malkmus of Pavement

I'm a pretty icy performer. I'm nice at the bottom of my heart, but I like the tough-love, bitchy-performer thing. People say you're arrogant and mean. It's not true. It's part of the act. **1997**

adam duritz of CountingCrows

Fortunately, I don't get stage fright. I just get rest-of-life fright. **1994**

tori amos You can't control your popularity; I know I'm an acquired taste—I'm anchovies. And not everybody wants those hairy little things. If I was potato chips, I could go a lot more places, but I'm not. **1998**

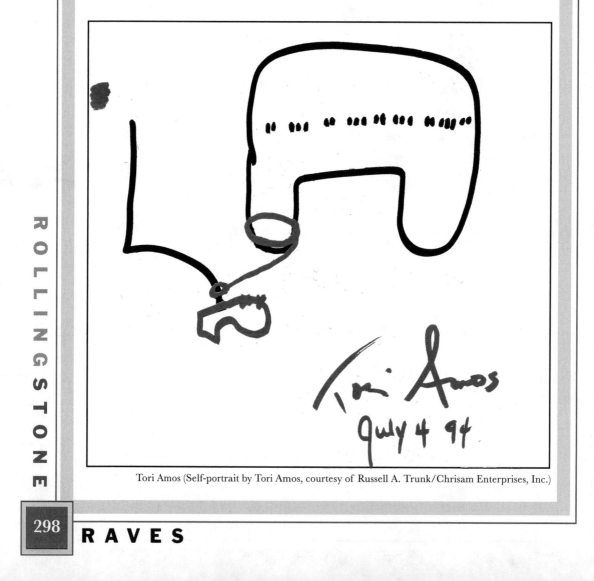

Tori Amos (Self-portrait by Tori Amos, courtesy of Russell A. Trunk/Chrisam Enterprises, Inc.)

johnny cash
You know my album cover [*American Recordings*] with the two dogs on it? I've given them names. Their names are Sin and Redemption. Sin is the black one with the white stripe; Redemption is the white one with the black stripe. That's kind of the theme of that album, and I think it says it for me, too. When I was really bad, I was not all bad. When I was really good, I could never be all good. There would always be that black streak going through. **1994**

steven tyler of Aerosmith
I'm kind of like Howard Stern. I confront people right away. It's gotten me in trouble. But it can be beneficial because people know what I'm thinking about. I let 'em know where I'm coming from. I kind of like that about me. **1994**

eddie van halen of VanHalen
I'm just a jeans-and-T-shirt normal guy. People that really know me say, "Boy, you're a boring asshole." **1998**

john lennon
I don't bother so much about the others' songs. For instance, I don't give a damn about how "Something" is doing in the charts—I watch "Come Together" [the flip side] because that's my song. **1970**

david bowie
I already consider myself responsible for a whole new school of pretension. Really. I'm quite serious about that. The only thing that seems to shock anybody anymore is something that's pretentious or kitsch. You have to hit people on the head, and pretension does the trick. It shocks as much as a Dylanesque thing did ten years ago. **1976**

noel gallagher of Oasis
I'm in the best band, and I've just written the best album. So as far as I'm concerned, everybody can fuck right off. Those other bands are not even in a position to string my guitar at the moment. Fucking wankers, all of 'em. **1996**

method man of Wu-TangClan
Tical 2000: Judgment Day is my second LP, right. T2. That's Tical Tical. Two thousand is two words that begin with T. T.T. You got Method Man—M.M. Millennium starts and ends with M. M.M. M is also one thousand in Roman numerals; two of them make two thousand. I'm just perfect with this LP right now. My sec-

ond LP, two thousand. The millennium is approaching, too, that's even better, man. People *need* this album right now. **1998**

paul mccartney
I've been told I'm the biggest Beatles fan of all. I'm proud of what we did. We were a great band. Name me one better. **1994**

yoko ono
No, I didn't know any of [the Beatles's music when I met John Lennon]. I had heard about the band, the mopheads or whatever. I knew that they were making a big impact on people, like a social phenomenon. I just never got around to listening to their music. **1992**

cher
I am multiphrenic. When you see *Cher*, it's not me. It's something I invented. . . . People thought I was sleeping with the entire Mormon Tabernacle Choir, but I was staying home watching TV. But people don't want to know that. They want to read that *Cher* has a wild life. They believe what they want to believe. . . . I wanted to be invited to wonderful parties. I wanted to be famous, but I didn't really know how to do anything. I had no skills. I couldn't even call information for my mother, but I still *wanted to be famous*. I even had my autograph down, the same way I do it today, when I was twelve. **1984**

nick cave
I have a certain way with words when it comes to violence. I just enjoy ruminating over the details. **1996**

robert smith of theCure
Is there a burning question no one's ever asked me? Okay. "Why are you so scarily good?" Well, it's just a natural thing. It's in the blood. It just happened that way. **1996**

sean lennon
I like to talk. On every report card I had, the teacher would say, "Sean likes to hear himself talk." **1998**

joni mitchell
I've always had a different perspective—an artist is a sideliner, not a joiner; they must have a certain clarity and depth, which is burdensome and really inconvenient for fun. **1998**

tricky
No one's as honest as me, and no one's as brave. There's not a better lyric writer in the world. I want to change people's lives, really. **1995**

pete townshend

I wanted my popularity to be real popularity. I wanted the real me to be appreciated, not the performing me. I didn't particularly want to be loved for the way I played the guitar. The way I played guitar was part of my angry side, my rebellious side. What my audience loved me most for was something that was only a small part of me. **1987**

van morrison

Sometimes it's an experience, and sometimes it's just a gig. Sometimes you get halfway there, sometimes you get all the way there. It's never the same. It's unpredictable. You work from the chaos. You work the material. There's no set pattern. What I do is just as much a mystery to me as it is to you. **1990**

whitney houston

People who go out and buy me, buy me for *me*. Furthermore, I came out first anyways [*laughs*]—anybody that's gonna come has definitely got to come after. They don't say I sound like Mariah Carey, they say Mariah Carey sounds like *me*, you dig what I'm saying? **1993**

foxy brown

Everybody has her gimmick. Lauryn [Hill] is very positive. Missy [Elliot] and Da Brat are sorta fun and hardcore. Then you have Foxy, who is, like, sex. I don't think my shit is a gimmick—I think it's real. It's what I am. Every woman has a Foxy Brown in her, meaning just that bad bitch who ain't takin' no shit. But if someone thinks it's a gimmick, you know what my motto is? "Just gimme my check." **1998**

tom petty

I didn't get into this to be a pinup. I wanted to be taken seriously as far as writing songs, making music. The other thing limits your run, really. Some people are so good-looking they can't help it. But I'm certainly not saddled with that problem. **1995**

cyndi lauper

Me, I always wanted to make world music—to say something that's worth sayin' and really touch humanity. That's why I'm here. There's a wonderful place that you go when you sing, there's a really good feeling. And it's wonderful to reach out and touch someone with it, because they touch you back. And sometimes that's worth the price of beans. **1984**

joey ramone of theRamones

We've always been our own breed of band. We concocted a unique sound and style all our own, a trademark. That's what everybody tries to achieve, but so few really do. I guess since the inception of rock & roll, there's only a handful of bands with such a distinct sound and style that you catch instantly; you know when you're hearing Led Zeppelin, you know when you're hearing the Beatles, and you know when you're hearing . . . the Ramones. For our style, it has always been "less is more" and that rock & roll was supposed to be fun. **1994**

neil diamond

I don't fit in. But you could put me in *any* show and I wouldn't fit in. You could put me in a rock show and I wouldn't fit in. You could put me in a country show and I wouldn't fit in. You could put me onstage with Sinatra and I wouldn't fit in. I just do *not* fit in . . . I'm sorry. I apologize to everybody. But I never tried to fit in, because that meant conforming what I could write or what I could do to a certain set of rules. . . . The last group I remember joining was the Boy Scouts, and *they* threw me out for nonpayment of dues. So I suppose you could say that I've always gone my own way. **1988**

thomas bangalter of DaftPunk

Our point of view is getting music to be more democratic. We just want to keep a low profile, where maybe the music will be the star itself, not us. We don't like showing our faces on cover art. It's just that everybody is afraid to break the rules, but we're not. We don't care about saying it's us. There's that image, by wearing masks we can keep control and say, hey, we're not big-headed. Maybe people will be thinking we're pop stars, and this is some fucking gimmick. Maybe they'll be impressed by the gimmick, but we don't want them to be impressed by ourselves, you know, that physical description. **1997**

michael stipe of R.E.M.

I have this reputation for being an incredibly serious person. And in interviews, I'm desperately trying to think of really good answers. So I come across as this reverent curmudgeon. But when I get in front of TV cameras, I come across like a chipmunk on speed. Cameras make me really animated. But it's weird being a media figure, to be recognized everywhere by somebody. It's like you walk into someplace and you're playing a game—it's a matter of time until someone whispers to someone else, they look at you and then whisper to someone else. **1992**

liam howlett of the Prodigy

So many people fall into the trap of making music written on computers sound mechanical. I try to have a certain amount of organicness to make it funk and roll more. Like "Breathe"—we met a death-metal band this weekend that does a cover of it. When you listen to it, it *could* be drums, a bass and a guitar. I don't want to bring the techno, mechanical side out in my music, I'm more into the roots of hip-hop and the breaks—that's where *I'm* from. **1997**

The Prodigy: Liam Howlett, Keith Flint, Maxim, Leeroy Thornhill (from left)
(Steve Gullick/XL Recordings)

tina turner

Mick [Jagger] is, and always has been, a *boy*. A boy that *I'd* be. Now, if I was male and you said, "Who would you want to be like?" I guess I could say I'd want to dance *better* than Mick. But I like how he does it. He's naughty; he's got a great boy inside of that man's body—no matter how old he gets, no matter what is happening to him visually. We're not together often, but when we are, it's as if we have known each other all of our lives. We laugh, we play—it's almost like kids, you know? **1997**

sting

There's no one else who sings like me. They might sing better than me, but no one sings exactly like me. My voice sticks out on the radio by a mile. And as long as I have this voice, what I do is original. **1988**

fred schneider of the B-52's

"Happy Birthday" is my favorite song. As long as it's being sung to me. **1996**

DON'TLOOKBACKINANGER

Memories light the corners of musicians' minds— when they have any at all, that is. When thinking back to the early days, some artists get misty: Steven Tyler, for instance, fondly recalls getting down in the Seventies. David Bowie, on the other hand, suffers from amnesia. Can it be that it was all so simple then, or has time rewritten every line?

steven tyler of Aerosmith

I'm still bummed I didn't get all the sex I could have had in the Seventies. The irony is I probably got more than I remember because I was having blackouts. But we never zeroed in on "Wow, let's get blow jobs on the bus." That was more for the road crew. We were more interested in the finer blends of cocaine from a shipment of dates that came in on the back of some camel with the stamp of a half-moon on it and the star of Lebanon, which, by the way, was laced with opium. We were real connoisseurs. That was much more important to me than some girl with big tits. **1990**

david bowie

Incredible losses of memory. Whole *chunks* of my life. I can't remember, for instance, any—*any*—of 1975. Not one minute! **1983**

bonnie raitt

When I got sober seven years ago, I also changed my diet, and it's really affected my energy. I never get sick. I've been healthy and less than healthy, and healthy's much better. Less than healthy's more fun, but healthy is better. **1994**

don henley of theEagles

We were deliberately minimalist, to a fault probably. We were accused by one critic of loitering onstage—which pissed us off then. Now we can laugh about it. That's what's great about being forty—that shit's funny now. **1990**

neil young

[Stephen Stills and I are] like brothers, you know? We love each other, and we hate each other. We resent each other, but we love playing together. I see and hear so much in Stephen that I'm frustrated when it isn't on record or something. There have been a lot of frustrations through our whole lives with each other, but there's also been a lot of great music. He continuously blows my mind with the ideas that he has for my songs. He's one of the greatest musicians I've ever met in my life. Great singer. Incredible songwriter. **1988**

beck

When I was living in Los Angeles and I had started playing guitar, I carried it everywhere. I was ready for any sudden jamboree that may befall me. There weren't too many happening, though. I used to practice down at Lafayette Park near where I used to live when I was a kid, and all the Salvadoran guys would be playing soccer nearby. I mostly practiced because where I lived was a one-bedroom kind of thing and a lot of us slept in there. So I'd go down to this park. I'd be practicing a Lead Belly song or something and the Salvadoran guys would be shaking their heads. Once in a while, a ball would sail over my head. I did that in New York, too, when I lived there. People always requested James Taylor songs and stuff, while I was steeping myself in some obscure Jimmie Rodgers song or a Delta blues song. They wanted to hear "Paradise City." It was hard not to feel defeated at the onset of my musical endeavors. Later on I busked. That's what being a successful street performer boils down to: "Hey Jude." Over and over. **1996**

john wozniak of MarcyPlayground

Back in the late Eighties and the early Nineties, "alternative" was just a bin in the record store. Back when I was buying records, it was a little bin in the corner. **1998**

art garfunkel I started playing our first album, the *Wednesday Morning*

album, and there's these sulky tunes which are just two voices and one guitar; I forgot how close we were and I had a very strong, very positive reaction. "Gee, these guys were breathing together." And I forgot that. It makes me feel that time, like geology, each strata of terrain covers over the past, you forget, you don't really see what's underneath unless you go digging. I forgot that we were remarkably tight in our day. And it was full of affection, you could not get that close to two people interpreting the song the same way and breathing together and singing with the same tonal sound, if there wasn't love. The word affection comes to mind. You feel like, "What an affectionate, sweet friendship these guys had because they really listened intimately to each other's vocal production." It was amazing. Then comes the rest of life. It makes that time an idyllic phase rather than a way of life. **1998**

ian mcculloch of EchoandtheBunnymen

I think if we had come out in 1990, we would have been a lot bigger. Instead, we were fighting the whole decade [the Eighties]. You know, there was so much crap there. We did have a reputation for being awkward and particularly coming over here the first few times, just telling everybody they were idiots—but a lot of them were. We did try and kind of do things differently and not be like all them other people that wanted to be stadium bands. So, I think our timing didn't help. The positive side of it is that we were burning light. Beacons. For me there are two meanings. That we have shone so very, very brightly and that we continue to emit. **1995**

susanna hoffs of theBangles

It was irritating in the early days particularly that people, the world, some journalists, or whatever, viewed us as a novelty because we were four women playing music together. I had so many role models all through my childhood who were female musicians. From singer/songwriters like Joni Mitchell and Bonnie Raitt and Carole King to the great vocalists of the Sixties like Dusty Springfield, Dionne Warwick and Petula Clark. We always thought it was kinda funny that we were always compared to the Go-Go's. Even though we loved the Go-Go's, it was just that the comparison was to another all-girl band. The old thing, like, they play pretty good for chicks. We got a lot of that in the early days. But we always thought of ourselves as a garage band, so we were determined to just do our thing and nothing was going to stop us. **1997**

Susanna Hoffs of the Bangles (Self-portrait by Susanna Hoffs, courtesy of Russell A. Trunk/Chrisam Enterprises, Inc.)

IKNOWTHISMUCHISTRUE

Wisdom is a hard-earned virtue. It falls from the lips of kings and fools, sages and babes, often heard and often unheeded. Confucius says, "The truly wise see wisdom all around, but always separate the rice from the stalk." We advise taking a grain of salt with the following rice.

david bowie John Lennon once said to me, "Look, it's *very* simple—say what you mean, make it rhyme and put a backbeat to it." And he was right: "Instant karma's gonna get you," boom. I keep comin' back to that these days. He was right, man. There is no more than that. There *is no more.* **1983**

johnny cash I think I had one voice lesson. The teacher told me not to take any more because it might affect my delivery. **1973**

k.d. lang I was grumbling about having to do a show, and this drummer said to me, "That's why you're out here; that's why you have to do interviews, why you have to ride the bus. Being onstage is the only moment of solace in your whole life, so turn it around—hate the interviews, hate riding the bus, hate the business, but love the stage." And ever since that day, it's been different for me. **1997**

mick jagger of **theRollingStones**
I don't think the lyrics are that important. I remember when I was very young, I read an article about Fats Domino which has really influenced me. He said, "You should never sing the lyrics out very clearly." **1968**

dick dale I live in the high desert, two thousand feet above Palm Springs, up in the mountains, where all the Indians and all the gold miners lived. All the big rockers come out to get a cranial enema. Clear your brain. Come out here to flush out your brain with silence. I've got a saying: "Wherever you go in life is where you're at. If you fall in a bucket of shit, tell yourself it's perfume, because you might have to stay there awhile." **1996**

busta rhymes Yeah, man, when I first signed my contract, December 12, 1989, I was seventeen years old, with a lot of money; we signed a six-figure deal. I was chillin'. Buyin' all types of clothes. Fuck class. I just wanted to be fly every day in school. And that wasn't the right way to be or no shit, but that's just how I was on it. You get caught up in the hype that you're gonna be on TV and on radio and paid for doin' shows and gettin' paid for little ideas you come up with in your bedroom. That feelin' is more powerful than anything else. When you're in that little age group, everything's like *Fantasy Island* to you and shit. That was one of the best moments for me, word up. Didn't have to ask Mom for nothin' for a minute. **1997**

fred schneider of theB-52's

I have several closets just filled with vinyl. There's thousands and thousands. It's taken over. But they're organized. I like a lot of the new CDs and all that, but I always like getting things on vinyl. It's cheaper! Get the vinyl version of a new CD and it's, like, six bucks cheaper. **1996**

d'arcy of SmashingPumpkins

You see, I have this thing, I know the meaning of my life. My purpose here on this earth. It's to learn to accept people, because I'm always forced, submerged into situations where I'm surrounded by people who I thought that I hated or did hate, and I'm forced into this situation until I learn to like them. Every time I say something bad about somebody, I always end up in a situation with them. So I have to be very careful about what I say. **1997**

sinéad o'connor

My best advice was from myself: to leave school and become a singer. I wish I'd listened to a teacher of mine who said, when "Nothing Compares 2 U" went to Number One, not to forget to leave the party before they all get drunk and start fighting. **1997**

tommy lee of MötleyCrüe

I love playing, so I hardly call it work. All the time, I'm looking up and thanking whoever it is up there that's responsible for where I'm at today and going, man, you know what, I love my life. I see so many people complaining about what they do for a living and I just go, "Man, don't fucking do it then." Life is too short, bro, to be unhappy doing what you don't want to be doing. I'm a lucky man. There's plenty of opportunity out there, that's for sure. **1997**

tina weymouth of TalkingHeads and TomTomClub

We always tell each other to get nervous before we go onstage. It's such a humiliating experience that you might as well just go for the whole feeling. It's terribly humiliating to go in front of people as this ordinary person trying to get across your music—you just have to psyche yourself. **1996**

wayne coyne of theFlamingLips

I like to sit around and talk and fuck with people, see what's going on. Everybody else would be glad to turn on the TV in the van and sleep. It's rare that you can get five people trapped in a room for ten hours at a time. You can get into some in-depth conversations, you know. I think it's fun. There are so many things you don't get to talk about. If you're in a room with someone you don't know, you don't say, "Do you believe in God? What do you think happens after you die?" Things that people can talk about for hours at a time. And I like that. I'm sure they like it or they wouldn't talk at all, but sometimes they're like, "I don't know the answers, quit buggin' me!" **1995**

beck
I try not to obsess about recording. I'm definitely the one who will leave all the mistakes—to have that balance between what's undone and done. I try to move on to the next thing. I have friends who have been working on the same song for five, six years. They just won't let the songs go. **1996**

usher
It's all about longevity. Age ain't nothing but a number. Gotta eat healthy, be healthy, think positive and work out. I work out every chance I get. Since I been on the road, I've been doing a lot of running across the stage. If you do a lot of cardiovascular—basketball, anything that makes you sweat—do it. That helps. But you got to eat healthy, too. It's all about abs—the abs of steel, baby. If you need a picture for that one, take a look at these. Women love abs. Do pull-ups, sit-ups, crunches, all of those. **1997**

herb alpert
It's the "it." I once introduced Stan Getz at a function, and I said that he had the "it." It's in the abstract. Some guys are playing and you're sitting there watching and listening and you know the guy just plays his ass off, but you're not feeling anything. Somebody else could come in and play three or four notes and you'll say, "Yeah, that's cool." That's the "it." It's like the George Harrison tune "Something"—you don't try to define that. **1997**

sean "puffy" combs a.k.a. Puff Daddy
Make God first in your life. Never have money. Treat others as you would want others to treat you. Have some fun while you're here. Don't listen to everything you hear. And love your mother. One of the rules I'm working out is trying to have some fun before it's time for me to get up out of here. I'm saying in the next hundred years I plan on taking a vacation. I ain't going away no time soon. But a hundred years, those go quick. Ask somebody who's a hundred years old. They'll say, "It seems like yesterday." But nah, I ain't going nowhere, I ain't havin' death premonitions. Nothing like that. A lot of writers be thinking like that. "Does he think this?" I've seen a lot of tragedies in my life, but it's God's will. I can't explain

everything. If it's His will, it's His will. For all I know, which I do know, it's probably better to not be here. Heaven is supposed to be and I believe that heaven is so much of a better place. Living on Earth, you probably look at it backwards. Probably when you get to heaven you say, "Oh, I shouldn't have been so upset after all." **1997**

rupaul
The new cool is really about being a sweet, wonderful person who loves yourself and is willing to share with other people. Not any of this boogie attitude shit. **1996**

rick nielsen of CheapTrick
My father's line years ago was, "Don't sweat the small stuff." He instilled that in me. If you do that, you waste half your time. So many people, that's what they do. "Well, look at this! The meat's not big enough for the bread!" If you're stressed about that, you can't even get to the real issues. I have a line that I use, "One box a day." If you have stuff accumulated for years, that's what you have to do. Old stuff will sit in the back of your mind or the back of your room and it'll shield you from going on to other things. You need to organize the things you hold on to that mean something to you. Little bit at a time. **1996**

meredith brooks
The best advice I've ever gotten about a relationship was, like, "Don't fight over the small stuff." If the guy you're with leaves the cap off the toothpaste, just put the cap back on the toothpaste. Don't argue over what movie you're going to go to, because if you want to see another movie, go with your girlfriend the next day. Don't argue over that kind of stuff. If you have a lot of good times living in a normal way, then when you do have a big bump, you can handle it and work it out so that you have memories of better times. I know *Don't Sweat the Small Stuff* is actually a book now, but that's what my father said: "Don't argue over the small things." This is advice he gave me a million years ago, before that book came out. **1998**

busta rhymes

There's a lot of things to deal with. Self-control, you know. I try to control my mood swings. Sometimes I can't. Sometimes I come off offensively because I'm speaking sincerely, sometimes. Not from a standpoint where I'm trying to blatantly disrespect people. But I don't mean it in a way that it might sound; I just mean it in its intensity. I'm dead serious about something. You have to learn how to discipline yourself, because you can. People try to justify things that they have total control of. You can't be held accountable for your actions sometimes, but you're always conscious of your actions. Even if you don't give a fuck, you have to still know what you're doing. **1998**

dave mustaine of Megadeth

It's really hard not to repeat all those terrible things that our parents say to us, but you know what? I read this story about this guy who said when he was four years old he thought his dad knew everything, when he was eight years old, he realized his dad didn't know so much. When he was fourteen, his dad didn't know anything. And when he was eighteen, he realized his dad kinda knew some stuff. When he was twenty-four, he realized his dad knew a lot, and when he was thirty, he wished his dad was still alive to tell him how much he really knew. And for me, I hope that's how it is for my son, because when my mom and dad were alive, they got divorced when I was four. My wife and I are still together, so my son still has a two-parent family at five, so he's outlasted myself. **1997**

mike d of theBeastieBoys

We're doing what we want to do, and that's why the kids respect us. We're not listening to older people. We're going to do it—if for nothing else, just because they told us we can't. . . . We are exercising our constitutional right to be fresh. **1987**

sean lennon

In the Sixties, you could stand on the earth and say, "Jimi Hendrix is alive. Janis Joplin is alive. Miles Davis is alive. John Lennon is alive. Brian Wilson is making *Smile*." I don't think any intelligent musician can possibly deny that was a special time. Bob Marley said, "You have to know your history." It's true. You've got to know your past to face the future. What makes the Beastie Boys and Beck so great is you know they listened to that shit, that they know all the music that's been made, inside and out. **1998**

bo diddley I would like to give a message to teenagers, the young and old: Be cool, don't do nothin' stupid. A dare is the worst thing in the world. Somebody dare you to jump off something, don't be no damn fool. Just don't do it. If it comes, don't do it. Just everybody be safe. Bo knows, okay. All right. Yeah. Bye-bye. **1998**

a rave from the compiler of the book's self-portraits

In February 1994, concluding an in-person interview with Nick Heyward of the Eighties band Haircut 100, I suddenly had an idea. Remembering what Nick had said about his artistic background, I proceeded to ask the lead singer to sketch his self-portrait. To my surprise, Nick drew a wonderful caricature of himself. This experience inspired me to consequently request all those I interview—ranging from Tori Amos and Jewel to Tool and "Weird Al" Yankovic—to create a self-portrait. The results have been tremendous. I now own more than 150 unique drawings, each of which reveals or highlights a fascinating detail about the artist.

—Russell A. Trunk

ARTISTBIOS

ote: *Artists who aren't solo performers are alphabetized under their band's name. However, artists who have been in more than one band are alphabetized by their own names.*

Aaliyah's debut album, 1994's *Age Ain't Nothing but a Number*, went platinum. The twenty-year-old R&B singer grew up in Detroit and learned to sing in her church choir.

Vocalist **Steven Tyler** and guitarist **Joe Perry** have been rocking & rolling for more than twenty-five years as the nucleus of riff-heavy **Aerosmith**.

The Afghan Whigs' **Greg Dulli** and **John Curley** argue the merits of their favorite films almost as heatedly as they cover Prince tunes in concert.

L.A. native **Herb Alpert** began playing trumpet at age eight and rose to fame in the Sixties with his south-of-the-border instrumental outfit, the Tijuana Brass. Alpert went on to cofound A&M records, signing the Carpenters, Carole King and, later, Janet Jackson. Alpert now co-operates Almo Sounds.

Tori Amos's dramatic piano playing, songbird vocal style and compellingly personal lyrics have won her critical acclaim and a devoted following since the 1992 release of her first solo album, *Little Earthquakes*.

Twenty-eight-year-old Englishman Richard James creates intricate, beat-centric electronic music under a variety of names, the best known being **Aphex Twin**. He lives and records in a former bank in London.

Alec Empire is the leader of **Atari Teenage Riot** and founder of the Digital Hardcore label. The German DJ/producer has stated that he formed his band and label to oppose hedonistic, fashion-conscious trends in dance music.

The B-52's debuted at a Valentine's Day party in 1977, and have been gleefully making music ever since. **Fred Schneider**, **Kate Pierson** and the band released a 1998 greatest-hits album and continue to tour.

Babyface, producer/songwriter (often with L.A. Reid) of countless hits for such artists as Boyz II Men, Bobby Brown, Michael Jackson and Whitney Houston, has garnered a few of his own solo hits as well.

Erykah Badu's soulful singing voice is most often compared to Billie Holiday's. The singer and proud mother of a two-year-old boy won a Grammy for her 1997 debut album, *Baduizm*.

Staten Island native **Joan Baez** is an icon of the early-Sixties folk revival. She achieved commercial success in the Seventies and has since remained politically and musically active.

Susanna Hoffs and **the Bangles** had everyone dancing funny in 1986 when the tom-tom beat of "Walk Like an Egyptian" hit Number One on the pop chart.

Part Marx Brothers, part "Weird Al" Yankovic, Canada's **Barenaked Ladies** made a splash in the States with the catchy 1998 hit "One Week." **Steven Page** is their lead singer.

The Beastie Boys—Mike D, **Adam "Ad Rock" Horovitz** and **Adam "MCA" Yauch**—began their career in a hardcore punk outfit called the Young and the Useless. By 1987, they had become the first successful white rap group. Their most recent album, *Hello Nasty*, remained at Number One on *Billboard*'s album chart for three weeks in 1998.

Beck Hansen shot to insta-fame in 1994 with the loopy "Loser," which spawned a horde of kitchen-sink imitators. A versatile musician with an encyclopedic knowledge of folk and blues, Beck is reinventing folk music for a new age.

Jeff Beck's wailing distortion, impossibly bent notes and hyperspeed fret work have influenced blues, psychedelia and heavy-metal guitar playing since the Sixties.

Big Wreck is a rock band who met at the esteemed Berklee School of Music in Boston. Frontman **Ian Thornley** is from Toronto, Canada.

Björk was part of Iceland's biggest rock band, the offbeat, atonal Sugarcubes, whose 1988 song "Birthday" won them American fans. She embarked on a solo career in 1993, and to date has released four well-received albums.

The Black Crowes, led by the skinny, scruffy brothers Rich and **Chris Robinson**, have kept freedom-rock alive and well since 1984. The unashamedly retro, pro-weed Atlanta outfit's most recent effort is 1999's *By Your Side*.

Blind Melon combined the big guitar sound of Seventies arena rock with the rootsiness of the Byrds. The band broke up after singer **Shannon Hoon** died from a drug overdose in 1995.

John Popper's lightning-quick harmonica and throaty vocals propelled **Blues Traveler** from the New York hippie scene that spawned them to mainstream success. Popper also founded the H.O.R.D.E. festival.

Tracy Bonham made waves in 1996 with her acerbic, resentful single "Mother Mother."

Annabella Lwin sang with England's **Bow Wow Wow**, whose biggest U.S. hit was 1982's "I Want Candy."

Born David Robert Jones, **David Bowie** (named after the knife) is the original musical chameleon—from glam rock to zoot suits, Bowie has done it. He is also an accomplished actor and visual artist.

Meredith Brooks's gotta-be-me anthem, "Bitch," landed her in the spotlight (and on the Lilith Fair lineup) in 1997.

Nineteen-year-old **Foxy Brown**'s platinum-selling 1996 debut, *Ill Na Na* (slang for her privates), was a big hit with rap fans of both sexes.

Junior Brown has redefined honky-tonk with his unique invention, the guit-steel. His masterful guitar playing, bass vocals and droll sense of humor distinguish his recordings from the contemporary country pack.

Jackson Browne has been making records since 1972. His introverted, highly observant songwriting took a turn from the romantic to the sociopolitical in the Eighties. He continues to write and perform.

Jeff Buckley released just two albums before his career was cut short by his accidental drowning in 1997. Posthumously released in 1998, *Sketches for My Sweetheart, the Drunk* was a testament to his untapped potential.

Busta Rhymes had already garnered widespread cred in underground rap circles before his gold-selling 1996 debut, *The Coming*, hit the streets.

After eighteen years, Texas's **Butthole Surfers**—including singer **Gibby Haynes**, guitarist **Paul Leary** and drummer **King Coffey**—are still the weirdest rock band around.

Candlebox hit the jackpot with its 1993 debut album, which soared to Number Seven. Lead singer **Kevin Martin** fronts the Seattle-based band.

Swedish pop outfit **the Cardigans** are second only to Abba in terms of success abroad. Their single "Lovefool," driven by **Nina Persson**'s cooing vocals, was their biggest U.S. hit.

Johnny Cash has combined rock and country since his beginnings at Sun Records in the 1950s. His straightforward guitar playing and deep, brooding vocals are outdone only by his adept songwriting.

Rosanne Cash, Johnny's oldest daughter, followed in her father's footsteps by writing country that's a little bit rock & roll.

Seventies teen idol **David Cassidy** made teenage girls swoon as Keith on *The Partridge Family* before embarking on a full-time music career. He released a greatest-hits album and an album of new material in 1998.

As leader of the Birthday Party and the Bad Seeds (and numerous offshoots), **Nick Cave** has honed his morose, brooding songwriting and vocal style. *The Best of Nick Cave and the Bad Seeds* was released in 1998.

Avid rare-guitar collector **Rick Nielsen** began playing in bands when he was still a teenager in Rockford, Illinois, before forming **Cheap Trick** in 1974. The power-pop godfathers' 1979 triple-platinum *Live at Budokan* endeared them to U.S. fans.

The Chemical Brothers—**Tom Rowlands** and **Ed Simons**— began DJ'ing at a friend's wedding when the hired help went on break. They went on to make their own furious funk on the albums *Exit Planet Dust,* 1997's Grammy-winning *Dig Your Own Hole* and 1999's *Surrender.*

Cher is equally at ease on stage, the screen both big and small, and in the studio. She's released countless albums, won an Oscar for her role in *Moonstruck* and has enjoyed four decades in show business.

Cibo Matto is **Yuka Honda** and Miho Hatori. Their 1996 debut album, *Viva! La Woman,* garnered rave reviews.

As a member of the Yardbirds, Cream and Derek and the Dominos, and as a solo artist, **Eric Clapton** has spent thirty years reinterpreting the blues. He has won several Grammys and was honored with an M.B.E. (Member of the British Empire) in 1995.

Paula Cole grew up in a small town in Massachusetts and polished her powerful vocal style at the Berklee School of Music. Her sophomore effort, 1997's *This Fire,* was nominated for eight Grammys.

Bootsy Collins's signature bass lines drove Parliament/Funkadelic's interplanetary excursions in the Seventies. He established himself as an artist in his own right with Bootsy's Rubber Band, and his work is among the most sampled in hip-hop.

Scottish singer/songwriter **Edwyn Collins** first made his mark in the punk band Orange Juice. As a solo artist, his biggest hit has been "A Girl Like You," from 1994's *Gorgeous George.*

Producer-turned-rapper **Sean "Puffy" Combs**, a.k.a. Puff Daddy, has dominated the charts in recent years. He has garnered praise for his drive (he started the multimillion-dollar Bad Boy Entertainment) and criticism for sampling former chart hits, almost in their entirety, as backing tracks.

Coolio was one of the early Nineties' biggest mainstream hip-hop stars. His laid-back West Coast–style earned his album *Fantastic Voyage* platinum sales in 1994.

Elvis Costello won international attention in the late Seventies as part of a new generation of singer/songwriters who infused the genre with the raw energy of punk. Throughout his career he has experimented with everything from chamber music to a 1998 collaboration with Burt Bacharach.

Counting Crows' rootsy multiplatinum debut, *August and Everything After,* brought them instant success in the early Nineties. **Adam Duritz** is their lead singer.

Fronted by **Scott Stapp**, **Creed** makes a big rock sound reminiscent of Pearl Jam. Their 1997 debut album, *My Own Prison,* went platinum.

David Crosby, **Stephen Stills** and **Graham Nash** have been singing high harmonies together since the late Sixties. Their soft-rock songs have won them fans of all ages.

Sheryl Crow began her professional career as a backup singer for Michael Jackson and Don Henley before stepping into the spotlight in 1993 with *Tuesday Night Music Club.*

Boy George and **Culture Club** scored a string of pop hits in the Eighties, including "Karma Chameleon" and "Do You Really Want to Hurt Me?" George then went on to a successful career as a DJ. The band reunited in 1998 for a tour.

Robert Smith formed **the Cure** in 1976, when he was seventeen. His introspective, dreamlike lyrics, tremulous vocals and spare guitar playing have won the band a slavish international following.

Thomas Bangalter is half of the French duo **Daft Punk**, whose house- and disco-flavored debut, *Homework,* was recorded in a bedroom and yielded several international dance hits.

King of the surf guitar **Dick Dale** has been blasting eardrums since the 1960s.

Terence Trent D'Arby's versatile vocal skills and rock-and-soul swagger earned him success in the late Eighties.

Deee-Lite lead singer **Lady Kier Kirby** brought East Village style and cool to the masses when her dance trio hit the Top Ten in 1990 with "Groove Is in the Heart."

Pop singer/songwriter **Neil Diamond** has released more than thirty-five Top Forty singles and nineteen platinum albums. His songs have been covered by everyone from Deep Purple to UB40 to Urge Overkill.

Bo Diddley's syncopated beat is virtually synonymous with rock & roll. For four decades he has toured with the trademark rectangular guitar he built himself and now resides with his family in Florida.

Ani DiFranco's music combines the honest expression of folk with the raw energy of punk. She has released a slew of albums on her own record label, Righteous Babe.

Rapper **DMX**'s gravelly voiced rhymes blasted him right to the top of the rap game in 1998, as hip-hop fans lapped up more than five million copies of his first two records.

After cofounding Throwing Muses and the Breeders, **Tanya Donelly** went on to form Belly, coupling her dark fairy-tale lyrics with pop song structures. She currently works as a solo artist.

The Donnas are an all-female teenage punk band from California who released their debut album in 1998.

The Doors embodied the dark side of psychedelia—unhinged, death-obsessed, sexual and excessive. Though he has been dead twenty-eight years, **Jim Morrison**'s shamanistic moves and rock-god swagger still influence lead singers and would-be Lizard Kings.

Duran Duran's fashionable mix of new wave and disco earned singer **Simon Le Bon** and the band five platinum albums and sold-out stadium tours throughout the Eighties.

Mike Simpson and his partner John King are best known as **the Dust Brothers**, the producers responsible for works of sampling genius like the Beastie Boys' *Paul's Boutique* and Beck's *Odelay*. In 1998 the Brothers started a record label, Nickel Bag (now Ideal Records).

The Eagles were the faces of Seventies California rock, merging country vocal harmonies with big guitar riffs. **Glenn Frey** and **Don Henley** have enjoyed success as solo artists, with Henley receiving Grammys in 1985 and 1989.

Echo and the Bunnymen's moody, atmospheric music fused punk, goth and the theatricality of the Doors. In 1995 founding members **Ian McCulloch** and **Will Sergeant** released an album as Electrafixion and in 1997 re-formed the original band.

Mark Eitzel led the American Music Club, a heralded underground Eighties band known for punk attitude, honky-tonk swagger and Eitzel's booze-fueled onstage antics.

A British pop-rock combo fronted by **Justine Frischmann** and reminiscent of underground Eighties bands like Wire and the Stranglers, **Elastica** scored a U.S. hit with "Connection" in 1995.

Missy "Misdemeanor" Elliot has become one of hip-hop's preeminent women artists and in 1998 was the first rap artist to tour with the Lilith Fair.

Eminem's gleefully violent, demented, cartoony style has earned the young white rapper an avid fan base of both MTV-addled teens and discriminating hip-hop heads.

Grammy-winning singer-songwriter **Melissa Etheridge** is known for her raspy voice, gritty delivery and bitter love songs.

Art Alexakis led the noisy pop-rock trio **Everclear** to platinum-selling success on their second album, 1996's *Sparkle and Fade*. Alexakis lives with his family in Portland, Oregon.

Perry Farrell launched his career with the punk-meets-Zeppelin outfit Jane's Addiction before going on to found Porno for Pyros and organize the alt-rock summit known as Lollapalooza.

Norman Cook, better known as **Fatboy Slim**, was the bassist for the sunny Eighties pop band the Housemartins before he became one of the most in-demand DJs and remixers around.

Wayne Coyne has led **the Flaming Lips** since the late Eighties. The band's psychedelic guitar sound, locomotive rhythms and quirky lyrics have won them a strong fan base as well as a hit with 1993's "She Don't Use Jelly."

Guitarist/songwriter **Lindsey Buckingham** contributed some of **Fleetwood Mac**'s most intriguing songs before embarking on a solo career.

Detroit native **Aretha Franklin** has been the reigning queen of soul since the 1960s. Her achingly beautiful voice encompasses the passion of gospel, the sensuality of R&B and the smooth cool of jazz.

Wyclef Jean and **the Fugees**' second album, *The Score*, was massively successful in the hip-hop field, while his solo effort, *The Carnival*, showcased the guitar-playin' rapper's taste for Spanish and South American music.

Fun Lovin' Criminals somehow mix George Benson, *Mean Streets* and Lynyrd Skynyrd into a funk-heavy groove. Frontman **Huey** (Criminals don't need last names) is one hell of a storyteller, on the record and off.

Led by Scottish flame-haired goddess **Shirley Manson**, **Garbage** is a boldly innovative pop band making music for the Twenty-first Century.

Art Garfunkel met Paul Simon in the sixth grade, and they recorded their first song in 1957. After becoming one of the Sixties' most popular acts, the duo split in the early Seventies, with both pursuing solo careers.

Goldfinger is a California ska band with a tubular bio, dude. Frontman **John Feldmann** worked in a Santa Monica shoe store with one of his future bandmates and met their drummer at a nearby Starbucks. Their original guitarist left the band for a pro surfing career. Rad!

Grant Lee Buffalo has released four unique albums that combine lush atmospherics with roots-rock elements topped by the sentimental and poetic lyrics of frontman **Grant Lee Phillips**.

With the **Grateful Dead**, vocalist **Jerry Garcia** and guitarist **Bob Weir** defined the Bay Area psychedelic scene of the late Sixties. The band became an institution known for its lengthy, improvisational live shows.

Green Day is a three-piece, three-chord, platinum-selling punk band from Berkeley, California. **Billie Joe Armstrong** is its singer and guitarist, as well as the proud papa of his son, Joey.

Guns n' Roses' hedonistic metal and fuck-it attitude translated into instant success upon the 1987 release of *Appetite for Destruction*. The band's reclusive, serpentlike frontman, **Axl Rose**, vanished from the spotlight in 1994 when the members took a break from the band to pursue solo projects.

Ben Harper is a folksy rock singer and guitarist from California.

Emmylou Harris helped to create country rock, singing harmonies on Gram Parsons's two albums before embarking on a solo career. She recently reunited with Dolly Parton and Linda Ronstadt, releasing *Trio II* in 1999.

Polly Jean Harvey's raw, introspective songwriting has won her a rabid following since the release of her debut, 1992's *Dry*, as P.J. Harvey.

After leaving beloved college-rock band the Blake Babies, **Juliana Hatfield** has garnered praise for her delicate vocals, assertive guitar playing and introspective lyrics.

Isaac Hayes was essential to the development of Sixties and Seventies soul and disco. He currently has a radio show on a New York City R&B station and is the voice of Chef on *South Park*.

As **Heart**, the hard-rockin' **Wilson** sisters, **Ann** and Nancy, sold millions of records in the late Seventies, only to outdo themselves with an Eighties comeback. They remain influential in the Seattle music scene: Pearl Jam, Alice in Chains and Soundgarden have all recorded at their Bad Animals studio.

New York rappers **Heavy D.** and the Boyz released two platinum-selling albums in the late Eighties.

Jimi Hendrix revolutionized modern rock guitar playing, making music that spoke a language of sounds as evocative as the blues and as expansive as Mozart.

Eccentric singer/songwriter **Robyn Hitchcock** has enjoyed cult status since his days with the Syd Barrett–influenced outfit the Soft Boys and with the Egyptians. He most recently was the subject of a Jonathan Demme feature film, released in 1998.

Hole began as a punk band in 1990. On 1998's *Celebrity Skin*, they tackled poppier terrain, still fronted by the ever-confrontational Courtney Love and rooted by the guitar-work of **Eric Erlandson**. Canadian **Melissa Auf der Maur** joined the band on bass in 1994.

John Lee Hooker's deep, raspy voice and rhythmic boogie guitar are unmistakable. The seventy-nine-year-old bluesman was inducted into the Rock and Roll Hall of Fame in 1991.

Darius Rucker started singing with **Hootie and the Blowfish** in bars in his hometown of Columbia, South Carolina. The group went on to sell fourteen million copies of their 1994 debut, *Cracked Rear View*.

Whitney Houston, daughter of renowned soul singer Cissy and cousin of Dionne Warwick, ascended to superstardom with a string of catchy ballads and dance pop singles. Her version of Dolly Parton's "I Will Always Love You" is one of the top-selling singles of all time.

Sneering pop-punk **Billy Idol** can boast four platinum albums and seven Top Forty hit singles from the mid-Eighties.

Former Australian soap-opera star **Natalie Imbruglia** tried her hand at singing in 1998 and recorded "Torn," a song that stayed at Number One in Great Britain for fourteen weeks and sent sales of her debut album, *Left of the Middle,* through the roof.

INXS began in 1977 in Sydney, Australia, and developed a danceable funk-rock sound that won it international stardom in the Eighties. Singer **Michael Hutchence** committed suicide in 1997.

English comedian **Eddie Izzard** is known for doing his hilarious, razor-sharp stand-up in drag. He's a talented actor as well, as seen in the art-house glam-rock film *Velvet Goldmine.*

Janet Jackson is a talented actress, dancer and pop vocalist. She has had roles on the sitcoms *Good Times* and *Diff'rent Strokes*, and has had a string of Top Forty singles and albums.

Jamiroquai is a pop-funk English outfit that learned a thing or two from Stevie Wonder. Frontman **Jay Kay** has an obscenely large collection of sports cars.

Brooklyn rapper/producer **Jay-Z** has achieved mainstream success without losing one iota of street cred.

David Yow fronts **the Jesus Lizard**, an industrial-strength noise outfit from Chicago.

Joan Jett got her start as leader of the all-female teen punk band the Runaways in 1975, but came into her own as a solo artist when three singles from her debut with the Blackhearts, *I Love Rock and Roll*, hit the Top Twenty.

The personal folk of **Jewel**'s debut, *Pieces of You*, made her a multiplatinum artist. She is the highest paid poet of all time, reportedly receiving 1.25 million for *A Night Without Armor* and a soon-to-be-published second book. Jewel also plans to star in films.

Billy Joel, the pride of Long Island, has forsaken rock & roll to write classical music but has left behind an impressive array of work spanning three decades. The piano man was inducted into the Rock and Roll Hall of Fame in 1999.

Mick Jones played guitar and sang in the legendary British punk band the Clash before forming Big Audio Dynamite in 1984. B.A.D. was well ahead of its time, combining rock, reggae and hip-hop into a danceable hybrid.

Fearless experimenter **Rickie Lee Jones**'s 1979 self-titled debut album made her an instant star. Her eclectic jazzy folk has won her a cult following that continues to grow. She released a trip-hop album, *Ghostyhead*, in 1997.

One of the pioneering women in rock, **Janis Joplin**'s tough-mama blues singing was unequaled in the Sixties. Her life was cut short by a 1970 heroin overdose.

Montell Jordan is an R&B singer with two platinum albums to his credit. His latest effort was 1998's *Let's Ride*.

California's **Korn** took their groove-heavy metal from grass roots to grandstands and breathed new life into the genre. **Jonathan Davis** is their wailing, moaning frontman.

Lenny Kravitz has taken the best of Sixties and Seventies rock and soul and given it his personal touch over the course of five successful albums.

Lawrence "Kris" parker, best known as **KRS-One**, is a rap philosopher who campaigns against violence and ignorance as heatedly as he rhymes.

L7 rock harder and snowboard better than any goddamned man can. **Donita Sparks** plays guitar with the group.

k.d. lang's country roots launched her career, but the Canadian-born singer's pop crooning on *Constant Craving* earned her a Grammy in 1990.

Cyndi Lauper's quirky Eighties pop made history: She was the first woman to score four Top Five singles from a debut album.

John Lennon left an indelible mark on rock & roll as a member of the Beatles, as a solo performer and in collaboration with his wife, Yoko Ono. In 1980 he was assassinated by a fan.

Sean Lennon's eclectic debut album, *Into the Sun*, placed free-form jazz alongside bossa nova and country & western.

Lil' Kim's Lilliputian skirts, sex-and-money rhymes and Technicolor wigs are as infamous as her affair with the late Notorious B.I.G.

Limp Bizkit is a Florida metal band that integrates hip-hop and punk into their caustic mix, but aren't above covering George Michael's "Faith." Frontman **Fred Durst** is a former tattoo artist.

Brown University alum **Lisa Loeb** wants to graduate from singer/songwriter to singer/songwriter/actress.

Formerly of Galaxie 500, **Dean Wareham** is the literate frontman of **Luna**, whose most recent album is 1997's *Pup Tent*.

Icon, actress, singer, blonde, brunette, redhead—**Madonna** has courted more controversy and pushed more buttons than any pop star since Elvis Presley. Arguably, she is the most famous woman in the world.

Hated by the Christian Right, beloved by his slavish fans, **Marilyn Manson**'s shock-rock theatrics made him a household name virtually overnight. *Mechanical Animals,* his 1998 foray into glam rock, won Manson new converts, while his wit and intelligence in interviews won him even more. **Twiggy Ramirez** plays bass for Manson's band.

Marcy Playground's languid "Sex and Candy" remained at the top of the Modern Rock Radio chart longer than any song ever. **John Wozniak**, the band's shy, affable frontman, used to follow the Grateful Dead.

The eldest child in a musically gifted family, **Ziggy Marley** appeared with the Melody Makers at the state funeral of his father, Bob Marley, in 1981. Marley runs the Ghetto Youth United label in Jamaica, and is politically active in several international organizations.

Rob Thomas fronts **Matchbox 20**, a high-drama rock band from Florida, whose debut, *Yourself or Someone Like You*, went multiplatinum.

South African–born **Dave Matthews** has led his multicultural, polyrhythmic jam band to international fame and platinum album sales.

Maxwell sounds like Marvin Gaye and dresses like Sly Stone—with male-model good looks. What else could a soul singer want?

Ex-Beatle Sir **Paul McCartney** was awarded a Knighthood in 1997 and was inducted into the Rock and Roll Hall of Fame as a solo artist in 1999.

Grammy-winning Canadian singer/songwriter **Sarah McLachlan** achieved national recognition for founding the Lilith Fair and critical recognition for her 1997 album, *Surfacing*.

Dave Mustaine cofounded Metallica before he was booted out for abusing drugs, booze and his band mates. He formed **Megadeth**, began playing faster and angrier, and quickly won a following.

Metallica's dense dueling guitars and thinking-man's lyrics were the antidote to Eighties high-hair metal. When vocalist **James Hetfield** and the rest of the band hit their forties in the Nineties, they celebrated by chopping off their locks and mixing alternative rock into their sonic stew.

The Mighty Mighty Bosstones are a Boston ska-punk band that has been together for more than ten years. Frontman **Dicky Barrett** is an avid suit collector, Rat Pack fan and reader of True Crime books.

When **Steve Miller** was but a wee four years old, he learned his first chords from jazzy maestro Les Paul. By the late Sixties, the Space Cowboy was a well-known Bay Area blues man who made the transition to pop star in the Seventies and Eighties.

Joni Mitchell's uncompromising vision and innovative work continue to earn the respect of musicians, music fans and critics. The Canadian singer/songwriter is in a class by herself.

Mix Master Mike has been cutting beats with the Beastie Boys and Invisibl Skratch Picklz for years. The DJ's first solo album, 1998's *Anti-Theft Device*, was a showcase of Mike's top-shelf turntable skills.

Techno DJ/punk rocker **Moby** is a distant relative of Herman Melville (hence the stage name). He was one of the first rave DJs to eschew anonymity for the limelight. The unabashed porn fan mixed gospel with techno on 1999's *Play*.

In 1995 **Alanis Morissette**'s gazillion-selling album, *Jagged Little Pill*, opened the door for a slew of tepid imitators. Her 1998 follow-up, *Supposed Former Infatuation Junkie*, is as honest and emotionally raw as its predecessor, with a decidedly Eastern musical bent.

An introverted and moody visionary, the Grammy-winning **Van Morrison** remains a prolific singer/songwriter adept at the blues, soul, rock and the Celtic vocal traditions of his native Belfast, Ireland.

Mötley Crüe updated Kiss's theatrics and parlayed furious songs of fast livin' into multiplatinum success. Drummer **Tommy Lee** launched an amateur film career in 1998.

Fronted by **Kevin Shields**, the late-Eighties Irish band **My Bloody Valentine**'s lush, layered guitars, wispy melodies and barely audible lyrics redirected rock toward dreamier terrain. Since the band's dissolution in the early Nineties, Shields has gained acclaim as a producer and remixer.

Mya's delicate birdsong soared in "Ghetto Superstar," Fugee rapper Pras's cut on the *Bulworth* soundtrack. The nineteen-year-old R&B vocalist grew up in Washington, D.C.

Dave Navarro played guitar in Jane's Addiction before joining the party-hearty Red Hot Chili Peppers. He left the Peppers in 1998 to pursue a solo career and recorded an album entitled *Spread*.

Singer/songwriter **Me'Shell Ndegéocello**'s funky bass playing has been featured on two solo albums to date.

The prolific **Willie Nelson** penned hits like "Crazy" for Patsy Cline and "Wake Me When It's Over" for Andy Williams before releasing his first album in 1962. 1998's *Teatro* features the talents of Daniel Lanois and Emmylou Harris, as well as Nelson's trademark wry vocals and understated delivery.

Stevie Nicks rose to fame with Fleetwood Mac before embarking on a thriving solo career while still in the band, beginning with the 1981 quadruple-platinum album *Bella Donna*.

Trent Reznor is the one-man mastermind behind the angst-driven industrial pop oeuvre of **Nine Inch Nails**. He is a classically trained pianist and a skilled composer and arranger. He discovered Marilyn Manson, whom he signed to his label, Nothing.

Gwen Stefani sings with the California ska-pop band **No Doubt**, whose second album, *Tragic Kingdom*, yielded three hit singles.

The Notorious B.I.G., a.k.a. Biggie Smalls, walked like a gangsta, talked like the daddy of the macks and had the rhyme skills to back all of it up. His murder in 1997 left a permanent void in the hip-hop world.

Gary Numan's robotic electro-pop frequently topped the English charts, while 1979's "Cars" remains his biggest hit among synthophobic Americans. Numan, a professional pilot, flew around the world in 1981.

Led by guitarist **Noel Gallagher** and his younger brother **Liam**, **Oasis** is the most popular British rock band of the Nineties. **Paul McGuigan** holds down bass duties.

Sinéad O'Connor's gut-wrenching delivery and otherworldly voice garner as much attention as her provocative public statements. During her heyday in the early Nineties, O'Connor's shaved head and shapeless clothing refuted the female-pop-star stereotype. In 1999 she became a priest in the Latin Tridentine order of the Catholic Church.

The Offspring is a Southern California rock band fronted by **Brian "Dexter" Holland**.

Yoko Ono is known for her career in avant-garde art and music, as well as for her marriage to John Lennon and the couple's musical collaborations and pro-peace political work.

Joan Osborne played Greenwich Village blues bars until the folky "One of Us" won her national attention in 1995, when her album, *Relish*, earned seven Grammy nominations.

Ozzy Osbourne and Black Sabbath drafted the Seventies' blueprint for heavy metal, replete with occult overtones and copious consumption, before

Osbourne embarked on a successful solo career. He has organized and headlined the metalpalooza known as Ozzfest since 1996.

Pavement's fractured, lo-fi guitar rock and frontman **Stephen Malkmus**'s literary, cryptic lyrics separate the group from the indie-rock pack; 1999's *Terror Twilight* is their latest, and possibly last, album.

Unlike many of its Seattle peers, **Pearl Jam** takes more from Seventies arena rock than punk. **Stone Gossard** plays guitar with the band, whose first two albums sold more than ten million copies.

Tom Petty parlayed heavy Byrds, Bob Dylan and Rolling Stones influences into a classic rock & roll sound. In the Eighties, Petty was invited to join Roy Orbison, George Harrison, Jeff Lynne and Dylan in the Traveling Wilburys, confirming his place in the rock canon.

Liz Phair burst onto the indie-rock scene with the frank sexuality and deft songwriting of her 1993 debut, *Exile in Guyville*. Her follow-up, *Whip-Smart,* is more introspective, while 1998's *Whitechocolatespaceegg* explores the emotional terrain of motherhood and married life.

Vermont's **Phish** started playing local bars more than a decade ago and has become America's favorite jam band. Frontman **Trey Anastasio** is a virtuoso guitarist, fluent in jazz, rock, funk and bluegrass, and capable of mimicking the Beastie Boys as well as the Beatles.

PM Dawn's psychedelic pop twist on hip-hop showcases the rapping and smooth harmonies of **Prince Be** over soundtracks that owe as much to Brian Wilson as Grandmaster Flash.

Iggy Pop predated punk rock by ten years, and grunge by thirty, but the shadow of his scarred, steak-smeared torso looms over both. His unhinged stage antics (rolling topless on busted glass, adorning his body with peanut butter, sporadic nudity, fire) assured him cult status and mainstream disgust.

Fronted by **Chris Ballew**, **the Presidents of the United States of America** were a Seattle power-pop trio best known for "Peaches," a catchy, whimsical ode to the fuzzy fruit. The band split up in 1997.

The Pretenders translated British punk's three-chord rhythms and satirical lyrics into huge commercial success in the Eighties. **Chrissie Hynde**'s tough stage persona and no-nonsense songwriting inspired generations of female rockers.

Primus has won itself a loyal audience with its bass-heavy sound, cartoony vocals and irreverant lyrics. **Les Claypool** is its bassist and lead singer.

Keyboard and sampler whiz **Liam Howlett** composed tracks in his bedroom under the pseudonym **the Prodigy** before forming the band/spectacle of the same name. The band's mix of punk, hip-hop and furious techno scored them an international hit in 1997 with "Firestarter."

Singer and lyricist **Jarvis Cocker** has been making music with **Pulp** since the early Eighties. Cocker's acutely satirical and insightful lyrics have won him critical acclaim and a mass following both at home in England and abroad.

Queen Latifah brought pro-woman activism to hip-hop in the early Nineties. The former high school basketball star was a human beatbox in her first group, Ladies Fresh, before launching her music career and moving into acting on the TV series *Living Single* and the films *Set It Off* and *Living Out Loud*.

Colin Greenwood plays bass and **Thom Yorke** sings with **Radiohead**. The band's beautiful, lush compositions and bleak lyrics of isolation are arguably the most innovative rock songs being written today.

Rage Against the Machine merge rap, thrash and leftist politics into a rafter-rattling live show. At the center of their sound is **Tom Morello**'s grating, eccentric and utterly grooving guitar playing.

Over the course of three albums in the early Eighties, vocalist **Ana da Silva** and the other **Raincoats** evolved from caustic and amateurish to graceful and folky. Longtime fan Kurt Cobain encouraged the band to re-form (which they did for an album and tour in 1994), and Nirvana's label, DGC, reissued their albums.

Bonnie Raitt incorporates blues, pop and folk into her songwriting, and has been a critics' darling since the release of her debut album in 1971. It was 1989's *Nick of Time* that brought Raitt her much-deserved commercial success.

The Ramones' fast, simple, solo-free songs, **Johnny Ramone**'s guitar riffs and **Joey Ramone**'s deadpan vocal delivery shaped the sound of both New York and British punk rock in the mid-Seventies. The band called it quits in 1996.

From Berkeley, California, **Rancid** burst on the scene in 1995, with the singles "Time Bomb" and "Ruby Soho." **Lars Frederiksen** plays guitar and sings.

Flea and **Anthony Kiedis** have been making zany rap-rock with the **Red Hot Chili Peppers** since 1983.

With the Velvet Underground, **Lou Reed** created passionate, bold music that continues to be an influence on rock & roll. As a solo artist, Reed has experimented with self-conscious commerciality, avant-garde noise and idiosyncratic folk rock.

Aaron Barrett and **Andrew Gonzales** are members of **Reel Big Fish**, a California ska band who can cover a-ha's "Take on Me" as well as they can do Lita Ford's "Kiss Me Deadly."

Roger Clyne and his Byrdsian band **the Refreshments** hail from Arizona and proffer witty, beery pop songs.

Fronted by **Michael Stipe**, **R.E.M.** rose from underground heroes to international superstars, influencing countless rock bands with their jangly guitars, cryptic lyrics and do-it-yourself aesthetic.

Reverend Horton Heat's punk-rock rockabilly is in a class by itself. **Jim "the Reverend" Heath** is a spitfire on the guitar and an ace at horseshoes, and he can fix a '56 Ford with his eyes closed.

Ex–Modern Lover **Jonathan Richman** was the troubadour in 1998's gross-out comedy *There's Something About Mary*.

Country phenom **LeAnn Rimes** had three albums in the Top Twenty simultaneously in 1997, when she was just fifteen years old.

Robbie Robertson began his career in the Sixties with the Band, linking American folklore and primal myths in a catalog of austerely precise arrangements. After the group's dissolution in 1976, Robertson composed film scores, acted and released well-received solo albums, the latest being 1998's *Contact From the Underworld of Redboy*.

The Rolling Stones turned a love affair with Chicago blues into a far-reaching and lucrative career spanning four decades. Now in their fifties, **Mick Jagger** and **Keith Richards** are still powerful in concert, as 1998's *No Security*, recorded during their Bridges to Babylon tour, proved in abundance.

The heavily tattooed, strongly opinionated **Henry Rollins** got his gig singing with California punks Black Flag by jumping onstage during one of their shows. After the band broke up, Rollins founded the Rollins Band and began a career as a spoken-word artist and book publisher.

Darryl "D.M.C." McDaniels is part of **Run-D.M.C.**, the group who introduced hip-hop culture to the masses in the mid-Eighties.

RuPaul's hit "Supermodel (You Better Work)" got his drag shtick out of the clubs and onto the charts, girl. Then Miss Thang got a fabulous talk show on VH1.

Shaun Ryder and the ecstasy-fueled acid-house grooves of **Happy Mondays** set the stage for the English rave scene in the Eighties. The band broke up in 1992, and in 1993 Ryder formed **Black Grape**, who broke up in 1998.

Michigan's **Bob Seger** plugged away on the local rock scene for years until he hit his stride in the late Seventies and began to turn out multiplatinum records full of that old-time rock & roll.

Semisonic's melodic pop-rock hit "Closing Time" put the Minneapolis band, fronted by **Dan Wilson**, on the map while giving barkeeps in college towns across the land a new way to say "last call."

Duncan Sheik is a singer/songwriter who cites Nick Drake and the arty English band Japan as two of his biggest influences.

Ben Gillies is one third of **Silverchair**, a grungy Australian rock trio who made it big before they could drive.

Jim Kerr formed **Simple Minds** in 1978 and was lauded by the British music press long before the group achieved U.S. success with epic synth-pop songs like "Don't You (Forget About Me)" and "Alive and Kicking" in the late Eighties.

Roni Size and the collective Reprazent are advancing dance music with their innovative, rapid-fire beats and fluid, hip-hop-laced live shows.

Sleater-Kinney is an all-female punk-rock band from Olympia, Washington, formed in 1994 and named after the road where their practice space was located. Singer/guitarist **Carrie Brownstein** is a classically trained pianist.

The retro surf psychedelia of "Walking on the Sun" was a big summer hit for **Steve Harwell** and **Smash Mouth** in 1997 and a departure from the band's brand of messy punk rock. Their latest album is *Astro Lounge*.

Smashing Pumpkins began as an arty-but-rockin' Chicago trio (singer **Billy Corgan**, bassist **D'arcy**, guitarist James Iha and a drum machine) in 1989. In 1996 *Mellon Collie and the Infinite Sadness* became the best-selling double album of all time.

Pat Smear, who played searing lead guitar with the L.A. punk outfit the Germs, accompanied Nirvana on the In Utero tour. After Cobain's death, Smear joined Foo Fighters, but tired of the busy tour schedule and amicably left the band in 1997.

Patti Smith's punk-rock poetry and shamanistic stage persona have inspired generations of musicians, including devotee Michael Stipe, who decided to form a band after hearing her debut album, *Horses*.

Social Distortion came hurtling out of the Eighties L.A. punk scene, surviving a breakup as well as frontman **Mike Ness**'s heroin addiction and outlaw antics before achieving major-label success ten years later.

Sonic Youth have been making noise since 1981. **Thurston Moore**'s discordant guitar paved the way for the alt-rock explosion of the mid-Nineties and influenced hordes of younger bands.

Over the course of a decade, founding members of Minneapolis's **Soul Asylum**—**Dave Pirner**, **Dan Murphy** and **Karl Mueller**—have grown from their trashy punk roots to polished anthems and ballads touched with jazz and country elements.

Soul Coughing is a New York band that combines live and sampled elements with frontman **M. Doughty**'s impressionistic lyrics and monotone rapping.

Soundgarden, named after a pipe sculpture in a Seattle park, brought together the raw power of Led Zeppelin and the dark broodings of Black Sabbath. **Kim Thayil** played guitar with the Grammy-winning band, which broke up in 1997.

The Jon Spencer Blues Explosion has been turning the blues on its ass for nine years now. **Jon Spencer**'s manic stage antics and the band's furious playing can tear down the house in any damn town, thank 'ya very much.

The Spice Girls' saccharine dance-pop seeped into the very fabric of humanity through song, film, doll, book and lollipop—earning the five British women up to $75 million a year. Soon after, **Geri "Ginger Spice" Halliwell** departed to start a solo career, leaving high-kicking **Sporty Spice** and the others behind.

The Spin Doctors are a rootsy, improvisationally inclined New York rock band, who landed their first hit in 1992 with "Little Miss Can't Be Wrong." **Chris Barron** is their lead singer.

Rock & roll's working-class hero, **Bruce Springsteen** has won multiple Grammys over the three decades of his career. *The Ghost of Tom Joad* is his most recent album of new material; *Tracks,* a comprehensive box set of his work, was released at the end of 1998.

After providing the Beatles' backbeat, **Ringo Starr** went on to a solo career.

Sting dissolved the Police at the peak of their popularity to pursue a solo career, incorporating jazz, Latin music and traditional English folk into his articulate and literary songwriting.

Stone Temple Pilots' hard-rock sound won them instant success in the early Nineties, but singer **Scott Weiland**'s heroin addiction plagued the band, causing recording delays and an unofficial split. Weiland embarked on a solo career and brief tour. STP reunited in 1998.

DJ Homicide and singer **Mark McGrath** are members of the noisy L.A. rock band known as **Sugar Ray**, who scored a hit in 1998 with the reggae-flavored "Fly" and another in 1999 with the similarly melodious "Every Morning."

Supergrass is an exuberant rock trio from England who have modernized the English Mod sound of the Sixties. **Gaz Coombes** is their lead singer.

Matthew Sweet plays power pop with muscle when he's not watching or reading Japanese animation and comics.

Talking Heads' innovative, rhythmic pop drew as much from African and South American music as from punk and new wave. Bassist **Tina Weymouth** and Chris Frantz, now married with children, released an album with Jerry Harrison as the Heads and continue to produce a variety of bands at their home studio.

Former *CBS News* and *Entertainment Tonight* anchor **John Tesh** left the small screen to pursue his dream of composing new age instrumentals. He sings and plays guitar and is now one of the genre's powerhouses.

Stephan Jenkins fronts **Third Eye Blind**, a tuneful four-piece rock band from San Francisco who achieved platinum sales with their 1997 eponymous debut.

Nick Hexum fronts **311**, a band from Omaha, Nebraska, that combines rapped vocals with bass-heavy rock.

Kristin Hersh formed **Throwing Muses** with her stepsister Tanya Donelly before embarking on a solo career.

Glen Phillips was the singer for **Toad the Wet Sprocket**, a mellow pop quartet that took its moniker from a Monty Python sketch. The group split up in 1998.

As Sixties Mods, Seventies punks, rock-opera pioneers and progressive Eighties rockers, **Pete Townshend** and the Who explored the inner and outer world with equal aplomb.

Q-Tip and **A Tribe Called Quest** paired witty rhymes with jazz samples and laid-back basslines, blazing a new trail in hip-hop in the early Nineties.

The elusive, gravelly voiced MC called **Tricky** came from the early-Nineties Bristol trip-hop scene. His albums have veered from cohesive and accessible to self-consciously jarring, but they've been consistently innovative.

Tina Turner got her start as an Ikette in the 1950s, before getting equal billing in the Ike and Tina Turner Revue. After years of marital abuse and a suicide attempt, Tina left husband Ike in 1976 and went on to Grammy-winning success by the mid-Eighties.

U2 dominated the Eighties with earnest, soaring rock & roll. Dave **"the Edge"** Evans's minimal reverb-saturated guitar lines and Paul **"Bono"**

Hewson's sensuous vocals have remained U2's poignant constant in the band's diverse twenty-one-years-and-counting career.

Usher Raymond's for-the-ladies R&B crooning and ubiquitous abs have made the nineteen-year-old no stranger to fan mobbings.

Thanks to **Eddie Van Halen**'s amazingly innovative, self-taught guitar style and the band's nearly two-decade string of multiplatinum albums, **Van Halen**'s keg-party metal is an American institution.

Luther Vandross made the rare transition from jingle singer to pop star: He's had ten Top Forty hits of his own, arranged for David Bowie, Ringo Starr and Barbara Streisand, and written songs for Aretha Franklin.

Brian Vander Ark fronts **the Verve Pipe**, a Michigan rock band of the Pearl Jam variety, who scored a Number Five hit in 1997 with "The Freshmen."

Rufus Wainwright's versatile, operatic singing voice and expert piano playing are the result of hard work and genetics. The Canadian singer/songwriter is the son of folk luminaries Loudon Wainwright III and Kate McGarrigle.

Jakob Dylan fronts the roots-rock band **the Wallflowers**. The group's platinum-selling sophomore album, *Bringing Down the Horse,* secured his reputation as a songwriter.

Weezer doled out quirky power-pop and unabashed geekiness over the course of two mid-Nineties albums. Bassist **Matt Sharp** went on to form the new-wave-y Rentals, whose latest album is 1999's *Seven More Minutes.*

Whale is an irreverent kitchen-sink outfit from Sweden. Pop, dance, rock—you name it, they do it, all with a dash of bizarre humor. **Cia Soro** is one its vocalists.

A chance meeting with Daniel Lanois landed blues rocker **Chris Whitley** a record deal and producer for his first album, the critically acclaimed *Living With the Law.*

Flannery O'Connor fan **Lucinda Williams** has released five critically acclaimed albums of country and blues since she dropped out of college to devote her life to music. Her 1998 album, *Car Wheels on a Gravel Road,* won a Grammy for Best Contemporary Folk Album.

Singer/songwriter, producer and arranger **Brian Wilson** has influenced generations of musicians. In the late Nineties, the eccentric visionary returned to performing and recently produced an album for his daughters, Carnie and Wendy.

Carnie Wilson didn't think of becoming a singer until 1986, when her friend Chynna Phillips (daughter of the Mamas and the Papas' Michelle Phillips) approached Carnie and her sister. The vocal-harmony trio Wilson Phillips recorded a string of hit singles

A truly gifted multi-instrumentalist and singer, **Stevie Wonder** has been a pop star ever since he hit puberty. His fusion of R&B, pop balladry, African rhythms and jazz is unique; his expert playing of virtually every instrument on his albums is amazing.

Wu-Tang Clan are the apex of modern hip-hop. Mastermind producer and rapper **RZA** has led the nine-member (and growing) rap collective from Staten Island, New York, to massive commercial and critical success. **Method Man** has become a star in his own right, known for his drafty voice, crafty raps and two multiplatinum solo albums. **Raekwon** has been rocking the hip-hop underground for years with his versatile rhyme skills .

Andy Partridge and **XTC** have been crafting innovative art pop since the late Seventies. They boast a heap of critical acclaim, a cult following and two new albums, *The Apple Venus, Vols. 1* and *2*.

The accordion-wielding madman called **"Weird Al" Yankovic** recorded a demented Knack parody, "My Bologna," in his bathroom, was discovered by long running oddity DJ Dr. Demento, and so began his career as a songwriter.

Neil Young's acoustic ballads, soft country rock and heavy hard rock, all complemented by his clear, high voice, have inspired a massive following for more than thirty years. The visionary singer/songwriter and avowed rock purist has consistently proved that simplicity is an art.

ZZ Top is a nitty-gritty blues-rock trio from Texas. **Billy Gibbons** has been slinging the band's guitar riffs since 1970.

index

contributors

Anthony Bozza graduated from Northwestern University, interned at ROLLING STONE, then joined the magazine's music staff in 1995. He compiled the Raves column before moving on to writing Random Notes and feature stories. Among his other accomplishments, he once made deli sandwiches for Martina Navratilova and Phish's bass player in the same day.

Shawn Dahl is the former senior editor of Rolling Stone Press, the book division of ROLLING STONE, where she worked for nine years following college graduation in 1989. While there, she coedited *Rolling Stone: The Seventies* and worked on dozens of other titles.Currently, as editor of the first edition of the guidebook *Time Out New York Eating & Drinking 2000*, she's reviewing many of New York City's culinary highs and lows. She also codesigned the illustrated book *Pornstar*, by Ian Gittler

An MTV and MTV2 veejay since 1995, **Matt Pinfield** is the host of the MTV shows *120 Minutes, Pinfield Suite, Pinfield Presents, Mattrock* and *Top Ten Breakdown*, among others. As a radio DJ in Asbury Park, New Jersey, he won the Gavin Radio Award for American Music Director in 1992 and in 1993.

A writer and photographer, **Russell A. Trunk** was born in Harefield, England, in 1966, and has written for *Orbit Magazine* and *Sur Music*, among other publications. He currently resides in Michigan, where he founded his own music and photojournalism company, Chrisam Enterprises, Inc. (named after his two children, Christopher James Russell, age eight, and Samantha Lisa, age fourteen). For more information about his artists' self-portraits, Trunk can be contacted via e-mail (chrisam1@flash.net).